Musical Beginnings

Musical Beginnings

Origins and Development
of Musical Competence

Edited by
IRENE DELIEGE
Unité de Recherche en Psychologie de la Musique (URPM)
Centre de Recherches Musicales de Wallonie
Université de Liège

and

JOHN SLOBODA
Unit for the Study of Musical Skill and Development
Department of Psychology
University of Keele

OXFORD
UNIVERSITY PRESS

OXFORD
UNIVERSITY PRESS

Great Clarendon Street, Oxford OX2 6DP

Oxford University Press is a department of the University of Oxford.
It furthers the University's objective of excellence in research, scholarship,
and education by publishing worldwide in

Oxford New York

Athens Auckland Bangkok Bogotá Buenos Aires Calcutta
Cape Town Chennai Dar es Salaam Delhi Florence Hong Kong Istanbul
Karachi Kuala Lumpur Madrid Melbourne Mexico City Mumbai
Nairobi Paris São Paulo Singapore Taipei Tokyo Toronto Warsaw

with associated companies in Berlin Ibadan

Oxford is a registered trade mark of Oxford University Press
in the UK and in certain other countries

Published in the United States
by Oxford University Press Inc., New York

A catalogue record for this book is available from the British Library

Library of Congress Cataloging in Publication Data
Musical beginnings : origins and development of musical competence /
edited by Irene Deliege and John Sloboda.
Simultaneously published in French under title: Naissance et
développement du sens musical.
1. Music—Psychology. 2. Musical ability. 3. Developmental
psychology. I. Deliège, Irène. II. Sloboda, John A.
ML3838.M95   1996   781'.11—dc20   95-9599
ISBN 0 19 852333 5 (Hbk)
ISBN 0 19 852332 7 (Pbk)

Printed in Great Britain
on acid-free paper by
Biddles Ltd., Guildford and King's Lynn

Preface

A full understanding of the cognitive bases of musical behaviour must be underpinned by an appreciation of the way in which musical competence develops from conception through childhood to adulthood. In the early stages of the development of music cognition as a mainstream subdiscipline there was little integration between the majority of researchers who looked at adult competence and a minority who studied development. In the main, developmental research contented itself with describing age-related changes, linked in many cases to a pseudo-Piagetian notion of inevitable and biologically determined stages which unfolded of their own accord at particular ages. The current volume shows a much more sophisticated awareness of the need to explain developmental changes with reference to the child's changing environment and context: from the uterus, through the intense and semi-exclusive infant–mother bond, to the wider contexts provided by family, school, and society at large. Such a perspective is capable of accounting for both the general commonalities observed between members of a culture, but also allows some explanation of individual differences in musical capacity, an increasing preoccupation of the 'adult' literature. There has never been a better prospect for the integration of developmental psychology of music with traditional adult-based approaches.

A further important integrative feature of the current volume is that its many authors show how musical development is related to, and impacts on, other forms of development, be they linguistic, motor, or artistic. On the other hand, this volume deals hardly at all with educational issues and not at all with the classroom. It has been the intention of the authors collected here to address fundamental research on development, rather than its applications in particular educational settings. All the authors are scientists rather than educators, and what we have hoped to provide is an account of what science has revealed about the musical capacities of the young human that is as up-to-date as possible. We hope that our compilation will provide a firm foundation for those who wish to use science to underpin their developments of educational policy or practice.

The different topics dealt with in this work are presented in four sections devoted to stages and particular aspects of child development, from the prenatal period until the beginning of the teenage years. In the first section, dealing with the fetal stage, Jean-Pierre Lecanuet summarizes current knowledge on prenatal auditory experience (Chapter 1). The author explains that a great number of sounds from the external environment and from maternal vocalization reach the uterus and stand out from the general background noise. The auditory system is capable of taking these in and of analysing them from the mid-gestation stage. At the end of gestation, the fetus is capable of responding to these and of processing significant acoustical signals. Prenatal exposure to sound stimuli contributes to the development and continuance of these capacities, at the morphological and physiological levels.

The following section comprises three chapters that concern the first months of the infant's life. First of all, Hanuš Papoušek discusses the emergence of musicality and its human significance (Chapter 2) and draws attention to the highly developed capacity of very young infants to process complex auditory signals. Moreover, the author shows the particular role of melodic and phonetic elements in the infant's vocal communication and the implications of those elements for affective aspects of early child care and for clinical applications.

The purpose of Chapter 3 by Christoph Fassbender is to review methodological aspects and general research procedures that may be applied to infants, with a focus on behavioural techniques. This chapter presents the current understanding of infants' capacities to discriminate frequency, intensity, pitch, and timbre. Implications for the perception of music are discussed.

Mechthild Papoušek (Chapter 4) focuses on the presence of musical elements in the infant's preverbal vocalizations. Infant-directed speech and music typically incorporate some adjustments so as to compensate for the infant's as yet undeveloped capacity to process musical materials. The early stages of preverbal communication are characterized by the perceptual salience of musical elements such as melody, rhythm, and dynamics in both parental speech and infant vocalization. During parent–infant interactions the elements of music function as a means of communication and as objects in vocal activity, reciprocal vocal matching, and creative play. They play a critical role in the development of children's vocal capacities.

The third section of the book is devoted to temporal dimensions. Viviane Pouthas treats the development of the perception of time and temporal regulation of action in infants and children (Chapter 5), focusing on activities that have a regulatory function and may subserve the acquisition of temporal control in infants and young children. The author shows how these capacities develop in relation to the perception of the temporal structure of events.

Finally, the fourth section focuses on several aspects related to development in school-age children. Musical and artistic development is discussed by David Hargreaves (Chapter 6). The chapter presents a descriptive model in which the artistic development of the child is seen as proceeding through five phases: the presymbolic, schematic, figural, rule-based, and metacognitive phases. Examples are given of the ways in which these phases exist in cognitive and aesthetic development, in children's drawing and writing, as well as in four specifically musical domains, namely, singing, musical representation, melodic perception, and composition. Issues concerning the young performing musician are raised by John Sloboda and Jane Davidson (Chapter 7). This chapter reviews the factors that influence the development of young people who have a long-term commitment to musical excellence. These factors include intrinsic motivation for, and enjoyment of, music; family conditions and the specific behaviours and attitudes of parents; relationship to early teachers; and the nature and amount of practice activities.

Finally, to close the volume, Michel Imberty draws a comparison between linguistic and musical aspects of the cognitive development of preschool and school-age children. The musical cognition of the child conforms, in its development, to stages in the formation of linguistic capacities and, more generally, to stages in the development of the child's conception of time to which it is tightly bound. The author examines these stages and suggests a model that describes and predicts the structures of the child's vocal and musical inventions, a model that constitutes an initial attempt to produce a theoretical 'musical grammar' for children's musical behaviour.

Liège and Keele   I.D.
October 1994   J.S.

Acknowledgements

This textbook is put together from revised and expanded versions of invited presentations that were made at the First Summer School, organized in London (City University) by the European Society for the Cognitive Sciences of Music (ESCOM).

The editors would like to acknowledge financial support for this project from a number of sources, including the European Communities (Task Force, Human Resources, Education, Formation and Youth), the British Council, the Ministry of Education and Scientific Research, the General Commissariat of International Relations, the Council of Music of the French Communities of Belgium, the Centre of Music Research from Wallonia, the Research Unit in Psychology of Music (University of Liège), and the SPES Foundation.

The general quality of the book owes a great deal to the collaboration of several colleagues who agreed to review drafts of the chapters. Hervé Abdi, Robert Abrams, Rita Aiello, Annabel Cohen, W. Jay Dowling, Helga Lejeune, Michael Lynch, Dirk Povel, and Sandra Trehub kindly agreed to take part in this difficult task. The editors and the authors are extremely grateful for their valuable assistance.

This book is being published in both English and French. The French edition will appear as *Naissance et développement du sens musical*, published by Presses Universitaires de France in the series Croissance de l'enfant, Genèse de l'homme, edited by René Zazzo.

Contents

PART III TIME AND CHILDHOOD

PART IV SCHOOL AGE

Contributors

Jane Davidson Music Department, University of Sheffield, Sheffield S10 2TN, UK

Irène Deliège Unité de Recherche en Psychologie de la Musique (URPM), Université de Liège, 5 Boulevard du Rectorat, B32, B-4000 Liège, Belgium

Christoph Fassbender University of Hamburg, Musikwissenschaftliches Institut, Neue Rabenstrasse 13, D-20354 Hamburg, Germany

David Hargreaves Department of Psychology, The University, Leicester LE1 7RH, UK and School of Music and Musicology, University of Göteborg, Box 5439, S-40229 Göteborg, Sweden

Michel Imberty President of the University of Paris X, 200 avenue de la République, F-92001 Nanterre Cedex, France

Jean-Pierre Lecanuet Laboratoire de Psycho-Biologie du Développement, EPHE-CNRS (URA-315), 41 rue Gay-Lussac, F-75005 Paris, France

Hanuš Papoušek Professor emeritus, Department of Developmental Psychobiology, University of Munich, Strassberger Str. 43, D-80809 Munich, Germany

Mechthild Papoušek Institute of Social Paediatrics, University of Munich, Heiglhosstrasse, 63, D-81377 Munich, Germany

Viviane Pouthas Laboratoire de Psycho-Biologie du Développement, EPHE-CNRS (URA-315), 41, rue Gay-Lussac, F-75005 Paris, France

John Sloboda Department of Psychology, University of Keele, Staffordshire, ST5 5BG, UK

PART I

The Fetal Stage

1

Prenatal auditory experience

Jean-Pierre Lecanuet

1 INTRODUCTION

It is reported (Castarède 1987) that, whilst she was pregnant of the future king of France Henry IV (1553), Jeanne d'Albret had a woman playing a musical tune every morning in her vicinity. This was done because people of this time believed, first, that the fetus in the womb was able to hear the music and, second, that listening to music would mould the temperament of the baby and thus prevent him from having a dark mood, that is, in the French language of this time prevent him from being 'rechigné' (having a 'bad' mood). According to the historians, Henry IV never lost his joviality . . . .

This story is one among the numerous legendary, ethnological, or historical reports that can be collected about prenatal audition from sources ranging from the Bible to nursing manuals at the onset of the twentieth century. However, it is only since the 1920s and 30s that obstetricians have begun to systematically investigate fetal responsiveness to sounds. Since that time, helped by the development of ultrasound techniques allowing observation of fetal behaviour, research on fetal audition has been widely extended.

This chapter aims to review the body of experimental evidence, stemming from various sources, that has been built up about fetal audition. Thus, in Section 2 the acoustical structure of the intra-uterine environment will be described. It will be shown that the uterus is not only a place where maternal noises and especially the heartbeat sounds can be found, but that various external sounds including musical ones can also be recorded there. Data obtained from animal studies, mostly performed on mammals, will provide data that cannot be obtained from human studies. Section 3 will summarize what is known about the maturation of the auditory system and the possible time of onset of its functioning. Section 4 will present experimental demonstrations of this functioning obtained at various levels. Attempts at defining fetal auditory competencies will be presented. Section 5 will give a broad survey of the consequences in the pre- and postnatal periods of prenatal functioning of the auditory system.

2 THE FETAL SOUND ENVIRONMENT

The first series of human intra-abdominal recordings was obtained with microphones covered with rubber membranes that were inserted into the vagina or the cervix nearest to the uterus in either pregnant (Bench 1968; Walker *et al.* 1971; Murooka *et al.* 1976) or non-pregnant women (Tanaka and Arayama 1969; Walker *et al.* 1971; Busnel 1979), or inside the amniotic cavity after rupture of the membranes during or after delivery (Johansson *et al.* 1964; Walker *et al.* 1971; Henshall 1972; Murooka *et al.* 1976). Except for the acoustic-band analysis of Murooka *et al.* (1976) and Busnel (1979), only global measures were performed in these studies. On the whole, they described a very noisy womb (72–96 dB sound pressure level (SPL); reference value, 20 μPa) with only very loud external low-frequency sounds being transmitted to the amniotic fluid. The considerable background noise was interpreted as originating from the maternal cardiovascular system. However, some authors recorded significantly lower SPL (between 30 and 50 dB) in non-pregnant women or after delivery (Bench 1968; Murooka *et al.* 1976).

2.1 Maternal background noise

In contrast to the findings from the initial studies, more recent ones, using hydrophones adapted to fluid impedance and narrowband analysis, have indicated that the womb is a relatively quiet place. When the mother is in a calm environment and when there are no abdominal gurgles, which clearly emerge with high SPLs from the background noise, the mean SPLs are comparable to those generally encountered externally (Querleu *et al.* 1988; Gerhardt 1989; Benzaquen *et al.* 1990; Graham *et al.* 1991). The recorded intra-uterine background noise is a composite of: (1) electronic noises from the hydrophone and amplifiers; (2) ambient external noises; and (3) various maternal and fetal noises (respiratory, movements, gastrointestinal, cardiovascular, laryngeal), principally composed of low frequencies under 500–700 Hz. Pressure levels show a regular and significant decrease as frequency rises. Frequency band analyses have demonstrated that the important global pressure levels previously obtained were due to infrasounds (Benzaquen *et al.* (1990) and Gagnon *et al.* (1992) measured 85–97 dB at 12.5 Hz) and/or very low frequencies below 50–60 Hz (Querleu *et al.* 1989; Benzaquen *et al.* 1990) for which human absolute auditory thresholds are very high. Peters *et al.* (1991) clearly showed that this high-energy peak represents resonances from the buildings in which the recordings were made. Therefore, contrary to long-held opinion, this high energy does not have a biological origin.

Low-pitched pulsation, recorded at frequencies above 50–60 Hz and under 500–700 Hz and interpreted as vascular sounds, was identified either as the maternal heartbeat (Walker *et al.* 1971; Murooka et al. 1976; Querleu *et al.* 1981), the umbilical artery (Graham *et al.* 1991), the uterine artery (Bench 1968), or uteroplacental blood flow (Querleu *et al.* 1988, 1989; Benzaquen *et al.* 1990).

All the recent data suggest that vascular sounds, occasionally present in the recordings, are not always present at the same SPL everywhere inside the human amniotic cavity. For instance, during delivery, Benzaquen *et al.* (1990) were able to record maternal cardiovascular sounds at the fetal neck level in only two of 10 mothers and never during uterine contractions. This was interpreted to mean that the sounds were of uteroplacental—not maternal—origin. When these pulsating noises could be recorded, their emergence from the background noise was only 19 dB SPL at 100 Hz and 2 dB SPL at 650 Hz.

Power spectrum analysis shows that, when considering intra-uterine components at or above 100 Hz, various values are found as a result of different transducers (best sensitivity in the low or in the high frequencies) and recording sites. Querleu *et al.* (1981, 1988), after several series of recordings far from or close to the placenta with different transducers, measured mean SPLs ranging from 65 to 28 dB SPL, the lowest value being obtained far from the placenta with only 20 dB SPL at 500 Hz and no more than 10 dB SPL at and above 700 Hz; an overall 25 dB SPL emergence of the maternal heartbeat was found. The authors suggested that noises from the placenta probably have a higher masking effect than cardiac noise. Gagnon *et al.* (1992), with another type of hydrophone located in a pocket of fluid near the fetal neck and, therefore, far from the placenta, measured 60 dB SPL at 100 Hz with less than 40 dB above 200 Hz. Thus, it now seems clear that the contribution of vascular sounds to the recorded background noise depends on the location of the transducer.

2.2 *In utero* attenuation of auditory stimuli

The most recent band analyses on the attenuation of airborne broad- and narrow-band noises and pure tones when emitted in close vicinity (less than 2 m from the maternal abdomen) show that there are variations in the *in utero* SPL in both the human (Nyman *et al.* 1991; Richards *et al.* 1992) and the ewe (Vince *et al.* 1982, 1985; Gerhardt 1989; Abrams 1992; Lecanuet, Gautheron, Locatelli, and Jacquet, in preparation). Some are systematic and related to the distance between the source and the transducer when the location of the transducer is changed *in utero*. Richards *et al.* (1991) and Lecanuet *et al.* (in preparation) found that the intra-uterine noise level in pregnant ewes decreased as the distance from the sound source increased, although Nyman *et al.* (1991) were unable to confirm this relationship in human subjects; Peters *et al.* (1993*b*) recently drew isopressure lines inside the uterus of a dead ewe filled with liquid and demonstrated that the attenuation of frequencies over 1000 Hz increased from the outside to the centre of the cavity suggesting a 'wrapping around' effect. Other sources of variation are less clearly defined and probably depend on maternal factors, such as the thickness of maternal tissue, and this may vary from subject to subject, according to the fetal position, the time of day at measurement (Vince *et al.* 1982, 1985), and the composition of the external ambient environment.

Major results—most of them obtained on sheep—can be summarized as follows.

1. The pressure levels of sounds at long wave lengths and low frequencies (<300 Hz), were generally comparable *in* and *ex utero*: *in utero* measurements showed some variability with several dB SPL attenuation or enhancement (at 50 and 63 Hz in the sheep for Peters *et al.* 1993*a*) depending on the research teams. When the wavelength of the frequency is longer than the diameter of an object reached by this frequency, the entire volume of the object may be set in motion by this frequency without sound absorption.

2. According to Peters *et al.* (1993*a*), *in utero* pressure loss in the ewe was moderate between 400 and 1000 Hz and grew by 6.5 dB/octave on average between 1000 and 8000 Hz, thus peaking at 20 dB. Lecanuet *et al.* (in preparation) found that this pressure loss started at around 300–500 Hz depending on the distance between the hydrophone and the abdominal skin of the ewe. In the human, Querleu *et al.* (1988) reported that a similar pressure drop of 20 dB developed at a rate of 6 dB/octave, while Richards *et al.* (1992) recorded a maximum attenuation of 10 dB at 4000 Hz. In all recent studies and in both species, maximum attenuation never exceeded 30–35 dB SPL up to 10 kHz.

3. A shift tendency has been found in the ewe at higher frequencies, the *in utero* pressure increasing and becoming even higher than the *ex utero* pressure, a phenomenon already seen in the measurements of Vince *et al.* (1982). Peters *et al.* observed this reversal from 12 500 Hz onwards and, because they used 1/3 octave band noise stimuli, they found it to be linear. Using sweeping pure tones, Lecanuet *et al.* (in preparation) has found such increases at as low a frequency as 4000 Hz, the frequency values depending again on the depth of the hydrophone in the sheep. These increases appeared as a series of pressure peaks of resonance and antiresonance probably due to standing waves caused by reflection of the short waves on the internal walls of the uterus.

2.3 Differentiation of speech from the background noise

Data on voice differentiation and attenuation *in utero* agree with the results presented above. Recent acoustical recordings revealed that the maternal voice as well as external speech located near the mother clearly emerged from the uterine background noise components at frequencies over 100 Hz. Recordings performed by Busnel (1979) and Querleu *et al.* (1988, with an SPL level of 60 dB) have shown that both the mother's and others' speech: (1) was muffled and significantly attenuated in the high-frequency components; (2) had well preserved prosodic character-istics, and (3) was somewhat intelligible since some phonemes (up to 30 per cent in Querleu *et al.* 1988) and words could be recognized by adults when the recordings were performed far from the placenta. This is also true of external voices recorded from the pregnant ewe by Vince *et al.* (1982, 1985) and Gerhardt (1989). In a recent work Griffiths *et al.* (1994) found that phonemes emitted by a male voice and recorded in a pregnant ewe had a mean intelligibility score of 55 per cent (61 per cent at 85 dB, 47 per cent at 75 dB, and 41 per cent at 65 dB), while they had only a 34 per cent mean score when emitted by a female voice. Com-pared to external recordings the intelligibility scores were respectively reduced by 29 and 50 per cent. Analysis of VCV (vowel, consonant, vowel) stimuli transmission showed that voicing information was better transmitted *in utero* than place or manner information, which was less preserved for a female than for a male speaker. *In utero* speech, in certain recording conditions, may even be clearly intelligible in the human (Benzaquen *et al.* 1990; Smith *et al.* 1990) or the ewe (Lecanuet *et al.*, in preparation, at 90 dB SPL).

Human studies of *in utero* speech transmission, performed with a hydrophone near the fetal head during delivery, have all shown that there is a significantly better transmission of the maternal voice than of the external voice. Querleu *et al.* (1988) and Benzaquen *et al.* (1990) measured an overall 20-dB SPL attenuation of external voices, with no significant difference between male and female voices. In contrast, there is only an 8-dB SPL attenuation of the maternal voice. Richards *et al.* (1992) recorded the maternal voice—which had an external 72-dB SPL level—5 dB SPL louder *in utero* than *ex utero*. External voices—emitted at 90 dB SPL—suffered almost no attenuation at all, namely 2 dB for male voices and 3 dB for female voices; this represents a mean difference of only 8 dB between the maternal voice and external ones in this experi-ment, which is therefore comparable to the 12-dB difference reported by Querleu *et al.* (1988). It is of interest to note that results related to *in utero* maternal bleats in the pregnant ewe are similar. Gerhardt (1989) re-corded no attenuation in their components at frequencies up to 300 Hz, while Vince *et al.* (1985) noted several dB SPL enhancement of these frequencies inside the uterus compared to simultaneous *ex utero* recordings; pressure loss started only at around 1700 Hz.

The higher *in utero* SPL of the maternal voice compared to the SPL of externally presented voices spoken at the same level can be readily explained by the particular mode of transmission *in utero* via two different pathways. On the one hand, the maternal voice is airborne and is transmitted like any other close external sound and may thus suffer from the same acoustic modifications. On the other hand, the maternal voice is internally transmitted via body tissues and bones. Petitjean's (1989) study confirmed the excellent bone conduction of the fundamental frequency and higher harmonics through the spine and the pelvic arch.

2.4 Sound isolation of the fetus

Transmission of external pressures to the fetal ear is controlled by two factors that compose the isolation from the sound environment: (1) attenuation due to the transmission to the amniotic cavity; and (2) transformation of the *in utero* pressures into cochlear displacements. While, as demonstrated above, the first factor has been quite extensively described, one does not know what proportion of the *in utero* pressures reaches the fetal internal ear. This depends on the transduction mode at fetal head level. It is either directly made through the external and middle ear fluids or via bone conduction in the fetal head. Up to now the pathways taken by acoustic pressures have not been defined.

Gerhardt *et al.* (1992) attempted to define the isolation of the fetal sheep cochlea—that is, the attenuation plus the biological transduction—by comparing the external pressure levels necessary to elicit identical cochlear potentials before and after delivery. Values of this isolation grew from 11 dB at 125 Hz to 45 dB at 2000 Hz. Abrams *et al.* (1995) concluded that the fetal ear is not protected from low (<125 Hz) frequency signals, an important finding if one remembers that low-frequency signals are coded in the fetus by cochlear cells that will code later for high frequencies and thus need to be protected to prevent future auditory deficits. Rubel and Ryals (1983) showed that the cochlear tonotopy (that is, the spatial distribution of frequency sensitivity in the cochlea) changes during maturation.

3 AUDITORY SYSTEM MATURATION

In postnatal life the middle ear transmits acoustic vibrations from the external ear to the inner ear. It has been suggested, and this will be developed below, that this middle ear functioning could be impaired by the *in utero* situation. Nevertheless, functional or not, ossicles develop from the eighth gestational week onwards and the tympanic membrane from the eleventh week. Middle ear development continues until the eighth gestational month.

In the inner ear, the cochlea develops from the otocyst, a structure appearing around the 28th day. It starts to curl by the sixth week, reaches its full morphological development—measuring 3 mm and curled in 2½ turns—by the tenth week, and its final adult size by the twentieth week. The organ of Corti, which bears the auditory receptors, develops within the cochlea from the eighth week onwards. The first auditory cells (inner hair cells) and the three rows of outer hair cells can be seen as differentiated types of cells by the eleventh week. None of them are functional at this age, nor at the fourteenth week when the cell positioning on the basilar membrane has reached its final state (Pujol 1993).

According to Pujol and Uziel (1986), who base their inference on the parallelism in the chronology of cochlear development in humans and in every studied mammal, the human cochlea seems functional by the twentieth week, while histological studies showed that the auditory receptors are not completely mature at this time. The first cochlear potentials can be recorded in all animal studies at the same developmental stage. It is by the twentieth week that the efferent innervation of the outer hair cells takes place, mature synapses being found between the 24th and 28th weeks (Pujol *et al.* 1991). Maturation of the inner ear probably ends during the eighth month with the organization of afferent and efferent synaptic connections.

At the onset of cochlear functioning auditory competencies, which are well characterized in animal studies, are poor. Electrophysiological responses can only be recorded for medium frequencies (1000–2000 Hz, depending on the species). Auditory thresholds are high (around 100 dB); there is no frequency discrimination and no temporal coding. However, these abilities improve rapidly: auditory thresholds decrease; temporal coding begins; frequency sensitivity widens, first in the low-frequency range and then at high frequencies; and then unit frequency selectivity sharpens. The first cochlear potentials are evoked by mid-frequencies, although the base of cochlea, which usually codes high frequencies when mature, is the first cochlear zone to develop (see Rubel and Ryals 1983).

It had been thought that residual embryonic mesenchyma and amniotic fluid, still present in the external and middle ear at birth, might impair *in utero* middle-ear functioning. However, the anatomical studies of McLellan *et al.* (1964) and the tympanometric studies of Keith (1975) showed that they do not induce ear drum and ossicle stiffness. Nevertheless, it can be assumed that the middle ear is not necessary for fetal audition since it is adapted to the amplification of acoustic stimuli in aerial life. Without this amplification, clinical studies show that there is an average loss of 30 dB from the aerial environment of the outer ear to the liquid environment of the cochlea. *In utero*, since the outer and middle ear are filled with amniotic fluid and since liquids, tissues and bones have close conducting properties, the acoustic energy inside the uterine cavity can reach the cochlear receptors with negligible energy loss, thus suppressing the need for an amplifying system. However, the middle-ear transmission might still be possible, but, as pointed out by Rubel (1985), its prenatal functioning is necessarily different from its postnatal one.

4   EVIDENCE OF PRENATAL AUDITORY FUNCTIONING

Data obtained in several mammalian species have provided electro-physiological and neurochemical demonstrations of prenatal auditory function. In the human, cardiac and motor responses to several vibro-acoustic and acoustic stimulations have been studied and some evoked potential measurements have been performed during labour.

4.1   Auditory evoked potentials

Fetal brainstem and cortical auditory evoked potentials have been extensively studied *in utero* in the chronically implanted guinea-pig (Scibetta and Rosen 1969) and sheep (Woods and Plessinger 1989). These potentials display the same characteristics and the same develop-mental course as those recorded *ex utero*. In the human, they have been recorded with electrodes placed on the fetal scalp during labour (Barden *et al.* 1968; Scibetta *et al.* 1971; Staley *et al.* 1990).

   In the premature baby, short, middle, and late latency evoked aud-itory responses have also been extensively examined. All three may be recorded, but are not consistently detectable at 24–25 weeks gestational age (GA). The detectability of major components increases progressively with age and is stable by 30–32 weeks (Starr *et al.* 1977; Krumholz *et al.* 1985; Pasman *et al.* 1991). Brainstem responses are consistent and repro-ducible, but, as previously inferred from animal studies (see above), with very high thresholds (100 dB SPL) at 25 weeks. Thresholds gradu-ally decrease with development and by 35 weeks GA are no more than 10–20 dB hearing level different from the threshold of adults. The five principal components showing neural activation from the cochlear nerve to the inferior colliculus are then regularly obtained but are still im-mature with regard to peak and interpeak latencies and amplitudes.

4.2 Neurochemical responses: local cerebral (14-C) 2-deoxyglucose (2-DG) uptake

This method, which allows the investigation of fetal brain activity *in utero* through cerebral glucose utilization (energy metabolism), has been used in two animal models, the fetal guinea-pig (Servières *et al.* 1986; Horner *et al.* 1987) and the fetal sheep (Abrams *et al.* 1993). Pure tones in guinea-pigs and vibroacoustic stimulation in sheep induce a marked increase in 2-DG uptake in auditory structures: in the brainstem in the guinea-pig and in all auditory structures, including the auditory cortex, in the fetal sheep. In the guinea-pig, frequency-specific auditory labelling has been obtained in response to loud, external free-field pure tones up to 20 kHz. The location of the labelling in the cochlear nucleus and in the inferior colliculus is a function of the frequency of the tones. The tonotopic organization of the structures has thus been demonstrated *in utero*.

4.3 Behavioural studies

4.3.1 *Fetal responses*

When obstetricians started to investigate fetal responsiveness, guided by the observation made by many pregnant women that their babies moved when a very loud noise occurred, they analysed motor and then cardiac fetal responses to loud rough and 'naturalistic' external sounds; examples of such stimuli are warning horns (Peiper 1925; Fleischer 1955) and wood claps (Forbes and Forbes 1927; Ray 1932; Spelt 1948).

Since the earliest observations, motor responses have been classified either as isolated, strong, and sudden or as a sustained increase in fetal activity. Inhibition of ongoing movements (Fleisher 1955; Tanaka and Arayama 1969; Vecchietti and Bouché 1976; Bouché 1981) was also described at a very early stage.

Mostly phasic heart-rate accelerations, but also sustained heart-rate modifications, such as tachycardia or a change in heart-rate variability, were described as cardiac responses. Some authors studied both motor and cardiac responses and showed that motor response rates were lower than cardiac acceleration rates (Tanaka and Arayama 1969; Grimwade *et al.* 1971).

4.3.2 *Mode of administration and structure of stimulation*

In the 1950s experimenters started utilizing carefully defined acoustic stimulation, such as pure tones and band noises. The airborne mode of stimulation was abandoned in favour of stimulation applied directly on the mother, near the fetal head, so as to avoid or minimize sound pressure loss. Two procedures were used.

1. Stimulation was directly transmitted to the maternal abdomen by the oscillatory source (vibroacoustic mode), generally a bone vibrator, a tuning fork, an electric toothbrush, or the electroacoustic larynx (EAL). The EALs, which were adopted in the 1980s, deliver broadband noises with highest pressure levels in the low frequencies (>135 dB SPL *in utero* in the sheep (Gerhardt 1989; Gagnon *et al.* 1992).

2. Stimulation was air-coupled, and in most cases the loudspeaker (usually part of headphones) was isolated from the mother's abdomen with a rubber or foam ring.

Vibroacoustic devices are designed to propagate sound pressure more efficiently through tissues and fluids than through air. Impedance mismatches are therefore avoided. However, such devices introduce non-auditory stimulation. They might activate fetal cutaneous receptors, which mature very early in development (Hooker 1952), and also possibly the sacculus. The latter, which is part of the vestibular system, matures 2 weeks earlier than the auditory apparatus (Pujol and Sans 1986) and is known to be activated by loud low frequencies in different species including the human (Cazals *et al.* 1983; Ribaric *et al.* 1991).

The air-coupled procedure is likely to result in an important alteration of stimulus if the loudspeaker is applied directly to the mother's abdomen. The loudspeaker membrane is partially blocked, thus producing frequency distortions and high-frequency amplification. In contrast, when the loudspeaker is coupled with a rubber or a foam ring, it is the low frequencies that are more likely to be amplified. Therefore, the conditions produced by the two procedures just described are very different from the conditions of fetal auditory activation by external everyday sounds.

This is probably why, in the 1980s, some investigators returned to the use of airborne stimulation by placing loudspeakers at various distances from the maternal abdomen (10 cm to 1 m) (Querleu *et al.* 1981, 1989; Granier-Deferre *et al.* 1983, 1985; Lecanuet *et al.* 1986, 1988; Kisilevsky *et al.* 1989; Kisilevsky and Muir 1991).

A survey of fetal studies shows that various types of stimuli were emitted via the different administration modes—airborne, air-coupled, or vibratory. Pure tones, various bandwidth frequency noises, high-pass filtered or unfiltered pink or white noises, and the EAL were delivered. Even though the SPL—measured at different *ex* or *in utero* sites— varied across a wide range (from 65 to 125 dB SPL), most studies, owing to the reasons mentioned above, were performed at or above 100 dB SPL. Responses to this stimulation level will be reported first.

4.3.3 Startling stimulation

Ontogeny of responses Vibroacoustic studies using **broad-band noises** have shown that, as early as 24 weeks GA in some fetuses (Leader *et al.* 1982; Birnholz and Benacerraf 1983; Crade and Lovett 1988; Kisilevsky *et al.* 1991) and in all subjects at 28 weeks GA (Querleu *et al.* 1981; Birnholz and Benacerraf 1983; Kuhlman *et al.* 1988; Groome *et al.* 1991) or 30 weeks GA(Leader *et al.* 1982; Divon *et al.* 1985; Crade and Lovett 1988; Druzin *et al.* 1989), motor responses are evoked. The developmental time course of phasic heart-rate accelerations compared to that of motor responses seems to be delayed by 2–3 weeks (Gagnon *et al.* 1987; Druzin *et al.* 1989; Kisilevsky *et al.* 1990). Using a 110-dB broad-band noise in an air-coupled situation, Shahidullah and Hepper (1993) recorded a diffuse motor response of slow latency as early as 20 weeks GA. By 25 weeks the response was an immediate startle-type response. According to the authors, the development of outer hair cells, or some other maturational process occurring within the auditory system, may contribute to this change in responsiveness.

Using **pure tones**, motor responses were first detected in vibroacoustic and air-coupled studies at 27–28 weeks (Vecchietti and Bouché 1976; Shenhar *et al.* 1982) or at around 7 months (Tanaka and Arayama 1969; Gelman *et al.* 1982). Cardiac accelerative changes were described as early as 5–6 months (Ogawa 1955), 26 weeks (Wedenberg 1965), 27 weeks (Vecchietti and Bouché 1976), 28 weeks (Shenhar *et al.* 1982), or 30 weeks (Tanaka and Arayama 1969). Because of important experimental design differences, no precise conclusions can be drawn about the ontogeny of fetal responses to pure tones. However, a gradual increase in responsiveness was observed with gestational age for both motor responses (Sontag and Wallace 1935; Tanaka and Arayama 1969; Vecchietti and Bouché 1976) and cardiac accelerative changes (Wedenberg 1965; Tanaka and Arayama 1969; Vecchietti and Bouché 1976; Jensen 1984*b*). According to Sontag and Wallace (1936), cardiac accelerations display larger amplitudes as fetuses get older. By 8 months, motor response and accelerative change rates found in most studies are between 70 and 90 per cent (Sontag and Wallace 1935; Fleischer 1955; Wedenberg 1965; Tanaka and Arayama 1969; Vecchietti and Bouché 1976). These discrepancies may be explained by differences in response detection procedures and also in stimulus characteristics. But no systematic studies have been performed to analyse the effect of frequency, intensity or duration of stimulation on the proportion and characteristics of early fetal responses.

In near-term fetuses (35–41 weeks GA), as in newborns, the responses that are evoked with loud vibroacoustic or airborne stimuli (over 105 dB SPL) are modulated by both the characteristics of the stimulus and the fetal state.

The effects of stimulus characteristics   The three groups of recent airborne studies mentioned above demonstrated that broad-band noise given at the same SPL, 110 dB, elicited much higher rates of accelerative changes and motor responses than pure tones or narrowband noises. This is in contrast to the air-coupled and direct vibratory conditions where high proportions of responses were obtained with pure tones. A probable explanation is that the SPL reaching the amniotic fluid are much greater in the latter condition.

As mentioned before, most studies were performed with loud stimuli (over 100 dB SPL) that induced—more or less reliably—a heart-rate acceleration usually accompanied by a motor response. In the airborne mode of stimulation Kisilevsky *et al.* (1989) found that the threshold intensity for a reliable heart-rate acceleration is somewhere between 100 and 105 dB. Lecanuet *et al.* (1988) found, while monitoring the fetal state, that relatively high percentages of heart-rate accelerative responses were elicited with octave-band noises presented at 100 dB in a high-variability heart-rate state: 50 per cent at 2000 Hz and 55 per cent at 5000 Hz, with an average amplitude of 18 beats/min for the two frequencies.

Whatever the stimulation mode, when the acoustic pressure level of the stimulus was enhanced, motor and cardiac response rates increased, as did acceleration amplitudes (Jensen and Flottorp 1982; Kisilevsky *et al.* 1989; Yao *et al.* 1990). A 5-dB SPL difference was sufficient to modify fetal responsiveness (Kisilevsky *et al.* 1989). This general increase was observed independently of fetal behavioural state. However, both cardiac and motor responsiveness were greater in a state of high heart-rate variability (active sleep) than in a state of low heart-rate variability (quiet sleep) (Schmidt *et al.* 1985; Lecanuet *et al.* 1986).

Contradictory results have been obtained in studies using pure tones (in air-coupled and vibratory modes of stimulation), response rates being higher for high-frequency than for low-frequency stimulation or vice versa. With broadband noises, given in the airborne mode of stimulation, higher pitched sounds induced more responses than lower ones (Lecanuet *et al.* 1988). Low frequencies, such as a 500-Hz centred noise, induced very few motor responses. When motor reactions were induced, the mean amplitudes of fetal heart-rate accelerations were higher (22 beats/min; ranging from 6 to 48 beats/min) than when there were no concomitant fetal movements (12.5 beats/min) thus reflecting a somato-cardiac effect.

The effects of fetal state   Since the publication of Nijhuis *et al.* (1982), four behavioural states have been described in the near-term fetus: active (2F) and quiet (1F) sleep; active (4F) and quiet (3F) wakefulness. In the 2F state (active sleep), both cardiac and motor responsiveness are greater and cardiac accelerations have higher amplitudes and are more often accompanied by a motor response than during the 1F state (quiet sleep) (Schmidt *et al.* 1985; Lecanuet *et al.* 1986, 1988). Schmidt *et al.* (1985) also found a greater reactiveness in quiet (3F) and active (4F) wakefulness compared to sleep states. When stimuli are above 110 dB SPL or vibroacoustical stimulation (VAS) response ratios seem to be no longer modulated by state, they induce, when given in quiet sleep, an immediate change to active sleep (state 2F) or wakefulness with movement (state 4F) (Gagnon 1989*a*; Visser *et al.* 1989; Kisilevsky *et al.* 1989).

4.3.4 *Non-startling airborne stimulation*

Sounds between 85 and 100 dB SPL *ex utero* do not induce startle responses or cardiac accelerations, but evoke moderate heart-rate deceleration, unaccompanied by movement. For example, Lecanuet *et al.* (1988) found that a 500-Hz octave-band noise emitted at 100 dB elicited only cardiac decelerations and that the deceleration had the same amplitude in quiet and active sleep (-10 beats/min). This type of response had been anecdotally mentioned by many authors (Bernard and Sontag 1947; Dwornicka *et al.* 1964; Tanaka and Arayama 1969; Grimwade *et al.* 1971; Goodlin and Schmidt 1972; Goodlin and Lowe 1974; Vecchietti and Bouché 1976; Jensen 1984*a*). Some of the decelerative responses were described as part of biphasic cardiac responses. Pilot studies confirmed that these cardiac decelerative responses: (1) could be reliably elicited in fetuses in quiet sleep (1F) by various types of continuous or rhythmic airborne stimuli emitted within this 85–100 dB range *ex utero*; and (2) quickly habituated to a repeated stimulus (given every 3–4 s). This made it feasible to examine the possibility of discriminative auditory capacities in the 36–40 weeks GA fetus. An habituation/dishabituation procedure derived from Clarkson and Berg's study (1983) on speech discrimination in the awakened neonate was used.

In a first study (Lecanuet *et al.* 1987) fetuses that were exposed every 3.5 s to a pair of syllables ([ba] and [bi] and [ba]) uttered in French by a female speaker and emitted at the same pressure level (95 dB) displayed a decelerative response. Reversing the order of the paired syllables after 16 presentations also reliably induced the same type of response. This response recovery suggested that the fetus discriminated between the two stimuli. This discrimination may have been performed on the basis of an intensity difference between the [ba] and the [bi], since the equalization of these syllables was done on the basis of the sound pressure level, not the hearing level.

In the next study (Lecanuet *et al.* 1992) a conservative data analysis procedure that took into account each subject's pre-stimulus heart-rate variability was developed. This procedure defined for each subject:

(1) whether the stimulus presentation and the modification of its acoustic structure induced a heart-rate change; (2) whether the direction of the heart-rate change was accelerative or decelerative; and (3) what its amplitude was. With this procedure it was demonstrated that near-term fetuses exposed to a short sentence, 'Dick a du bon thé', uttered by a male voice (minimum fundamental frequency $F_0 = 83$ Hz) or a female voice (minimum $F_0 = 165$ Hz) at the same hearing level (90–95 dB SPL) and at 3.5-s intervals, reacted with a high proportion of decelerative responses (77 per cent to the male voice, 66 per cent to the female voice) within the first 10-s of stimulation as compared to a group of non-stimulated subjects. After return to a stable heart-rate pattern the initial voice (male or female) was either replaced by the other voice or continued (in a control condition). A majority (69 per cent) of the experimental subjects displayed a heart-rate deceleration in response to the change, while 43 per cent of the control subjects displayed a weak amplitude acceleration (Lecanuet *et al.* 1993).

The presence of these significant novelty responses showed that near-term fetuses may perceive a difference between the voice characteristics of two speakers, at least when they are highly contrasted in F_0 and timbre. These results cannot be generalized for all female and male voices or for all utterances. It should be emphasized that in this experiment fetal heart-rate change occurred within the first seconds of exposure to the novel stimulus, thus suggesting that only a short speech sample is needed for the fetal auditory system to detect an acoustically relevant change in speaker. Since the most obvious acoustic cues for the discrimination are fundamental frequency and timbre, near-term fetuses in quiet sleep may perform pitch discrimination as was found during quiet sleep in the newborn by Alho *et al.* (1990) based on analysis of the electroencephalogram (EEG).

4.3.5   *Fetal responses to musical stimuli*

Almost every pregnant woman has noticed that the baby she carries seems to react differentially according to the type of music emitted in the environment. Data described above suggest that various other factors than the type of music, namely, its loudness, its pitch, and, to a large extent, the behavioural state of the baby, may control the reaction of the fetus. Thus, the differential average increase of heart-rate variability measured on a group of 20 subjects exposed to the air-coupled presentation of two distinct sequences of classical music by Olds (1985*b*) may partly be due to such effects. A global increase of the number of heart-rate accelerations and movements is expected in response to the presentation of any loud sequence of stimulus, a response observed by Olds triggered by the emission of 5 min of singing or piano music.

An air-coupled presentation by Woodward (1992) of 15 s. of a sample of Bach's organ prelude given at 100 dB induced a high percentage of heart-rate acceleratory responses (93 per cent) in a high-variability state —much more than in a low-variability state. Almost all these responses started within 5 s of presentation of the stimulation.

Finally, one has to consider some potential indirect effects of music on the fetus: those induced by the maternal response to this music. This is a very difficult task since the psychobiological impact of music on an adult depends not only on the style of the music but on the personal history of the subject. Zimmer *et al.* (1982) played 25 min of music to future mothers via headphones (classical or pop music) and found that the fetuses of these mothers showed more body movements and fewer respiratory movements than during a silent period. This effect was more significant when the mother's favourite music was played. Conversely, no modification of fetal heart-rate was found by Olds (1985*a*) during a presentation of music to the mother through headphones.

5 CONSEQUENCES OF AUDITORY PRENATAL EXPERIENCE

Prolonged exposure—for several weeks and even months—of a maturing auditory system to a large variety of external and/or maternal sounds has several types of effects. They can be described first at structural and functional levels and second at a behavioural level where they represent more or less specific learning. Fetal learning can be demonstrated pre- and postnatally. It can be inferred from a peculiar sensitivity to the presentation of a fetal stimulation or the demonstration of a clear preference for this stimulation when given in a choice situation. Some of the auditory abilities reported above can be seen as consequences of a prenatal exposure to auditory stimulation.

5.1 Prenatal consequences of sound exposure

5.1.1 *Structural and functional effects*

Animal studies performed on species in which the auditory function starts after birth (mouse, rat, gerbil, cat, guinea-pig) have shown that afferent input is necessary to establish and maintain a correct functioning of the auditory system and to partially control sound integration in the brainstem.

Bilateral auditory deprivation starting before or during the period of appearance of cochlear potentials causes the same anatomical alterations, but to a smaller extent, as those caused by a bilateral destruction of the cochleas: (1) a reduction in the number and size of the neurones and dentritic arborization along the auditory relays of the brainstem acoustic pathway; (2) higher electrophysiological auditory thresholds; and (3) a reduction in the ability to discriminate complex rhythmic structures.

Monaural deprivation causes neuronal and electrophysiological alterations affecting mostly ipsilateral structures dealing with binaural interactions. Some experiments show that sound deprivation would mainly induce a delay in the development of auditory sensitivity: impairment can be reversible if the deprivation does not extend to a critical period (review in Ruben and Rapin 1980; Conlee and Parks 1981; Moore 1985; Clopton 1986). Such deficits impair auditory spatial localization (Clements and Kelly 1978; Knudsen *et al.* 1982). On the other hand, prolonged exposure to selectively enriched sound environments—which do not induce any acoustic trauma—stimulates local dendritic growth (Smith *et al.* 1983), modifies the reactivity of central acoustic units (Clopton and Winfield 1976, Sanes and Constantine-Paton 1983), and seems to facilitate some discriminative auditory tasks. Thus, it can be hypothesized that sounds reaching the fetal ear might contribute to the structural and functional shaping of the auditory pathway.

5.1.2 *Behavioural effects*

Habituation Experiments reported above have shown that repetition at a short interval (every 3–4 s) of a 92–95 dB acoustic stimulus led to the disappearance of a decelerative cardiac response that had been induced by the first presentation of this stimulus, thus indicating an habituation to this stimulus (Lecanuet *et al.* 1992).

Due to their interest for the fetal diagnosis of potential neural defects, a large number of studies have been—and still are—performed to analyse the fetal ability to habituate to loud stimuli. These studies indicate that the number of stimulus presentations required to obtain habituation depends on: (1) the type of observed response (motor or cardiac); (2) the defined habituation criteria (that is, the number of trials inducing no response, and the use or not of a dishabituation stimulus); (3) the characteristics of the stimulus (spectral organization and duration, interstimulus time interval); and (4) the fetal behavioural state.

With **airborne auditory stimulation** at or lower than 110 dB SPL *ex utero*, motor startle responses significantly decrease or disappear after only 2–4 stimulations (Peiper 1925; Fleischer 1955; Goupil *et al.* 1975; Birnholz and Benacerraf 1983; Lecanuet *et al.* 1986; Kisilevsky and Muir 1991). As in the premature or term newborn, the fetal cardiac response is slower to habituate than the motor response. Significant reduction or disappearance of this response is obtained after two to seven stimulations (Goodlin and Lowe 1974; Lecanuet *et al*. 1986; Kisilevsky and Muir 1991). The amplitude of the cardiac acceleration also diminishes after a few repetitions of the stimuli (Bench *et al*. 1967; Bench and Mentz 1978; Lecanuet *et al*. 1986). Using a classical habituation/dishabituation procedure, Kisilevsky and Muir (1991) have obtained a significant decrement of both cardiac accelerative and movement responses to a complex noise, at 110 dB SPL, followed by a recovery of these responses when triggered by a novel stimulus, a vibroacoustic one. Fetal state interferes with habituation; this process is faster during the quiet sleep state than during active sleep state (Lecanuet *et al*. 1986).

When applying *vibroacoustic stimulation*, a strongly startling stimulation as stated before, motor response rate decrements occur much more slowly than with airborne auditory stimulation. It takes at least 6–40 stimulations to occur depending on fetal age and habituation criteria (Leader *et al*. 1982, 1988; Madison *et al*. 1986; Kuhlman *et al*. 1988). The authors did not notice any difference as a function of fetal state. Kisilevsky and Muir (1991) did not observe any statistically significant fetal heart-rate accelerative response decline after eight vibroacoustic stimulation trials, but only a trend in that direction.

Conditioning Two controversial attempts at establishing a classical conditioning have been conducted (Ray 1932; Spelt 1948). A non-startling conditional stimulus (a low-frequency vibration) was repeatedly presented before an unconditional startling sound stimulus until it was able to evoke this startle response. Apparently, such a conditioning would have been erased and reinstated after a 3-week delay. More recently, Feijoo (1981) claimed to have associated the musical theme of *Peter and the Wolf* by Prokofiev (given at 60 dB SPL) with a state of deep maternal relaxation (presented as an unconditional stimulus inducing fetal movements) several times a week during the sixth, seventh, and eighth months of pregnancy. When tested at the thirty-seventh week, trained fetuses responded immediately with movements to the presentation of the musical theme, while non-exposed fetuses moved only 6–10 min later. Backwards presentation of the sequence did not have any effect on trained subjects.

Effects of mere exposure to the maternal voice Thirty-six weeks GA, fetuses showed no ability to discriminate between their mother's voice and that of a stranger played to them via an air-coupled loudspeaker placed on the abdomen but did discriminate between their mother's voice as played to them by the loudspeaker and the mother's voice produced by her speaking, showing less movements in response to the direct speaking voice (Hepper *et al*. 1993). According to the authors, the latter discrimination may be due to the presence of internally transmitted components of speech which the fetus perceives when the mother is speaking but which are not present when the tape recording of the mother's voice is played.

Effects of mere exposure to a spoken sentence   Airborne presentation at 85 dB to 37-week GA fetuses of a story repeatedly played twice a day during the previous month induced a transitory heart-rate decelerative response while another story spoken by the same female voice did not induce any significant change, thus suggesting a prenatal recognition of the familiar story (DeCasper *et al.* 1994).

5.2   Postnatal effects of prenatal sound exposure

Prenatal auditory experience may result in general and/or specific learning the effects of which are evidenced in various postnatal situations. Familiar stimuli or classes of stimuli may—more or less selectively— soothe the crying newborn or elicit orienting responses from the quiet one. If they are frightening ones, they may have lost this capacity after the baby has been exposed to them during fetal life. More convincingly, familiar stimuli or classes of stimuli can be preferred to unfamiliar ones in choice test situations like the non-nutritive sucking one.

5.2.1   Soothing and orienting effects

Maternal heartbeat and other internally generated sounds   Salk (1960, 1962) found that newborn babies daily exposed to the sound of an adult heartbeart emitted at 72 beats/min—a sound supposedly familiar from the earliest fetal period—were soothed by this sound and slept sooner and gained weight more rapidly than non-stimulated babies. Following Salk, there was a wide array of investigation of the effects of maternally generated internal noises. Initially, these studies were largely restricted to an examination of the soothing impact of maternal cardiac noises on the neonate. Probably as a result of differences in experimental design, such as the use of different types of stimuli and different observation timing (short-term or long-term), results were ambiguous with some describing a soothing effect that others did not confirm (Takemoto 1964; Tulloch *et al.* 1964; Brackbill *et al.* 1966; Roberts and Campbell 1967; Brackbill 1970, 1973; Palmqvist 1975; Smith and Steinschneider 1975; Murooka *et al.* 1976; Schmidt *et al.* 1980; Kato *et al.* 1985).
  Murooka and colleagues (1976) comparing various stimuli, including recordings of the intra-uterine background noise (that is, recorded close to the placenta and thus including loud maternal cardiovascular components; see above the discussion on the acoustic structure of internal sounds), concluded that any noise having an acoustical structure similar

to that noise—and not only this very stimulus—had a short-term pacifying effect. This effect has been confirmed by Kato *et al.* (1985) and by Asada *et al.* (1987) who recorded heart-rate and respiration modifications of soothed crying babies. Yoshida *et al.* (1988) report a similar effect on irritable babies, lasting at least for the first 7 postnatal days. Yoshida and Chiba (1989) showed that the intra-uterine noise emitted at 75 dB lowered the F_0 of crying and elicited positive facial mimics. Using a non-nutritive sucking choice procedure De Casper and Sigafoos (1983) demonstrated that the Murooka heart-beat sound had a reinforcing value for 3-day-old babies.

Speech sounds and musical episodes It has been mentioned above that speech sounds, especially those spoken by the maternal voice, were not masked by the intra-uterine background noise. Thus, prolonged exposure of the human fetus to such stimuli may have postnatal effects.

Natural or synthetic speech sounds seem particularly attractive to the newborn who shows transient decelerative responses to the onset of their presentation (Ashmead and Lipsitt, quoted by Fifer 1981; Brazelton *et al.* 1974; Eisenberg *et al.* 1974), an effect that may, however, be induced by many other auditory low-pitched, moderately intense stimuli (Hutt and Hutt 1970; Turkewitz *et al.* 1972). Many studies conducted during the last 25 years have suggested that newborns process speech stimuli in a specific way different from the method they apply to other auditory stimuli (see review in Aslin *et al.* 1983). This is usually seen as a consequence of an inherited human sensitivity to linguistic sounds (Chomsky 1975) rather than as the effect of a prenatal exposure to speech sounds. However, the explanations are not mutually exclusive.

The particular attractiveness of **the mother's voice** on less than 2-week old neonates has been described by several authors (André-Thomas 1966; Wolff 1969; Hammond 1970; Brazelton 1978). The explanation could be postnatal association of this voice with positive reinforcers more than prenatal learning. Conflicting evidence is presented below.

About **musical sequence**, Feijoo (1981), in the delivery room, and Hepper (1988), studying 4–5 day-old babies, observed that the infants were significantly soothed and attentive to music their mothers listened to daily during the last 3 months of pregnancy. Feijoo played the bassoon part of Prokofiev's *Peter and the Wolf*; in Hepper's study it was the musical theme of the mothers' favourite British television series, *Neighbours*, that was the target.

5.2.2 *Long-term habituation to startling stimuli*

Prenatal learning is suggested by two studies of long-term habituation. Human and guinea-pig neonates are significantly less disturbed by a startling sound if they have been repeatedly exposed to it prenatally. The longer the prenatal exposure of a human neonate—living in the Osaka airport neighbourhood—to aeroplane noises, the better he slept as compared to babies whose mothers had lived in the airport neighbourhood for shorter times during pregnancy (Ando and Hattori 1970, 1977). Similarly, neonate guinea-pigs were less responsive (no significant heart-rate change) to the vocalization of a Bantam hen than control animals, who had not been exposed to this sound during gestation (Vince 1979).

5.2.3   Demonstration of auditory preferences

The maternal voice   Studies performed with young babies, 2–4 day-old neonates using a selective interburst (of sucks) interval (IBI) duration reinforcement procedure of non-nutritive sucking demonstrated that the mother's voice was not only attractive to newborns as mentioned above but was also preferred to another female voice (DeCasper and Fifer 1980; Fifer 1981). The possibility of a very fast postnatal acquisition was again argued. The authors then compared the preference for airborne versions of these voices to preference for their 'intra-uterine', low-pass filtered versions. No particular preference was demonstrated by Spence and DeCasper (1987). (While the newborns did prefer an airborne version of another woman's voice, this was considered to be a demonstration of a prenatal contribution to the neonates' general preference for the mother's voice.) Finally, Fifer and Moon (1989) and Moon and Fifer (1990), using a modified version of the 'intra-uterine' mother's voice (either mixed or not with maternal cardiovascular sounds), found that newborns preferred an 'intra-uterine' form of their mother's voice over an airborne version. In addition, DeCasper and Prescott (1984) found that 2-day-old babies did not prefer their father's voice to another male voice even after 4 to 10 hours of postnatal contact with their father; this postnatal contact was thus insufficient to induce a preference to this voice. Taken together, these results suggest that the absence of a preference for the father's voice is probably due to less prenatal experience with the father's voice than with the mother's voice.

Newborns' prenatal familiarity with the maternal voice may explain why Hepper *et al.* (1993) found, through an analysis of their movements, that they discriminate normally intoned speech from 'motherese' intoned speech (with exaggerated contours) only on the maternal voice. Subjects, however, discriminated the maternal voice from a strange female voice.

Speech sequence   DeCasper and Spence (1986) showed, using the non-nutritive IBI contingent sucking procedure, that 2–3-day-old newborns preferred hearing a story their mother had read out loud for 6 weeks before birth to one that they had never heard. Because no difference was found during testing if the story was read by the mother or another woman's voice, prenatal learning of some acoustic features of the story, probably prosodic, is suggested.

Musical sequences Using the non-nutritive sucking procedure, Panneton (1985) showed that newborns whose mothers had been singing a melody—using the syllable 'la' instead of the words of the song—changed their pattern of sucking in order to turn on a recording of this melody more often than the recording of an unfamiliar melody, where both melodies contained the same segmental information (the syllable 'la') and the same individual notes but where the temporal order, duration, and relative number of the notes were different in each melody. With a different sucking procedure, that is, prenatally presented music being contingent to a sucking pause (an IBI) and novel music being contingent to the onset of a burst of sucks in one test condition and vice versa in another condition, Woodward (1992) found that newborns lengthened the pauses (reinforced by the 'familiar' music) and had a smaller number of bursts in the second part of a 10-min test than in a silent pre-test period in the first condition type of test. Babies had been exposed from 34 weeks GA onwards either to a sequence of classical music or to a sequence of jazz music (depending on the future mother's own preference).

A speech sequence sung by the mother's voice In one experiment performed by Satt (1984) with the DeCasper's non-nutritive sucking test 3 days after birth, babies had to choose between two recorded lullabies, both sung by their mother. They preferred the lullaby to which they had been repeatedly exposed during the end of their fetal life to the unfamiliar one.

Maternal language In the following studies, the neonates had some postnatal experience with the maternal language before they were tested, either for a specific preference for this language or for their capacity to discriminate between the maternal language and another one. Using a non-nutritive sucking choice procedure, Moon *et al.* (1993), with both Spanish- and English-speaking women, demonstrated that 2-day-old newborns preferred their mother's language to the other one. Demonstration of a preference for the mother's language at such an early age favours an interpretation of the data of Mehler *et al.* (1986, 1988) in terms of a prenatal familiarization. In the latter studies, 4-day-old babies discriminated between two languages (French/Russian or English/Italian) only if one of them was the mother's language. Moreover, babies born of French-speaking mothers showed a higher average sucking rate per minute during the habituation phase if the non-contingent speech emitted during this period was French than if it was Russian, both languages being spoken by a bilingual woman. Such a behaviour persisted when babies were exposed to low-pass ($<400\,Hz$) filtered versions of the two languages, which kept only prosodic cues of the spoken sentences. In addition, babies born of mothers speaking neither French nor Russian were unable to discriminate between those two languages as if the absence of any familiar prosodic cue rendered impossible the perception of differences. Thus, such data may reflect either a prenatal familiarization to a specific language, augmented by 3–4 days of postnatal exposure to this language, or fast learning occurring during this neonatal period.

6 CONCLUSION

The studies reviewed in this chapter show that: (1) a large variety of acoustical stimulation, speech sounds—especially maternal ones—but also external sounds naturally present in the daily environment of the pregnant woman, musical ones being of course included in that list, emerge from the intra-uterine background noise and are loud enough to stimulate the fetal auditory system; (2) the human auditory system is functional 3–4 months before birth; (3) fetuses beyond 28–30 weeks of gestation reliably react to external sounds—including speech at a later stage—displaying either startle responses with heart-rate accelerations or heart-rate decelerative responses as a function of the structure of the stimulation and of their behavioural state; (4) prenatal exposure to acoustical stimulation may exert structural and functional effects on the human auditory system nervous pathway as it does in animals at the same stage of auditory development. Prenatal familiarization to specific sounds or classes of sounds may contribute to the development of a particular sensitivity to these stimuli and to the formation of a preference for: (1) a given speaker (mother); (2) some particular prosodic sequence when read or sung by the mother during the last weeks of her pregnancy; (3) some particular musical sequence; (4) a given language (maternal).

A decade of research has shown that, in spite of its relative immaturity, the mammalian fetal brain is able to perform learning that will control postnatal behaviour. Thus, in order to end the way we started in the world of anecdotes collected in everyday life, one might consider that data reviewed above may account for facts episodically reported by professional musicians born to musician parents. They recalled having a feeling of familiarity when listening to or starting to study a novel tune that appeared—after a family investigation—to have been a repetitive part of their prenatal environment, a tune played by their mother during the period they carried this future musician. Anyway, it can be said that prenatal musical experience as well as—and some readers will say more than—any structurally organized acoustic stimulation may contribute to shaping auditory abilities and to developing long-term preferences or general sensitivity to the type of sounds experienced.

ACKNOWLEDGEMENTS

Parts of the materials presented in this chapter have been adapted from previous publications written in co-operation with Drs C. Granier-Deferre and M-C. Busnel. The author wishes to express his gratitude to these persons and to Mrs A-Y Jacquet for her help in the preparation of the references.

REFERENCES

Abrams, R. M., Peters, A. J. M., Gerhardt, K. J., and Burchfield, D. J. (1993). Vibroacoustic stimulation in fetal sheep: effect on cerebral glucose utilization and behavioural state. *Journal of Developmental Physiology*, **19**, 171–7.

Abrams, R. M., Gerhardt, K. J., and Peters, A. J. M. (1995). Transmission of sound and vibration to the fetus. In *Fetal development: a psychobiological perspective* (ed. J.-P. Lecanuet, N. Krasnegor, W. P. Fifer, and W. P. Smotherman), pp. 315–30. Lawrence Erlbaum Associates, Hillsdale, New Jersey.

Alho, K., Sainio, K., Sajaniemi, N., Reinikainen, K., and Näätänen, R. (1990). Event-related brain potential of human newborns to pitch change of an acoustic stimulus. *Electroencephalographs and Clinical Neurophysiology*, **77**, 151–5.

Ando, Y. and Hattori, H. (1970). Effects of intense noise during fetal life upon postnatal adaptability (statistical study of the reactions of babies to aircraft noise). *Journal of the Acoustical Society of America*, **47**, 1128–30.

Ando, Y. and Hattori, H. (1977). Effects of noise on sleep of babies. *Journal of the Acoustical Society of America*, **62**, 199–204.

André-Thomas, A. S. (1966). *Locomotion from prenatal life*. Spastic Society, Heinemann, London.

Asada, M., Minagawa, J., Yamada, T., Ohmichi, M., and Hasegawa, T. (1987). Neonates' response to music. *Obstetrics and Gynecology Proceedings*, **36**, 1749–56.

Aslin, R. N., Pisoni, D. B., and Jusczyk, P. (1983). Auditory development and speech perception in infancy. In *Handbook of child psychology*, Vol. II *Infancy and developmental psychobiology* (ed. M. M. Haith and J. J. Campos), pp. 527–687. Wiley, New York.

Barden, T. P., Peltzman, P., and Graham, J. T. (1968). Human fetal electro-encephalographic response to intrauterine acoustic signals. *American Journal of Obstetrics and Gynecology*, **100**, 1128–34.

Bench, R. J. (1968). Sound transmission to the human fetus through the maternal abdominal wall. *Journal of Genetic Psychology*, **113**, 1172–4.

Bench, R. J. and Mentz, D. L. (1978). Neonatal auditory habituation and state change. *Quarterly Journal of Experimental Psychology*, **30**, 355–62.

Bench, R. J., Mittler, P. J., and Smyth, C. N. (1967). Changes of heart rate in response to auditory stimulation in the human fetus. *Bulletin of the British Psychology Society*, **20**, 14a.

Benzaquen, S., Gagnon, R., Hunse, C., and Foreman, J. (1990). The intrauterine sound environment of the human fetus during labor. *American Journal of Obstetrics and Gynecology*, **163**, 484–90.

Bernard, J. and Sontag, L. W. (1947). Fetal reactivity to tonal stimulation, A preliminary report. *Journal of Genetic Psychology*, **70**, 205–10.

Birnholz, J. C. and Benacerraf, B. B. (1983). The development of the human fetal hearing. *Science*, **222**, 516–18.

Bouché, M. (1981). Echotomographic evaluation of fetal sound stimulation. *Ultrasons*, **2**, 339–41.

Brackbill, Y. (1970). Acoustic variations and arousal level in infants. *Psychophysiology*, **6**, 517–26.

Brackbill, Y. (1973). Continuous stimulation reduces arousal level: stability of the effect over time. *Child Development*, **44**, 43–6.

Brackbill, Y., Adams, G., Crowell, D., and Gray, L. (1966). Arousal level in neonates and preschool children under continuous auditory stimulation. *Journal of Experimental Child Psychology*, **4**, 178–88.

Brazelton, T. B. (1978). The remarkable talents of the newborn. *Birth and the Family Journal*, **5**, 4–10.

Brazelton, T. B., Koslowski, B., and Main, M. (1974). The origins of reciprocity in mother–infant interaction. In *The effect of the infant on its caregiver* (ed. M. Lewis and L. A. Rosenbloom), pp. 178–96. Wiley, New York.

Busnel, M-C. (1979). Mesures intravaginales du niveau et des distorsions acoustiques de bruits maternels. *Electrodiagnostic Therapie*, **16**, 142.

Busnel, M. C. and Granier-Deferre, C. (1983). And what of fetal audition? In *The behaviour of human infants* (ed. A. Oliveirio and M. Zappella), pp. 126–30. Life Sciences Collection, Plenum Press, New York.

Castarède, M-F. (1987). *La voix et les sortilèges*. Les Belles Lettres, Paris.

Cazals, Y., Aran, J-M., and Erre, J-P. (1983). Intensity difference thresholds assessed with eighth nerve and auditory cortex potentials: compared values from cochlear and saccular responses. *Hearing Research*, **10**, 263–8.

Chomsky, N. (1975). *Reflections on language*. Pantheon Books, New York.

Clarkson, M. G. and Berg, W. K. (1983). Cardiac orienting and wowel discrimination in newborns: crucial stimulus parameters. *Child Development*, **54**, 162–71.

Clements, M. and Kelly, J. B. (1978). Auditory spatial responses of young guinea pigs (Cavia Porcellus) during and after ear blocking. *Journal of Comparative Physiological Psychology*, **92**, 34–44.

Clopton, B. M. (1986). Neural correlates of development and plasticity in the auditory, somatosensory and olfactory systems. In *Developmental neuropsychobiology* (ed. W. T. Greenough and J. M. Juraska), pp. 256–78. Academic Press, London.

Clopton, B. M. and Winfield, J. A. (1976). Effect of early exposure to patterned sound on unit activity in rat inferior colliculus. *Journal of Neurophysiology*, **39**, 1081–9.

Conlee, J. W. and Parks, T. N. (1981). Age and position dependent effects of monaural acoustic deprivation on nucleus magnocellularis of the chicken. *Journal of Comparative Neurology*, **202**, 373–4.

Crade, M. and Lovett, S. (1988). Fetal response to sound stimulation: preliminary report exploring use of sound stimulation in routine obstetrical ultrasound examinations. *Journal of Ultrasound Medicine*, **7**, 499–503.

DeCasper, A. J. and Fifer, W. P. (1980). Of human bonding: newborns prefer their mother's voice. *Science*, **208**, 1174–6.

DeCasper, A. J. and Sigafoos, A. D. (1983). The intra uterine heartbeat: a potent reinforcer for newborns. *Infant Behavior and Development*, **6**, 19–25.

DeCasper, A. J. and Prescott, P. A. (1984). Human newborns' perception of male voices: preference, discrimination, and reinforcing value. *Developmental Psychobiology*, **17**, 481–91.

DeCasper, A. J. and Spence, M. J. (1986). Prenatal maternal speech influences newborn's perception of speech sounds. *Infant Behavior and Development*, **9**, 133–50.

DeCasper, A. J., Lecanuet, J-P., Busnel, M-C., Granier-Deferre, C., and Maugeais, R. (1994). Fetal reaction to recurrent maternal speech. *Infant Behavior and Development*, **17**, 159–64.

Detterman, D. K. (1978). The effect of heart beat sound on neonatal crying. *Infant Behavior and Development*, **1**, 36–48.

Divon, M. Y., Platt, L. D., Cantrell, C. J., Smith, C. V., Yeh, S. Y., and Paul, R. H. (1985). Evoked fetal startle response: A possible intrauterine neurological examination. *American Journal of Obstetrics and Gynecology*, **153**, 454–6.

Druzin, M. L., Edersheim, T. G., Hutson, J. M., and Bond, A. L. (1989). The effect of vibroacoustic stimulation on the nonstress test at gestational ages of thirty-two weeks or less. *American Journal of Obstetrics and Gynecology*, **161**, 1476–8.

Dwornicka, B., Jasienska, A., Smolarz, W., and Wawryk, R. (1964). Attempt of determining the fetal reaction to acoustic stimulation. *Acta Otolaryngologica, Stockholm*, **57**, 571–4.

Eisenberg, R. B., Marmarou, A., and Giovachino, P. (1974). Infant heart rate changes to a synthetic speech sound. *Journal of Audiological Research*, **14**, 20–8.

Feijoo, J. (1981). Le foetus, Pierre et le Loup. In *L'Aube des Sens*, Cahiers du Nouveau-né (ed. E. Herbinet and M-C. Busnel), pp. 192–209. Stock, Paris.

Fifer, W. P. (1981). Early attachment: maternal voice preference in one- and three-day-old infants. Unpublished D. Phil. thesis. University of Greensboro, North Carolina.

Fifer, W. P. and Moon, C. (1989). Psychobiology of newborn auditory preferences. *Seminars in Perinatology*, **13**, 430–3.

Fleischer, K. (1955). Untersuchungen zur Entwickllung der Innenohrfunktion (Intra-uterine Kinderbewegungen nach Schallreizen). *Zeitschrift für Laryngologie und Rhinologie*, **3**, 733–40.

Forbes, H. S. and Forbes, H. B. (1927). Fetal sense reaction: hearing. *Journal of Comparative Physiological Psychology*, **7**, 353–5.

Gagnon, R. (1989a). Acoustic stimulation: effect on heart rate and other biophysical variables. *Clinics in Perinatology*, **16**, 643–60.

Gagnon, R. (1989b). Stimulation of human fetuses with sound and vibration. *Seminars in Perinatology*, **13**, 393–402.

Gagnon, R., Campbell, K., Hunse, C., and Patrick, J. (1987). Patterns of human fetal heart rate accelerations from 26 weeks to term. *American Journal of Obstetrics and Gynecology*, **157**, 743–8.

Gagnon, R., Benzaquen, S., and Hunse, C. (1992). The fetal sound environment during vibroacoustic stimulation in labor: Effect on fetal heart rate response. *Obstetrics and Gynecology*, **79**, 950–5.

Gelman, S. R., Wood, S., Spellacy, W. N., and Abrams, R. M. (1982). Fetal movements in response to sound stimulation. *American Journal of Obstetrics and Gynecology*, **143**, 484–5.

Gerhardt, K. J. (1989). Characteristics of the fetal sheep sound environment. *Seminars in Perinatology*, **13**, 362–70.

Gerhardt, K. J., Abrams, R. M., and Oliver, C. C. (1990). Sound environment of the fetal sheep. *American Journal of Obstetrics and Gynecology*, **162**, 282–7.

Gerhardt, K. J., Otto, R., Abrams, R. M., Colle, J. J., Burchfield, D. J., and Peters, A. J. M. (1992). Cochlear microphonics recorded from fetal and newborn sheep. *American Journal of Otolaryngology*, **13**, 226–32.

Goodlin, R. C. and Lowe, E. W. (1974). Multiphasic fetal monitoring: a preliminary evaluation. *American Journal of Obstetrics and Gynecology*, **119**, 341–57.

Goodlin, R. C. and Schmidt, W. (1972). Human fetal arousal levels as indicated by heart rate recordings. *American Journal of Obstetrics and Gynecology*, **114**, 613–21.

Goupil, F., Legrand, H., Breard, G., Le Houezec, R., and Sureau, C. (1976). Sismographie et réactivité foetale. 5e Journées Nationales de Médecine Périnatale (ed. O. Dubois and R. Renaud), pp. 262–6. Arnette, Paris.

Graham, E. M., Peters, A. J., Abrams, R. M., Gerhardt, K. J., and Burchfield, D. J. (1991). Intraabdominal sound levels during vibroacoustic stimulation. *American Journal of Obstetrics and Gynecology*, **164**, 1140–4.

Granier-Deferre, C., Lecanuet, J-P., Cohen, H., and Busnel, M-C. (1983). Preliminary evidence on fetal auditory habituation. In *Noise as a public health problem* (ed. G. Rossi), pp. 561–72.

Granier-Deferre, C., Lecanuet, J-P., Cohen, H., and Busnel, M-C. (1985). Feasibility of prenatal hearing test. *Acta Otolaryngolica, Stockholm* (Suppl.) **421**, 93–101.

Griffiths, S. J., Brown, W. S. Jr, Gerhardt, K. J., Abrams, R. M., and Morris, R.J. (1994). The perception of speech sounds recorded within the uterus of a pregnant sheep. *Journal of the Acoustical Society of America*, **96**, 2055–63.

Grimwade, J. C., Walker, D. W., Bartlett, M., Gordon, S., and Wood, C. (1971). Human fetal heart rate change and movement in response to sound and vibration. *American Journal of Obstetrics and Gynecology*, **109**, 86–90.

Groome, L. J., Gotlieb, S. J., Neely, C. L., Waters, M. D., and Colwell, G. D. (1991). Development of the fetal response decrement. *American Journal of Obstetrics and Gynecology (SPO Abstracts)*, **164**, 361.

Hammond, J. (1970). Hearing and response in the newborn. *Developmental Medicine and Child Neurology*, **12**, 3–5.

Henshall, W. R. (1972). Intrauterine sound levels. *Journal of Obstetrics and Gynecology*, **112**, 577–8.

Hepper, P. G. (1988). Fetal 'soap' addiction. *Lancet*, **1**, 1147–8.

Hepper, P. G., Scott, D., and Shahidullah, S. (1993). Newborn and fetal response to maternal voice. *Journal of Reproductive and Infant Psychology*, **11**, 147–53.

Hooker, D. (1952). *The prenatal origin of behavior*. University of Kansas Press, Lawrence, Kansas.

Horner, K., Servières, J., and Granier-Deferre, C. (1987). Deoxyglucose demonstration of in utero hearing in the guinea-pig fetus. *Hearing Research*, **26**, 327–33.

Hutt, S. J. and Hutt, C. (1970). *Direct observation and measurement of behavior*. C.C. Thomas. Springfield, Ill.

Jensen, O. H. (1984*a*). Fetal heart rate response to controlled sound stimuli during the third trimester of normal pregnancy. *Acta Obstetrica Gynecologica Scandinavica*, **63**, 193–7.

Jensen, O. H. (1984*b*). Accelerations of the human fetal heart rate at 38 to 40 weeks' gestational age. *American Journal of Obstetrics and Gynecology*, **149**, 918.

Jensen, O. H. and Flottorp, G. (1982). A method for controlled sound stimulation of the human fetus. *Scandinavian Audiology*, **11**, 145–50.

Johansson, B., Wedenberg, E., and Westin, B. (1964). Measurement of tone response by the human fetus. A preliminary report. *Acta Otolaryngologica, Stockholm*, **57**, 188–92.

Kato, Y., Tanaka, S., Tabata, T., and Takeda, S. (1985). The responses of neonates to intrauterine sound, with special reference to use for screening of hearing impairment. *Wakayama Medical Report*, **28**, 9–14.

Keith, R. W. (1975). Middle ear function in neonates. *Archives of Otolaryngology*, **101**, 376–9.

Kisilevsky, B. S. and Muir, D. W. (1991). Human fetal and subsequent newborn responses to sound and vibration. *Infant Behaviour and Development*, **14**, 1–26.

Kisilevsky, B. S., Muir, D. W., and Low, J. A. (1989). Human fetal response to sound as a function of stimulus intensity. *Obstetrics and Gynecology*, **73**, 971–6.

Kisilevsky, B. S., Muir, D. W., and Low, J. A. (1990). Maturation of fetal heart rate and movement responses to vibroacoustic stimulation. In *Proceedings of the 7th International Conference on Infant Studies*, p. 456. Ablex, Norwood, New York.

Kisilevsky, B. S., Killen, H., Muir, D. W., and Low, J. A. (1991). Maternal and ultrasound measurements of elicited fetal movements: A methodologic consideration. *Obstetrics and Gynecology*, **77**, 89–92.

Knudsen, E. I., Knudsen, P. F., and Esterly, S. D. (1982). Early auditory experience modifies sound localization in barn owls. *Nature*, **295**, 238–40.

Krumholz, A., Felix, J. K., Goldstein, P. J., and McKenzie, E. (1985). Maturation of the brain-stem auditory evoked potential in premature infants. *Electroencephalography and Clinical Neurophysiology*, **62**, 124–34.

Kuhlman, K. A., Burns, K. A., Depp, R., and Sabbagha, R. E. (1988). Ultrasonic imaging of normal fetal response to external vibratory acoustic stimulation. *American Journal of Obstetrics and Gynecology*, **158**, 47–51.

Leader, L. R., Baillie, P., Martin, B., and Vermeulen, E. (1982). The assessment and significance of habituation to a repeated stimulus by the human fetus. *Early Human Development*, **7**, 211–83.

Leader, L. R., Stevens, A. D., and Lumbers, E. R. (1988). Measurement of fetal responses to vibroacoustic stimuli. Habituation in fetal sheep. *Biology of the Neonate*, **53**, 73–85.

Lecanuet, J-P., Granier-Deferre, C., Cohen, H., Le Houezec, R., and Busnel, M-C. (1986). Fetal responses to acoustic stimulation depend on heart rate variability pattern, stimulus intensity and repetition. *Early Human Development*, **13**, 269–83.

Lecanuet, J-P., Granier-Deferre, C., DeCasper, A. J., Maugeais, R., Andrieu, A-J., and Busnel, M-C. (1987). Perception et discrimination foetale de stimuli langagiers, mise en évidence à partir de la réactivité cardiaque. Résultats préliminaires. *Compte-Rendus de l'Academie des Sciences de Paris*, **305** (Série III), 161–4.

Lecanuet, J-P., Granier-Deferre, C., and Busnel, M-C. (1988). Fetal cardiac and motor responses to octave-band noises as a function of cerebral frequency, intensity and heart rate variability. *Early Human Development*, **18**, 81–93.

Lecanuet, J-P., Granier-Deferre, C., Jacquet, A-Y., and Busnel, M-C. (1992). Decelerative cardiac responsiveness to acoustical stimulation in the near term foetus. *Quarterly Journal of Experimental Psychology*, **44b**, 279–303.

Lecanuet, J-P., Granier-Deferre, C., Jacquet, A. Y., Capponi, I., and Ledru, L. (1993). Prenatal discrimination of a male and a female voice uttering the same sentence. *Early Development and Parenting*, **2**, 217–28.

McLellan, M. S., Brown, R. J., Rondeau, H., Soughro, E., Johnson, R. A., and Hale, A. R. (1964). Embryonal connective tissue and exudate in ear. *American Journal of Obstetrics and Gynecology*, **108**, 164–70.

Madison, L. S., Adubato, S. A., Madison, J. K., Nelson, R. M., Anderson, J. C., Erickson, J., Kuss, L. M., and Goodlin, R. C. (1986). Fetal response decrement: true habituation? *Journal of Developmental & Behavioural Pediatry*, **7**, 14–20.

Mehler, J., Jusczyk, P., Lamberz, G., Halsted, N., Bertoncini, J., and Amiel-Tison, C. (1988). A precursor of language acquisition in young infants. *Cognition*, **29**, 143–78.

Moon, C. and Fifer, W. P. (1990). Newborns prefer a prenatal version of mother's voice. *Infant Behavior and Development*, **13**, 530 (special ICIS issue).

Moon, C., Cooper, R. P., and Fifer, W. P. (1993). Two-days-old prefer their native language. *Infant Behavior and Development*, **16**, 495–500.

Moore, D. R. (1985). Postnatal development of the mammalian central auditory system and the neural consequences of auditory deprivation. *Acta Otolaryngologica, Stockholm*, (Suppl.) **421**, 19–38.

Murooka, H., Koie, Y., and Suda, D. (1976). Analyse des sons intrautérins et de leurs effets tranquillisants sur le nouveau-né. *Journal de Gynécologie Obstétrique et de Biologie de la Reproduction*, **5**, 367–76.

Nijhuis, J. G., Prechtl, H. F. R., Martin, C. B., and Bots, R. S. G. M. (1982). Are there behavioural states in the human fetus? *Early Human Development*, **6**, 177–95.

Nyman, M., Arulkumaran, S., Hsu, T. S., Ratnam, S. S., Till, O., and Westgren, M. (1991). Vibroacoustic stimulation and intrauterine sound pressure levels. *Obstetrics and Gynecology*, **78**, 803–6.

Ogawa, G. (1955). The audiovisual sensories of fetus. *Journal of Obstetrics and Gynecology, Hokkaido*, **6**, 60–5.

Olds, C. (1985*a*). *A sound start in life*. Runwell Hospital, Wickford, Essex.

Olds, C. (1985*b*). Fetal response to music. *Midwives Chronicle*, **98**, 202–3.

Palmqvist, H. (1975). The effect of heartbeat sound stimulation on the weight development of newborn infant. *Child Development*, **46**, 292–5.

Panneton, R. K. (1985). Prenatal auditory experience with melodies: effects on postnatal auditory preferences in human newborns. Unpublished D. Phil. thesis, University of North Carolina at Greensboro, North Carolina.

Pasman, R. L., Näätanen, R., and Alho, K. (1991). Auditory evoked responses in prematures. *Infant Behavior and Development*, **14**, 129–35.

Peiper, A. (1925). Sinnesempfindugen des Kinder vor Seiner Geburt. *Monatsschrift Kinderheilkunde*, **29**, 236–41.

Peters, A. J. M., Abrams, R. M., Gerhardt, K. J., and Burchfield, D. J. (1991). Vibration of the abdomen in non-pregnant sheep: effect of dynamic force and surface area of vibrator. *Journal of Low Frequency Noise and Vibration*, **10**, 92–9.

Peters, A. J. M., Abrams, R. M., Gerhardt, K. J., and Griffiths, S. K. (1993*a*). Transmission of airborne sounds from 50–20,000 Hz into the abdomen of sheep. *Journal of Low Frequency Noise and Vibration*, **12**, 16–24.

Peters, A. J. M., Gerhardt, K. J., Abrams, R. M., and Longmate, J. A. (1993*b*). Three dimensional intraabdominal sound pressures in sheep produced by airborne stimuli. *American Journal of Obstetrics and Gynecology*, **169**, 1304–15.

Petitjean, C. (1989). Une condition de l'audition foetale: la conduction sonore osseuse. Conséquences cliniques et applications pratiques envisagées. Unpublished MD thesis, University of Besançon.

Pujol, R. (1993). Développement et plasticité du système auditif de l'enfant. *Communiquer*, **111**, 13–16.

Pujol, R. and Sans, A. (1986). Synaptogenesis in the cochlear and vestibular receptors. In *Advances in neural and behavioral development*, Vol. 2 (ed. R. E. Aslin), pp. 1–18. Auditory Development, Ablex, Norwood, New York.

Pujol, R. and Uziel, A. (1986). Auditory development: peripheral aspects. In *Handbook of human biological development* (ed. P. F. Timiras and E. Meisami). CRC Press, Boca Raton, Florida.

Pujol, R., Lavigne-Rebillard, M., and Uziel, A. (1991). Development of the human cochlea. *Acta Otolaryngologica, Stockholm*, **482**, 7–12.

Querleu, D., Renard, X., and Versyp, F. (1981). Les perceptions auditives du foetus humain. *Medecine et Hygiène*, **39**, 2101–10.

Querleu, D., Renard, X., Versyp, F., Paris-Delrue, L., and Crépin, G. (1988). Fetal hearing. *European Journal of Obstetrics and Reproductive Biology*, **29**, 191–212.

Querleu, D., Renard, X., Boutteville, C., and Crepin, G. (1989). Hearing by the human fetus? *Seminars in Perinatology*, **13**, 430–3.

Ray, W. S. (1932). A preliminary study of fetal conditioning. *Child Development*, **3**, 173–7.

Ribaric, K., Bleeker, J. D., and Wit, H. P. (1991). Perception of audio-frequency vibrations by profoundly deaf subjects after fenestration of the vestibular system. *Acta Otolaryngologica, Stockholm*, **112**, 45–9.

Richards, D. S., Abrams, R. M., Gerhardt, K. J., and McCann, M. E. (1991). Effects of vibration frequency and tissue thickness on intrauterine sound levels in sheep. *American Journal of Obstetrics and Gynecology*, **165**, 438–42.

Richards, D. S., Frentzen, B., Gerhardt, K. J., McCann, M. E., and Abrams, R. M. (1992). Sound levels in the human uterus. *Obstetrics and Gynecology*, **80**, 86–190.

Roberts, B. and Campbell, D. (1967). Activity in newborns and the sound of a human heart. *Psychonomic Science*, **9**, 339–40.

Rubel, E. W. (1985). Auditory system development. In *Measurement of audition and vision in the first year of postnatal life a methodological overview* (ed. G. Gottlieb and N. Krasnegor), pp. 53–90. Ablex, Norwood.

Rubel, E. W. and Ryals, B. M. (1983). Development of the place principle: acoustical trauma. *Science*, **219**, 512–14.

Ruben, R. J. and Rapin, I. (1980). Plasticity of the developing auditory system. *Annals of Otology, Rhinology, and Laryngology*, **89**, 303–11.

Salk, L. (1960). The effects of the normal heartbeat sound on the behavior of newborn infant: implications for mental health. *World Mental Health*, **12**, 1–8.

Salk, L. (1962). Mother's heartbeat as an imprinting stimulus. *Transactions of the New York Academy of Sciences*, Series 2, **4**, 753–63.

Sanes, D. H. and Constantine-Paton, M. (1983). Altered activity patterns during development reduce normal neural tuning. *Science*, **221**, 1183–5.

Satt, B. J. (1984). An investigation into the acoustical induction of intra-uterine learning. Unpublished D. Phil. thesis. Californian School of Professional Psychologists.

Schmidt, K., Rose, S. A., and Bridger, W. H. (1980). Effect of heartbeat sound on the cardiac and behavioural responsiveness to tactual stimulation in sleeping preterm infants. *Developmental Psychobiology*, **3**, 175–84.

Schmidt, W., Boos, R., Gniers, J., Auer, L., and Schulze, S. (1985). Fetal behavioural states and controlled sound stimulation. *Early Human Development*, **12**, 145–53.

Scibetta, J. J. and Rosen, M. G. (1969). Response evoked by sound in the fetal guinea-pig. *Obstetrics and Gynecology*, **33**, 830–6.

Scibetta, J. J., Rosen, M. G., Hochberg, C. J., and Chick, L. (1971). Human fetal brain response to sound during labor. *American Journal of Obstetrics and Gynecology*, **109**, 82–5.

Servières, J., Horner, K., and Granier-Deferre, C. (1986). Mise en évidence de l'activité fonctionnelle du système auditif in utero du foetus de cobaye autoradiographie au (14C) 2-désoxyglucose. *Compte rendu de l'Académie des Sciences, Paris*, **302** (série III), 37–42.

Shahidullah, S. and Heffer, P. H. (1993). The developmental origins of fetal responsiveness to an acoustic stimulus. *Journal of Reproductive and Infant Psychology*, **11**, 135–42.

Shenhar, B., Da Silva, N., and Eliachor, I. (1982). Fetal reactions to acoustic stimuli: a clinical trial, pp. 186–8. Paper presented at the XVIth International Congress of Audiology, Helsinki.

Smith, C. R. and Steinschneider, A. (1975). Differential effects of prenatal rhythmic stimulation on arousal states. *Child Development*, **46**, 574–8.

Smith, C. V., Satt, B., Phelan, J. P., and Paul, R. H. (1990). Intrauterine sound levels: intrapartum assessment with an intrauterine microphone. *American Journal of Perinatology*, **7**, 312–15.

Smith, Z. D. J., Gray, L., and Rubel, E. W. (1983). Afferent influences on brain stem auditory nuclei of the chicken: nucleus laminaris dendritic length following monaural acoustic deprivation. *Journal of Comparative Neurology*, **220**, 199–205.

Sontag, L. W. and Wallace, R. F. (1935). The movement response of the human fetus to sound stimuli. *Child Development*, **6**, 253–8.

Sontag, L. W. and Wallace, R. F. (1936). Changes in the rate of the human fetal heart in response to vibratory stimuli. *American Journal of Disabled Children*, **51**, 583–9.

Spelt, D. K. (1948). The conditioning of the human fetus in utero. *Journal of Experimental Psychology*, **38**, 338–46.

Spence, M. J. and DeCasper, A. J. (1987). Prenatal experience with low frequency maternal voice sounds influences neonatal perception of maternal voice samples. *Infant Behavior and Development*, **10**, 133–42.

Staley, K., Iragui, V., and Spitz, M. (1990). The human fetal auditory evoked brainstem. *Electroencephalography and Clinical Neurophysiology*, **77**, 1–3.

Starr, A., Amlie, R. N., Martin, W. H., and Sanders, S. (1977). Development of auditory function in newborn infants revealed by auditory brainstem potentials. *Pediatrics*, **60**, 831–9.

Takemoto, Y. (1964). Sleep induction by heartbeat rythm. *Folia Psychiatrica Japonica* (suppl.) **7**, 347–51.

Tanaka, Y. and Arayama, T. (1969). Fetal responses to acoustic stimuli. *Practical Otology, Rhinology, and Laryngology*, **31**, 269–73.

Tulloch, J. P., Brown, B. S., Jacobs, H. L., Prugh, D. G., and Greene, W. A. (1964). Normal heartbeat sound and behavior of newborn infants, a replication study. *Psychosomatic Medicine*, **26**, 661–70.

Turkewitz, G., Birch, H. G., and Cooper, K. K. (1972). Patterns of responses to different auditory stimuli in the human newborn. *Developmental Medicine and Child Neurology*, **14**, 487–91.

Vecchietti, G. and Bouché, M. (1976). La stimulazione acustica fetale: indagni preliminari sul significato delle reazioni evocate. *Attualita Ostetrica Ginecologica*, **22**, 367–78.

Vince, M. A. (1979). Postnatal consequences of prenatal sound stimulation in the guinea-pig. *Animal Behavior*, **27**, 908–18.

Vince, M. A., Armitage, S. E., Baldwin, B. A., Toner, Y., and Moore, B. C. J. (1982). The sound environment of the fetal sheep. *Behaviour*, **81**, 296–315.

Vince, M. A., Billing, A. E., Baldwin, B. A., Toner, J. N., and Weller, C. (1985). Maternal vocalisations and other sounds in the fetal lamb's sound environment. *Early Human Development*, **11**, 164–70.

Visser, G. H. A., Mulder, H. H., Wit, H. P., Mulder, E. J. H., and Prechtl, H. F. R. (1989). Vibro-acoustic stimulation of the human fetus: effect on behavioural state organization. *Early Human Development*, **286**, 296–312.

Wedenberg, E. (1965). Prenatal test of hearing. *Acta Otolaryngology* (Suppl.), **206**, 27–30.

Walker, D. W., Grimwade, J. C., and Wood, C. (1971). Intrauterine noise: a component of the fetal environment. *American Journal of Obstetrics and Gynecology*, **109**, 91–5.

Wolff, P. H. (1969). The natural history of crying and other vocalizations in early infancy. In *Determinants of infant behavior*, Vol. 4 (ed. B. M. Foss), pp. 81–109. Methuen, London.

Woods, J. R. and Plessinger, M. A. (1989). Fetal sensory sequencing: application of evoked potentials in perinatal physiology. *Seminars in Perinatology*, **13**, 380–92.

Woodward, S. C. (1992). The transmission of music into the human uterus and the response to music of the human fetus and neonate. Unpublished D. Phil. thesis. University of Cape Town, South Africa.

Yao, Q. W., Jakobsson, J., Nyman, M., Rabaeus, H., Till, O., and Westgren, M. (1990). Fetal responses to different intensity levels of vibroacoustic stimulations. *Obstetrics and Gynecology*, **75**, 206–9.

Yoshida, A. and Chiba, Y. (1989). Neonate's vocal and facial expression and their changes during experimental playbacks of intra-uterine sounds. *Journal of Ethology*, **7**, 153–6.

Yoshida, A., Horio, H., Makikawa, Y., Chiba, Y., Asada, M., Hasegawa, T., Minami, T., and Itoigawa, N. (1988). Developmental changes in neonates' response to intra-uterine sounds. *Abstracts of IX Biennal Meetings of International Society for the Study of Behavioural Development*, p. 303.

Zimmer, E. Z., Divon, M. Y., Vilensky, A., Sarna, Z., Peretz, B. A., and Paldi, E. (1982). Maternal exposure to music and fetal activity. *European Journal of Obstetrics and Gynecology and Reproductive Biology*, **13**, 209–13.

PART II

From the Baby to the Infant

2

Musicality in infancy research: biological and cultural origins of early musicality

Hanuš Papoušek

1 INTRODUCTION: PERSPECTIVES OF INFANCY RESEARCH

Surprising as it may seem, the helpless, fragile human infant, incapable of speech, has inspired a considerable amount of successful research relevant to all developmental periods of human life. Methodological and conceptual difficulties, typical of interpretations of human infancy prior to the Second World War, seem to have sharpened interest in precise methods, interdisciplinary co-operation, and strict verification of former speculative concepts. New interpretations of human infancy pay more respect to evolutionary adaptation, interactions between biological and sociocultural factors, functional interrelationships, and dynamic processes. Infancy researchers have, on the one hand, profited from technological and conceptual progress in related sciences and, on the other hand, have themselves stimulated with relevant arguments developmental approaches in these sciences.

Musicologists may be interested to note that present-day infancy research pays increasing attention to the early perception, processing, and production of melodic sounds. The history of this interest is short; yet its objects represent some fundamental aspects of the arts, education, and culture that are going to be explained in the present chapter and explicitly documented in Chapter 4 by M. Papoušek. Although the relationship of any musical competence to early infancy may seem remote, predispositions for this competence are, in fact, related to those capabilities that differentiate humans from other animals, develop from both genetic and environmental factors, and emerge prior to the birth.

The musicological aspects of development have been historically neglected in comparison with those capabilities that humans share with other animals and that justify the use of animal models in studies on human development. Two circumstances have helped to bridge the resulting gaps. First, progress in neurosciences has brought about new interpretations of the hemispheric differentiation of functions in the brain in relation to the development of speech and consciousness. Second, being influenced by biologists' experience that development of a species can hardly be explained without studying species-specific means of evolutionary adaptation, infancy researchers have turned their attention to the ontogeny of human forms of communication, consciousness, and culture.

Speech, as a uniquely human form of communication, represents an unusually effective means of biological adaptation. It has allowed unprecedented possibilities in accumulation, integration, and distribution of information, it has enabled the development of specific forms of culture, and it has provided opportunities to overcome biological constraints (see Section 4 of this chapter). Yet, its beginnings during preverbal infancy have long remained unexplored. The former view of human infants as altricial organisms delayed in locomotion has been revised. Infants are now considered precocious due to their unique achievement in communicative development (Papoušek and Papoušek 1984). Interestingly, musicality has been found to play an important role in this development.

Communication develops in intimate connection with integrative abilities in infants, such as learning and cognition. Human forms of verbal symbolization participate in sociocultural integration and co-determine its higher levels, including the linguistically conscious and the culture-dependent levels of self-regulation. The transition from stimulus–response studies on infants to interactional research on infants within social and cultural environments has elucidated the importance of communicative development and the role of environmental support for this development. Parents—and caregivers in general—have been found to function as competent teachers of the mother tongue and mediators of cultural impacts (Papoušek and Papoušek 1984, 1987). The most relevant contributions to the development of communicative and integrative capacities in infants occur in non-conscious, intuitive educational interventions. Elucidation of these interrelations has confirmed the validity of the biological expectation that species-specific means of evolutionary adaptation are based on the coevolution of universal predispositions in both parental and filial populations, function early during ontogeny, and are controlled by non-conscious subsystems of behavioural regulation. The use and modifications of caregivers' infant-directed speech may serve as a typical example (Papoušek and Papoušek 1987; M. Papoušek, Chapter 4).

This perspective subsumes communicative development into a complex frame of the evolution of human mind and culture. At the same time, it points towards the biological origins of the aforementioned specific means of human adaptation. Comparative research has made it evident that partial predispositions for speech and rational thinking have precursors in the animal world, and that humans are unique in the possession of all the predispositions that otherwise exist as isolated capacities in other species. Humans are also unique in the ways in which their culture has exploited the potentials of abstract symbolization in permanent records of written information and the establishment of institutions for further improvement of communication. It is also important that crucial milestones of communicative and integrative capacities occur during the preverbal period of infancy. The involvement of musicality in these early developmental processes indicates that their interpretation may open new perspectives for speculations on the evolutionary origins and adaptive significance of human musicality. Moreover, the evidence of predispositions for musicality and of integrative competence in infants may also reopen the question of pedagogical utilization of early musical competence.

This chapter serves as an attempt, in the following three sections, to review contemporary evidence on the development of infant capacities, which may relate to the very beginning of human communication, thinking, or cultural integration, and to examine how far musicality (sensitivity for music, predispositions for processing musical experiences, and expressions of musical skills) is involved. The elucidation of its involvement may facilitate the detection of the biological roots of musicality since at least some may be common or parallel. For this reason, musicologists may profit from advances in studies on communication between infants and caregivers or on early mental development. Only recently, new empirical observations have indicated when and how a transition from biologically determined rearing interventions to culture-dependent interventions occurs. This new and difficult area of infancy research is going to be discussed in relation to its potential educational consequences.

2 EARLY MUSICALITY AND HUMAN COMMUNICATION

Communication is a universal characteristic of living organisms. If human musicality is involved in the ontogeny of communication, it might have been involved in a common process of evolutionary selection and share the following consequences with communication as well: innate anatomical and behavioural predispositions; universal presence across age, sex, or culture; functioning early during ontogeny; participation of non-conscious, intuitive forms of regulation allowing efficient performance; and coevolution of supportive behavioural programmes in social counterparts. Of course, any attempt to reconstruct the pre-historical past of music and musicality represents a step into a poorly documented realm of research where a lack of reliable evidence can often be compensated only with logical deductions and analogies. It seems potentially fruitful, however, to explore such a reconstruction because it could lead to useful theoretical insights.

Music has commonly been conceptualized in an intimate connection with emotionality because musical experience, perceptual or productive, can mediate human feelings even in cases where a verbal mediation fails. If musical sounds are produced by animals or even physical forces in the nature, interpretations have to be more cautious. Sounds elicited by movements of water or air can be perceived as information about physical circumstances by one listener but as nature's caprice by another. According to information theory, the information content in a signal primarily depends on the listener's capacity for perceiving and processing that signal. According to psychological theories, identical sounds can elicit different emotional feelings in the listener depending on previous experience, current context, state of mind, and attributable values. Eliciting sounds as such may have nothing in common with communicative intentions or emotional feelings as in the case of sounds produced by wind or water. Conversely, the physical qualities of sounds may play important roles in communication, because some qualities may be more suitable for communication across large distances whereas other qualities may allow rapid and fine patterning in proximal communication.

Thus, the role of musical elements in communication among living organisms depends on the physical and ecological circumstances under which some particular forms of acoustic communication have been selected in individual species. Infrasonic vocal sounds in large mammals (elephants or whales) enable communication across enormously large distances, whereas high-pitched signals are advantageous for proximal communication among birds in noisy coastal environments or among monkeys in tropical rain forests (Wilson 1975). Melodic contours penetrate through sound-absorbing spaces more successfully than phonetic elements. Auditory signals offer obvious advantages for communication under conditions that do not allow sufficient visual contact between communicating partners and such—vocal or non-vocal—signals can be produced in various frequency zones, rhythms, spectral structures, and melodic patterns. Combinations of these qualities are rich enough to allow species-typical signals and individual identification, as in the case of voiceprints. Vocal marking is only part of a universal communicative repertoire including chemical, electrical, tactile, or visual forms of marking that allow telling individuals apart. Vocal signals enable a particularly flexible, rapid, and complex communication, generated from a single organ and producible with lower energetic investment than behavioural displays in visual communication, which often require extensive movements of the entire body (Wilson 1975).

During evolution, individual species, including humans, have utilized the physical potentials of auditory communication for specific needs, such as a division of living space, foraging, reproduction, social organization, or care for progeny. For the perception and production of auditory signals, adequate organs and neural structures have been selected according to both universal, biological principles and specific adjustments to ecological conditions (Mayr 1971). Vocal sounds mostly function in intimate interrelationship with visually perceivable patterns of movement, particularly in the communication among birds or primates. In contrast to reptiles, the participation of vocal sounds in communication increased during the evolution of birds and mammals (McLean 1990). New structures in the brains and vocal tracts of these animals offered predispositions for the production of finely differentiated vocal sounds, for their processing, and for their use as differential symbols—verbal or musical—for various events, needs, risks, or social interchanges. Thus, the evolutionary background should not be disregarded in interpretations of the cultural significance of sounds perceived as musical by humans, nor in speculations on a predestined significance of certain musical elements in expressions of emotional states.

Communicative sounds in speechless individuals—non-human animals and human infants—have often been considered merely as expressions of affective states. However, every such signal carries three levels of information (Bühler 1934): expression of affective state; representation of communicative context; and an appeal addressed to the social environment. Recent studies of animal communication have led to similar interpretations (Marler *et al.* 1992). The capacity of the nervous system determines to what degree each of the levels is utilized for communicative purposes. In contrast to reptilian brains, additional limbic and hippocampal structures in mammalian brains link communication with more complex forms of care for progeny, including emotional bonding, the use of separation calls, and elementary forms of playful behaviour (McLean 1990). The complexity of related behavioural expressions varies among mammalian species and reaches a particularly high level of complexity and plasticity in primates. The adaptive significance of vocal communication has resulted not only in innate anatomical predispositions but also in a strong intrinsic motivation for its use in primates, including humans with their cultural interests in vocal music.

The use of musical sounds as supplemental parallels to verbal communication persists in modern time, for instance, in the use of hunting horns, post horns, military trumpets, or drums for communication across distances that are too large to allow broadcasting of phonetic elements. Loud yodelling in the Alps or yelled–sung messages in the Carpathians serve similar purposes and enable vocal communication across hundreds of metres (Busnel and Classe 1976). Similarly, rhythm and tuning of drums are used by natives in the African savannahs, and whistled languages (Silbos) among Mexican indians or natives on the Canary Islands. The Mazateco indians of Oaxaca use tone features in their Silbo that are similar to those of their tonal language. In contrast, natives in La Gomera use an articulated Silbo, consistent with their dialect of Spanish which is a stress language (Busnel and Classe 1976).

Vocal sounds can be modified in the same qualities for both communicative or musical purposes, namely, in pitch, intensity, timbre, melody, rhythm, and harmony. Human speech includes additional phonetic qualities that enable production of consonants and syllables. All the resulting components may then be concatenated according to grammatical or syntactical rules. Human speech and vocal music may seem to represent two different categories; however, the intimate inter-relationships between them make separation difficult. It is also difficult to say which of them appeared earlier during human evolution. Although both language and music subserve communication and share analogous characteristics, such as arranging sound patterns in time, there is no reason for the conclusion that processes underlying music and language are homologous. Conversely, analogies often function as pointers for further research and may indicate where to search for evolutionary origins. One obvious link between language and music is the dual function of the human vocal tract: it serves both as a speech organ and as a musical instrument. For this reason, its early functioning attracts increasing attention in infancy research.

The qualities of vocal sounds can be richly varied independently of words or other forms of abstract symbolization as is typical for some non-human animals, birds in particular. Listening to bird songs, we may find them musical, although birds may perceive them as mere information on the partner's territorial claims and reproductive competence, on available food, or as alarming signals of environmental dangers. Mammalian vocal communication may also sound melodic and yet its meaning may be as limited as in bird songs. Among primates, for instance, singing exists in gibbons, but their songs convey information as rigid as that in bird songs (Marshall and Marshall 1976), and there is no evidence that gibbons playfully modify songs or attribute musicality to them.

During human evolution, the aforementioned predispositions have been selected in a particularly advantageous combination. Brain functions have reached an unparalleled level of complexity, allowing both complex cognitive operations with words and playful or creative modifications of acoustic elements in vocal music. With such flexibility, humans can create an internal world of symbolic representations where all aspects of life experience and accumulated information are segregated and integrated into novel concepts, expressed in verbal or musical symbols, and shared with the social environment. The human vocal tract includes adequate space in its supralaryngeal parts for rapid and subtle modulation of vocal sounds (Lieberman 1984). In addition, a comparable co-ordination of hand and finger movements allows parallel expressions in non-vocal forms, such as in sign languages or in written or otherwise coded forms of communication. Consequently, humans can use combinations of vocal sounds with bodily movements for an infinite repertoire of expressions. This advantage undoubtedly contributed to the evolution of human cultures, including the sciences, the arts, morals, and religions, for which no parallels are known in other animals.

Musical elements participate in the process of communicative development very early; in fact, recent research has suggested that they pave the way to linguistic capacities earlier than phonetic elements can do so (Papoušek *et al.* 1985). A brief outline of the development of human vocalization may elucidate this conjecture (see also M. Papoušek, Chapter 4).

The newborn comes with a fully developed, innate capacity for crying, but speech-related vocal sounds develop later and have to be learned from scratch. Crying—a long-distance signal of distress—is comparable to distress cries characterizing mammalian newborns with a considerable universality, and consists of a pre-programmed pattern, including adequately prolonged expiration. Speech sounds only partly depend on innate predispositions during preverbal development; relatively soon (around 4 months, according to de Boysson-Bardies *et al.* 1984), they are influenced by environmental language or singing, and through them by two pillars of human culture—rational thought and artistic creation. Although the infant always learns the language of its cultural niche, those whose language is to be acquired are rarely able to explain how they can mediate the cultural impact to infants incapable of speech. This enigma was solved when researchers concentrated on those parental predispositions for caregiving that coevolved in forms of non-conscious behavioural tendencies (Papoušek and Papoušek 1978, 1982, 1987). Parents display them in the presence of an infant unconsciously without rational decisions.

Microanalyses of the parents' supportive interventions reveal universal patterns of behaviour in which parents offer models of vocal sounds, encourage and reward their imitation in infants, and didactically adjust interventions to the momentary level of infant progress in vocalization (for details see M. Papoušek, Chapter 4). Parents consistently guide the infant towards at least three levels of vocal expertise that gradually emerge during preverbal vocal development in infants (H. Papoušek 1994). The first level is achieved when the initial fundamental voicing, superimposed on the unmodified momentary rate of breathing, has developed into prolonged, euphonic cooing sounds at around the age of 8 weeks, that is, when the infant has become capable of producing and modulating the earliest melodic vocal sounds. They have often been interpreted as mere expressions of emotional states; however, interactional research has revealed an important facet of communicative and cognitive development in them (Papoušek and Papoušek 1981, 1987). Two-month-old infants start phrasing vocalization with the help of such modulations, according to Lynch and co-workers (1995).

In infant-directed speech, parents intuitively guide infant vocalization towards melodic modulations, display prominent models for them (Papoušek and Papoušek 1981; Fernald and Simon 1984), and use the melodic profile of infant-directed speech as the first categorical messages about the infant's momentary vital circumstances. Thus, parents support the processes of abstraction and prepare the infant for the future use of verbal categorical messages (Papoušek *et al.* 1985). However, the infant can also use melodic modulations for vocal play and, later on, for singing (Papoušek and Papoušek 1981). This may be the reason why melodic modulations remain in the infant's vocal repertoire even after the acquisition of words (Papoušek 1992). Parents intuitively support infant use of melodic contours for vocal play as well and often sing nursery rhymes or lullabies. Under favourable conditions, preverbal infants develop a capacity of imitating nursery songs or improvising their own melodies, and start learning songs with lyrics when they can use words and simple sentences (Papoušek and Papoušek 1981).

The second level of infant vocal expertise concerns the production of consonants and the segmentation of the vocal stream into syllables. Learning results in the appearance of a distinct developmental milestone: the production of reduplicated canonical syllables (Oller 1986). Mothers facilitate this development by increasingly stimulating infants with rhythmic games and combining them with superimposed rhythmic melodies (Papoušek and Papoušek 1991). These forms of intuitive intervention can influence both speech acquisition and the development of musicality.

Canonical syllables seem to signal to parents that the time has come for a new type of didactic intervention concerning the third level of vocal expertise, namely, the declarative function of vocal symbols and the acquisition of words (Papoušek and Papoušek 1987). Whereas prior to canonical syllables parents intuitively and almost exclusively supported procedural aspects of speech and taught infants how to produce proper vocal sounds or use proper dialogic skills, they now immediately take canonical syllables as potential protowords, attribute them meanings, and use them in a declarative manner for naming persons, objects, and events in the infant's microenvironment (Ferguson 1964; Papoušek and Papoušek 1981; Locke 1986; M. Papoušek 1994). When the infant can speak the first distinct words, parents start using rational explanations and instructions more and more frequently; conscious, rational thinking and cultural impact become increasingly evident in parental support of the infant's verbal competence.

Several studies confirm the effectiveness of such parental interventions. A significant delay in the onset of canonical syllables in deaf, otherwise normally developing infants in comparison with hearing infants (Oller and Eilers 1988) illustrates the environmental facilitation of maturational processes. Specifically designed comparisons of twins with singletons (Bornstein 1985) examine an interesting natural experiment; they reveal a significant deficit in maternal didactic interventions in 5-month-old twins, and a significant delay in verbal communication and cognitive capacities in 13-month-old twins. Although it is hardly possible to convincingly separate interventions in intuitive parenting that specifically support only speech acquisition, playfulness or musicality in preverbal infants, these directions appear to diverge under the influence of cultural factors at the beginning of verbal communication.

3 EARLY MUSICALITY AND THE HUMAN MIND

Incompetent in locomotion and foraging as they are at birth, human infants master the first words and sentences in 1 or 2 years and become capable of communication in a complexity that surpasses that of all animal forms. Such an achievement is not plausible without adequate progress in infant learning and cognitive abilities. Initial studies of infant conditioning documented both capacities and constraints in very early learning, and showed that learning capacities quickly improved during the first months of life as a result of both maturation and practice (Papoušek 1967). A closer look at the infant's typical microenvironment revealed few favourable physical circumstances but plenty of social interactions in which the infant could practise integrative abilities. Interactional dialogues include innumerable episodes in which caregivers make themselves predictable, controllable, and contingent, initiate instrumental learning, and affectively reward successful learning (Papoušek and Papoušek 1984).

Studies on infant perception and production of speech sounds elucidate the supportive potentials of vocal interchanges in additional details and confirm the early involvement of musical elements. The human newborn enters the social world with an adult-like hearing organ—the inner ear—and with some intra-uterine acoustic experience that allows the newborn, for instance, to recognize the sound of a familiar voice (DeCasper and Fifer 1980), story (DeCasper and Spence 1986), or melody (Cooper and Aslin 1989). Studies of prenatal perception (for more details see J.-P. Lecanuet, Chapter 1) show that near-term fetuses can perceive a difference between female and male voices, most probably due to differences in pitch, and that fetuses display learning abilities in the form of habituation while processing voice signals (Granier-Deferre *et al.* 1992). Melodic modulations of vowels have a higher chance of being perceived by fetuses than consonants and phonetic parameters (Busnel and Granier-Deferre 1983). Two-day-old newborns already show a preference for their native language, probably due to prenatal rather than postnatal experience with intonation patterns (Moon *et al.* 1993).

Since the introduction of reliable measures, such as the head-turning method (Papoušek 1961; Fantz 1963), differential sucking (Sameroff 1965), or auditory evoked brainstem responses and cortical evoked potentials (Hecox 1975), it is possible to study auditory sensitivity, absolute thresholds, and their age-dependent changes. Available data suggest that human newborns are much more sensitive than previously thought (Olsho *et al.* 1987) and that young infants are less sensitive to low frequencies than to high frequencies, both in absolute terms and as compared to adults (Trehub *et al.* 1980; Schneider *et al.* 1980; Sinnott *et al.* 1983). At frequencies above 4000 Hz, infants perform even better than adults. Infants detect frequency changes of 2 and 1 per cent for low and high frequencies, respectively, are sensitive to increments of loudness by 3 dB, and perceive pitch and timbre similarly to adults. Such competence is not specific to humans as it exists even in animals with less complex nervous structures. Conversely, sophisticated methods have already enabled approaches to questions as complex as the participation of the Gestalt principle of frequency proximity in perceptual segregation (Demany 1982; Fassbender 1993). A detailed survey of this new area of research is presented in Chapter 3 by C. Fassbender.

A very careful search for the factors of early mental development has recently revealed 'exploratory competence' as a predictive factor different from those subserved by verbal—representational abilities (Tamis-LeMonda and Bornstein 1993). Analyses indicate a genetic basis of this factor on the one hand, and a relation to competent play on the other. At the same time, they clearly illustrate how important it is to keep concepts of mental development open to consideration of infant play; it may be relevant to the evolution of both culture and music in humans. Playful integration of experience seems to be based upon processes underlying not only play but also creativity, discovery, or humour in later life, according to the author's view (Papoušek 1979). Playfulness has not been documented in insects, fishes, amphibians, and reptiles but serves an important role in the socialization of mammals: the more intelligent and social the species, the more elaborate the play (Wilson 1975).

Biological or behavioural definitions of play are rather difficult. Animal play is often viewed as one form of activity in which the young train to acquire future adult skills without immediate risks or responsibilities. Students of human play attribute various degrees of functional significance to it: some authors stress observable structures (Hutt 1966); others consider play as a crucial factor in the evolution of cultures (Huizinga 1955) or as a process parallel to exploration and problem-solving (Bruner 1968).

The present author conceptualizes infants' playfulness as a particular capacity, supplementary to the fundamental integrative processes of learning and cognition (Papoušek 1979). When confronted with a novel event, the infant tries to accumulate enough information on it in order to conceptualize it as 'known'. The initial concepts may only be crude assumptions, sometimes based upon false premises or superstitions; yet, they can protect the infant against fear of the 'unknown'. With time, initial concepts may become boring and the infant may show the capability of reopening them for further exploration under pressure-free conditions to avoid boredom. Modifications and transformations of existing trivial concepts move away from triviality towards innovation, creativity, or humorous surprise. These higher-level operations are perhaps homogeneous during infancy but may be attributable and essential to play, artistic creativity, discovery, inventiveness, or humour later in life.

The author's concept on a higher level of integrative processes essential to playfulness subsumes: participation of emotions (indicating intrinsic motivation); universality (indicating adaptive significance); relation to the precursors in animal play (indicating biological origins) and to artistic or scientific competencies in adult humans (indicating culture-specific adaptation); and coping with internal states of fear or boredom (indicating human-specific forms of self-regulation). From this perspective, infant play may be an early manifestation of capacities playing important roles in human life and should not be underestimated.

Consequently, if musicality can be encompassed, this concept of playfulness may point the way to verifications of some fundamental aspects of human musicality, such as its biological roots, adaptive significance, intrinsic motivation, involvement in crucial aspects of biological and cultural adaptation, and self-regulatory efficiency. A similar approach has been helpful in the case of human communication where it revealed a functional involvement of musical elements in initial forms of vocal communication between preverbal infants and caregivers (Papoušek and Papoušek 1987).

Unlike that of animals, playfulness in humans is characterized by its striking independence of developmental periods and the behavioural skills necessary for survival. With a remarkable freedom, humans can play at all ages and literally with everything including intrinsic symbols, musical elements, mathematical formulae, or daydreams. They can develop any amount of play situations with various sets of rules and degrees of complexity. Eventually, they can professionalize or commercialize play, or even become addicted to it and disregard vital needs. In psychology, the stress-free, playful refinement of one's current concepts with its Attic salt and creative or inventive potentials has been under-researched, due to the overestimation of rational thinking and IQ tests. In contrast to academic psychology, the layperson's concepts of intelligence consistently embody practical problem-solving, creativity, and social skills in addition to rational knowledge (Sternberg *et al.* 1981). Thus, in terms of child-rearing and formal education, both theoretical and practical reasons point to the necessity of bridging current gaps in knowledge.

As explained in the preceding section, rich melodic modifications characterize dialogues between infants and caregivers and appear under circumstances that lend parent–infant interchanges features of teacher–pupil interchanges. During the first 2–3 months, the infant's repertoire develops from brief grating or harsh sounds to longer euphonic musical sounds approximating pure, harmoniously voiced tones (Papoušek and Papoušek 1981). In the parent's—and generally in every caregiver's—infant-directed speech, strongly accentuated prosodic elements, intonational contours, stress, and rhythmicity give the voice prominent features of musical qualities (Garnica 1977; Fernald 1984). Melodies are strikingly expressive with repetitions, frequent glides, prevalence of basic harmonic intervals (thirds, fourths, fifths, and octaves), and sometimes dramatic changes in intensity. Large numbers of repetitions allow even young infants to conceptualize, predict, anticipatorily answer, and control such elementary pieces of parental music. However, as soon as the infant's attention decreases, parents tend to modify patterns, re-capture infant attention, and guide the infant to reopening and enriching the original concepts. Microanalyses reveal many such episodes of integrative practising, both in parent–infant dialogues, and in infant monologues (Papoušek and Papoušek 1981). Practising concerns simple vocal play during the first postpartum months and more complex patterns of nursery rhymes and songs after the sixth month; it is mostly based upon intuitive predispositions, the biological origins of which were explained in Section 2. This situation changes with the infant's first words; they seem to open the way for verbal, rational, conscious, and culture-dependent guidance.

4 EARLY MUSICALITY AND HUMAN CULTURE

Culture is neither an entirely human, nor an entirely language-dependent phenomenon; its precursors—and indicators of biological origins—have been documented in other primates. Precultural phenomena in the Japanese macaque involve manual skills that rapidly spread mainly among the young due to observational learning and imitation, for instance, innovative washing of sand from potatoes (Kawai 1963), 'placer mining' of wheat, or digging up peanuts (Tsumori 1967). In humans, cultures function with high degrees of freedom and independence of real-life situations and in close interrelationships with languages and symbolic representation; thus, they reach unprecedented levels of complexity and adaptive significance.

The use of abstract and hierarchically integrable words—spoken or permanently recorded—enables an accumulation and systematic integration of vast amounts of information. Most human cultures have institutions that purposefully collect and distribute information in various areas of human activities, including musical engagement and education, and thus enormously facilitate the learning of skills and acquisition of knowledge. The possession of collective knowledge lends human culture a new level of self-regulation surpassing that of an individual. Human ontogeny advances from elementary autonomic or vagal (Porges 1991) self-regulation, through prelinguistic and preconscious regulation, toward conscious linguistic and rational self-regulation, and finally towards cultural integration in which individuals may subordinate themselves to more competent institutions. Along the way, infants profit not only from parental experience but also from the entire cultural heritage in ways that are not available to any other species.

Expressions of early musicality have been recently approached in studies on the early perception of musical patterns and on infant-directed singing. According to Trehub's review (1990), infants can detect changes in melodic contours, temporal patterning, pitch, and timbre. They discriminate different melodic patterns on the basis of relational information at the age of 5 or 6 months (Chang and Trehub 1977; Lynch and Eilers 1992), differentiate rising and falling two-tone sequences with as small a difference as one semitone (Thorpe 1986), and sensitively detect violations of contours but not transpositions or contour-preserving transformations of contours. The infant's representation of melodies is abstract, with contour playing a critical role. Infants can also, like adults, discriminate between contrasting temporal and rhythmic sequences (Morrongiello 1984), inasmuch as they impose rhythmic patterning on melodic sequences of equal duration of tones and intertone intervals

(Thorpe and Trehub 1989) and tend to group sequences on the basis of Gestalt principles.

Infants also discriminate between contrasting timbres based on variable energy distribution across the overtones of a complex sound (Trehub *et al.* 1990). According to Clarkson and Clifton (1985), infants respond equivalently to distinct tonal complexes that signal common pitch for adults, but differentially to those that adults perceive as contrasting pitches. In general, infants detect subtle changes in musical patterns by means of the same global and relational principles of perceptual organization used by adult listeners. Because these principles are universal across age and sex, and function early during ontogeny, they seem to be based upon biological predispositions.

As explained in relation to preverbal communication, parents tend to utilize musical elements to support the acquisition of speech in infants. However, melodic contours in infant-directed speech may also affect behavioural/emotional states in infants, enhance the attractiveness of nursery games, and specifically support the development of musicality (Papoušek and Papoušek 1981). Thus, it is legitimate to ask what kind of music would be suitable for infants. Trehub (1990) comes to the hypothetical conclusion that such music should be similar to what infants most frequently hear under natural, everyday circumstances, namely, the voice of young females or children in infant-directed speech or nursery songs. Accordingly, such auditory enrichment should correspond to an optimum in infant perceptual competence for simple unidirectional contours with few changes in rise–fall pitch direction, modal values ranging from 233 to 587 Hz, and temporal structures based on a rate of 2.5 tones per second with intervals of 0.8 to 1.4 second. Trehub considers the human voice to be more suitable for infants than other musical instruments, and occasional minor modifications in individual parameters as desirable to capitalize on the infants' ability to differentiate between contrasting patterns.

In addition to Trehub's recommendations, Papoušek and Papoušek (1981, 1987) stress the didactic aspects of musical stimulation provided by caregivers directly and with respect to feedback cues from infants. Such stimulation is contingent on infant signs of interest, adjusted to infant attention, and easy for the infants themselves to conceptualize, predict, and control. Importantly, it also fulfils the aforementioned guidance towards playfulness and creativity. Parents sensitively respond to changes in infant emotional/behavioural state and modify singing or musical elements in their speech so as to either maintain quiet and active waking states in infants or to facilitate transitions to sleep. Thus, they reduce the proportion of transitory infant states characterized by upset and a poor level of integrative and communicative abilities (Papoušek and Papoušek 1987). These aspects of support to early musicality cannot be sufficiently replaced by reproduced music.

Trehub and co-workers document a distinctive style in infant-directed singing, some aspects of which are recognizable across cultures and musical systems (Trehub *et al.* 1993*a*). Although the structure of songs across cultures provides little evidence of musical universals, adult listeners can differentiate infant-directed songs from those performed in the infant's absence. The discrimination is better in relation to songs from the listener's own culture but still significant in relation to songs from a foreign culture. Notably, women perform better than men in these discriminations.

Lullabies are particularly suitable for studies of the universal qualities of infant-directed songs because they are performed under comparable conditions and in intimate interactional situations. In comparative studies, adult listeners successfully differentiated lullabies from other songs across four foreign cultures as long as they listened to 'typical' lullabies; however, they misidentified 'atypical' lullabies (Trehub *et al.* 1993*b*). The crucial parameter of 'typicality' appeared to be a higher 'simplicity' score. The identification of typical lullabies was successful even with the lyrics and voice quality electronically removed from the songs.

A better understanding of the intimate interrelationship between the musical qualities of vocal sounds in songs and speech may supersede the question as to which of the two capacities appeared first during evolution. In human cultures, both music and languages are continually evolving and supposedly carry adaptive potentials; therefore, it may be more important to prove the relevance of those potentials and derive conclusions for the sake of adequate care for the next generations of infants.

ACKNOWLEDGEMENTS

The author's research and preparation of this publication have been kindly supported by the Alexander von Humboldt Foundation. Annabel Cohen and Michael P. Lynch reviewed the manuscript and contributed valuable recommendations.

REFERENCES

Bornstein, M. H. (1985). How infant and mother jointly contribute to developing cognitive competence in the child. *Proceedings of the National Academy of Sciences, USA*, **82**, 7470–3.

Bruner, J. S. (1968). *Processes of cognitive growth: infancy*. Barre Publishers, Barre, Massachusetts.

Bühler, K. (1934). *Sprachtheorie*. Fischer, Jena.

Busnel, R. G. and Classe, A. (1976). *Whistled languages*. Springer-Verlag, Berlin.

Busnel, M. C. and Granier-Deferre, C. (1983). And what of fetal audition? In *The behavior of human infants* (ed. A. Oliveiro and M. Zapella), pp. 93–126. Plenum Press, New York.

Chang, H. W. and Trehub, S. E. (1977). Auditory processing of relational information by young infants. *Journal of Experimental Child Psychology*, **24**, 324–31.

Clarkson, M. G. and Clifton, R. K. (1985). Infant pitch perception: evidence for responding to pitch categories and the missing fundamental. *Journal of the Acoustic Society of America*, **77**, 1521–8.

Cooper, R. P. and Aslin, R. N. (1989). The language environment of the young infant: implications for early perceptual development. *Canadian Journal of Psychology*, **43**, 247–65.

de Boysson-Bardies, B., Sagart, L., and Durand, C. (1984). Discernible differences in the babbling of infants according to target language. *Journal of Child Language*, **11**, 1–15.

DeCasper, A. J. and Fifer, W. P. (1980). Of human bonding: newborns prefer their mothers' voices. *Science*, **208**, 1174–6.

DeCasper, A. J. and Spence, M. J. (1986). Newborns prefer a familiar story over an unfamiliar one. *Infant Behavior and Development*, **9**, 133–50.

Demany, L. (1982). Auditory stream segregation in infancy. *Infant Behavior and Development*, **5**, 261–76.

Fantz, R. L. (1963). Pattern vision in newborn infants. *Science*, **140**, 296–7.

Fassbender, C. (1993). *Auditory grouping and segregation processes in infancy*. Kaste Verlag, Norderstedt, Germany.

Ferguson, C. A. (1964). Baby talk in six languages. *American Psychologist*, **66**, 103–14.

Fernald, A. (1984). The perceptual and affective salience of mothers' speech to infants. In *The origins and growth of communication* (ed. L. Feagans, D. Garvey, and R. Golinkoff), pp. 5–29. Ablex, Norwood, New Jersey.

Fernald, A. and Simon, T. (1984). Expanded intonation contours in mothers' speech to newborns. *Developmental Psychology*, **20**, 104–13.

Garnica, O. K. (1977). Some prosodic and paralinguistic features of speech to young children. In *Talking to children: language input and acquisition* (ed. C. E. Snow and C. A. Ferguson), pp. 63–88. Cambridge University Press, Cambridge.

Granier-Deferre, C., Lecanuet, J.-P., Jacquet, A.-Y., and Busnel, M.-C. (1992). Prenatal discrimination of complex auditory stimulations. Poster presentation at the 8th Meeting of the International Conference on Infant Studies, Miami.

Hecox, K. (1975). Electrophysiological correlates of human auditory development. In *Infant perception: from sensation to cognition*, Vol. 2. *Perception of space, speech and sound* (ed. L. B. Cohen and P. Salapatek), pp. 151–91. Academic Press, New York.

Huizinga, J. (1955). *Homo ludens*. Beacon, Boston.

Hutt, C. (1966). Exploration and play in children. *Symposia of the Zoological Society of London*, **18**, 61–81.

Kawai, M. (1963). On the newly acquired behaviors of the natural troop of Japanese monkeys on Koshima Island. *Primates*, **4**, 113–15.

Lieberman, P. (1984). *The biology and evolution of language*. Harvard University Press, Cambridge, Massachusetts.

Locke, J. L. (1986). The linguistic significance of babbling. In *Precursors of early speech*, Wenner-Gren International Symposium Series, Vol. 44 (ed. B. Lindblom and R. Zetterström), pp. 143–60. Macmillan, Hampshire.

Lynch, M. P. and Eilers, R. E. (1992). A study of perceptual development for musical tuning. *Perception and Psychophysics*, **52**, 599–608.

Lynch, M. P., Oller, D. K., Steffens, M. L., and Buder, E. (1995). Phrasing in prelinguistic vocalizations. *Developmental Psychology*, **28**, 3–25.

Marler, P., Evans, C. S., and Hauser, M. D. (1992). Animal signals: motivational, referential, or both? In *Nonverbal vocal communication: comparative and developmental aspects* (ed. H. Papousek, U. Jürgens, and M. Papousek), pp. 66–86. Cambridge University Press, Cambridge.

Marshall, J. T. and Marshall, E. R. (1976). Gibbons and their songs. *Science*, **199**, 235–7.

Mayr, E. (1971). *Population, species and evolution*. Belknap Press of Harvard University Press, Cambridge, Massachusetts.

McLean, P. D. (1990). *The triune brain in evolution: role in paleocerebral functions*. Plenum Press, New York.

Moon, C., Cooper, R. P., and Fifer, W. P. (1993). Two-day-olds prefer their native language. *Infant Behavior and Development*, **16**, 495–500.

Morrongiello, B. A. (1984). Auditory temporal pattern perception in 6- and 12-month-old infants. *Developmental Psychology*, **20**, 441–8.

Oller, D. K. (1986). Metaphonology and infant vocalizations. In *Precursors of early speech*, Wenner-Gren International Symposium Series, Vol. 44 (ed. B. Lindblom and R. Zetterström), pp. 21–35. Macmillan, Hampshire.

Oller, D. K. and Eilers, R. E. (1988). The role of audition in infant babbling. *Child Development*, **59**, 441–9.

Olsho, L. W., Koch, E. G., Halpin, C. F., and Carter, E. A. (1987). An observer-based psychoacoustic procedure for use with young infants. *Developmental Psychology*, **23**, 627–40.

Papoušek, H. (1961). Conditioned head rotation reflexes in infants in the first months of life. *Acta Paediatrica Scandinavica*, **50**, 565–76.

Papoušek, H. (1967). Experimental studies of appetitional behavior in human newborns and infants. In *Early behavior: comparative and developmental approaches* (ed. H. W. Stevenson, E. H. Hess, and H. L. Rheingold), pp. 249–77. Wiley, New York.

Papoušek, H. (1979). From adaptive responses to social cognition: the learning view of development. In *Psychological development from infancy: image to intention* (ed. M. H. Bornstein and W. Kessen), pp. 251–67. Erlbaum, Hillsdale, New Jersey.

Papoušek, H. (1994). Emergence of musicality and its adaptive significance. In *Music, speech and the developing brain* (ed. C. Faienza), pp. 111–35. Guerini e Associati, Milan.

Papoušek, H. and Papoušek, M. (1978). Interdisciplinary parallels in studies of early human behavior: from physical to cognitive needs, from attachment to dyadic education. *International Journal of Behavioral Development*, **1**, 37–49.

Papoušek, H. and Papoušek, M. (1982). Integration into the social world: survey of research. In *Psychobiology of the human newborn* (ed. P. M. Stratton), pp. 367–90. Wiley, London.

Papoušek, H. and Papoušek, M. (1984). Learning and cognition in the everyday life of human infants. In *Advances in the study of behavior*, Vol. 14 (ed. J. S. Rosenblatt), pp. 127–63. Academic Press, New York.

Papoušek, H. and Papoušek, M. (1987). Intuitive parenting: a dialectic counterpart to the infant's integrative competence. In *Handbook of infant development* (2nd edn) (ed. J. D. Osofsky), pp. 669–720. Wiley, New York.

Papoušek, M. (1992). Early ontogeny of vocal communication in parent–infant interactions. In *Nonverbal vocal communication: comparative and developmental aspects* (ed. H. Papoušek, U. Jürgens, and M. Papoušek), pp. 230–61. Cambridge University Press, Cambridge.

Papoušek, M. (1994). *Vom ersten Schrei zum ersten Wort. Anfänge der Sprachentwicklung in der vorsprachlichen Kommunikation.* [From the first crying to the first word. The beginnings of speech development in the preverbal communication.] [In German.] Verlag H. Huber, Berne.

Papoušek, M. and Papoušek, H. (1981). Musical elements in the infant's vocalizations: their significance for communication, cognition and creativity. In *Advances in infancy research*, Vol. 1 (ed. L. P. Lipsitt), pp. 163–224. Ablex, Norwood, New Jersey.

Papoušek, M. and Papoušek, H. (1991). Preverbal vocal communication from zero to one: preparing the ground for language acquisition. In *Perspectives on infant development: contributions from German-speaking countries* (ed. M. E. Lamb and H. Keller), pp. 299–328. Erlbaum, Hillsdale, New Jersey.

Papoušek, M., Papoušek, H., and Bornstein, M. H. (1985). The naturalistic vocal environment of young infants: on the significance of homogeneity and variability in parental speech. In *Social perception in infants* (ed. T. Field and N. Fox), pp. 269–97. Ablex, Norwood, New Jersey.

Porges, S. W. (1991). Vagal tone: an autonomic mediator of affect. In *The development of emotion regulation and dysregulation* (ed. J. Garber and K. A. Dodge), pp. 111–28. Cambridge University Press, Cambridge.

Sameroff, A. J. (1965). An apparatus for recording sucking and controlling feeding in the first days of life. *Psychonomic Science*, **2**, 355–6.

Schneider, B. A., Trehub, S. E., and Bull, D. (1980). High-frequency sensitivity in infants. *Science*, **207**, 1003–4.

Sinnott, J. M., Pisoni, D. B., and Aslin, R. M. (1983). A comparison of pure tone auditory thresholds in human infants and adults. *Infant Behavior and Development*, **6**, 3–17.

Sternberg, R. J., Conway, B., Ketron, J., and Bernstein, M. (1981). People's conceptions of intelligence. *Journal of Personality and Social Psychology*, **41**, 37–55.

Tamis-LeMonda, C. S. and Bornstein, M. H. (1993). Antecedents of exploratory competence at one year. *Infant Behavior and Development*, **16**, 423–39.

Thorpe, L. A. (April 1986). Infants categorize rising and falling pitch. Paper presented at the 5th International Conference on Infant Studies, Los Angeles.

Thorpe, L. A. and Trehub, S. E. (1989). The duration illusion and auditory grouping in infancy. *Developmental Psychology*, **25**, 122–7.

Trehub, S. E. (1990). The perception of musical patterns by human infants: the provision of similar patterns by their parents. In *Comparative perception*, Vol. 1. *Basic mechanisms* (ed. M. A. Berkley and W. C. Stebbins), pp. 429–59. Wiley, New York.

Trehub, S. E., Schneider, B. A., and Endman, M. (1980). Developmental changes in infants' sensitivity to octave-band noises. *Journal of Experimental Child Psychology*, **29**, 283–93.

Trehub, S. E., Endman, M., and Thorpe, L. A. (1990). Infants' perception of timbre: classification of complex tones by spectral structure. *Journal of Experimental Child Psychology*, **49**, 300–13.

Trehub, S. E., Unyk, A. M., and Trainor, L. J. (1993*a*). Maternal singing in cross-cultural perspective. *Infant Behavior and Development*, **16**, 285–95.

Trehub, S. E., Unyk, A. M., and Trainor, L .J. (1993*b*), Adults identify infant-directed music across cultures. *Infant Behavior and Development*, **16**, 193–211.

Tsumori, A. (1967). Newly acquired behavior and social interactions of Japanese monkeys. In *Social communication among primates* (ed. S. A. Altmann), pp. 207–19. University of Chicago Press, Chicago.

Wilson, E. O. (1975). *Sociobiology. The new synthesis*. The Belknap Press of Harvard University Press. Cambridge, Massachusetts.

3

Infants' auditory sensitivity towards acoustic parameters of speech and music

Christoph Fassbender

1 INTRODUCTION

Human perception is faced with the task of achieving accurate and meaningful mental representations of the objects and events in the environment. Distal acoustical objects and events provide information that is encoded in the form of sound waves. The sound waves, as proximal stimuli, reach our senses and yield information about our environment. Perception has to use this information to construct a valid mental representation of the outer world. In the auditory domain, many interwoven sounds reach the human ear at the same time. Nevertheless, one perceives an organized and ordered auditory environment. Sound sources are perceived as distinct from each other and placed at certain locations. One is able to follow and understand the linguistic message of a speaker even when it is very noisy and even in situations where many people are talking. In order to achieve a valid mental representation for higher processes to work on, perceptual processes must group together those sounds, for example, that emanate from one speaker and that contain the linguistic message and they must group these sounds separately from all those that emanate from other locations and that do not belong to the linguistic message. There are many cues in the proximal stimulus that can be used to achieve an accurately organized perceptual representation as long as the organism is sensitive to these cues. For example, binaural cues, such as interaural-time differences, interaural-intensity differences, and interaural-phase differences, all yield information about the location of a sound source in the environment.

The literature on infants' abilities to localize sounds reveals great developmental improvements in several areas of this ability (Muir *et al.* 1979; Clifton *et al.* 1981, 1984; Morrongiello and Rocca 1987*a,b*; Nozza

1987; Clifton 1992). Newborns turn their head in response to sound sources, but before they are 6 months old this behaviour does not occur with precision and reliability. Motor development certainly contributes to this improvement but it is assumed to reflect primarily the maturation of higher, cortically located processes (Morrongiello and Rocca 1987*a*). Thus, newborns and very young infants may not be able to use the acoustic cues that signal location, at least not to the same degree as adults. Newborns and young infants also lack knowledge about, for example, the syntactic structure and semantic content of a linguistic message. Knowledge about the syntax and semantics of language guide human adults in their perception of spoken language.

In general, because of physical constraints, sound sources in the natural environment do not emit sounds that vary across a broad range. Rather, they emit sounds that temporarily cohere in their frequencies, amplitudes, and spectral content. A perceptual system that is sensitive to the temporal coherence of these stimulus attributes and to the acoustic cues that indicate location should be able to form sound elements coming from one source into a coherent stream of information and separate it from other sound elements that come from different sources. The question here is whether or not infants are sensitive to the temporal coherence of stimulus attributes. Without such abilities, how could an infant follow the mother's voice and filter out linguistic aspects relevant for language acquisition such as prosodic contours, phrases, words, phonemes, and vowels, for example? And how could an infant follow music and discriminate aspects relevant for musical acculturation and learning such as melodic countour, diatonic structure, and musical and rhythmic phrases?

In the following attempt to provide answers to this question, or at least to certain aspects of it, I will review the literature on infants' auditory sensitivity concerning absolute thresholds, masked thresholds, and relative thresholds for frequency as well as for sensitivity to changes in pitch and timbre of complex sounds. When these stimulus attributes are available to the infant, they may play an important role in the perceptual organization of the auditory environment. Second, therefore, I will review research on auditory grouping and segregation processes and discuss which auditory streaming factors are available to the infant for organizing the perceptual space. Third, I will discuss the role that auditory grouping and the segregation process may play in infants' perception of speech and music.

2 AUDITORY SENSITIVITY IN INFANTS

Research on auditory sensitivity in infants before the 1970s had mainly observed overt reactions to sound stimulation and therefore yielded only rough estimates of infants' sensitivity to sound (for review, see Fassbender 1993). For example, sucking was inhibited in newborns and 2–5-month-old infants when stimulated with various sounds produced by organ pipes, a harmonica, and a whistle of less than 70 dB SPL (Bronshtein *et al*. 1958, cited in Eisenberg 1976).

Unfortunately, these early studies could not be easily compared with one another. They used many different behavioural responses to investigate responses to auditory sounds, such as general behavioural arousal (for example, Brackbill 1970), the auropalpebral reflex (for example, Wedenberg 1956), the startle reflex (for example, Suzuki *et al*. 1964), heart-rate changes (for example, Bartoshuk 1962; Berg and Berg 1979), sucking (for example, Sameroff 1968), and even finger movements (for example, Turkewitz *et al*. 1971). The common underlying assumption was that a change in response frequency or intensity within each of these response systems reflected equally well a simultaneous change in the stimulating sound. The various measures were thought to be interchangeable indices of auditory sensitivity. It is now thought, however, that the function that relates sound perception to a response varies widely from response system to response system (see Schneider and Trehub 1985). Investigations into the response equivalence for the same stimulus material also provided ambiguous results (Miller and Byrne 1983; Turkewitz *et al*. 1971). In addition, the early studies used a wide variety of stimuli, such as rattle sounds (for example, Bronshtein *et al*. 1958), musical tones (for example, Dearborn 1910), pure tones (for example, Kaye 1966), and speech stimuli (for example, Eimas 1974), and stimuli were presented at intensity levels ranging from about 60 dB (Sameroff 1967) to 104 dB (Kaye and Levin 1963). Such uncontrolled variation in the stimuli contributed to the incompatibility of the results and made valid interpretation and comparison very difficult.

2.1   Methods

In the past two decades, increasing efforts have been made to develop more precise and reliable methods to investigate infants' auditory sensitivity and to control for confounding effects that are due to the infants' limited response repertoire and their limited attentional resources. Visual reinforcement of head-turning responses has been a preferred method, since motor control of the eyes and the head precedes motor control of the trunk and the extremities (Moore *et al*. 1975; Moore and Wilson 1978). In this procedure, head turns in the presence of a specific sound are reinforced with the presentation of an interesting visual event (for example, illumination and activation of a mechanical toy), whereas head turns during the absence of the specific sound are not reinforced. When the infant has learned the response contingencies, the infant's sensitivity thresholds can be estimated by varying stimulus parameters such as sound intensity or sound frequency and by observing the level at which the infant stops to respond or does not make reliable head turns in the correct direction.

This technique is known as visual reinforcement audiometry (VRA). VRA studies have revealed that the method of stimulus presentation appears to have a consistent influence on infant detection thresholds (Werner 1992). Infants' pure-tone thresholds were lower (5 dB at 2000 Hz, 2 dB at 8000 Hz) when sounds were presented via headphones than when they were presented in a free sound field (Berg and Smith 1983). Developmental aspects of the acoustical properties of the infant's external ear most probably contribute to this difference (Werner 1992). Reinforcement and motivational factors seem to have a substantial impact on infants' thresholds as well (see Schneider and Trehub 1992; Werner 1992). Most critical, however, is the fact that visual reinforcement audiometry involves a location rather than a detection task. Since localization ability can be expected to develop with age, the results gained with these methods may also be confounded because stimuli differ in their salience and hence in their ease of localization (see Schneider and Trehub 1992; Fassbender 1993).

Variants of VRA first described by Moore *et al.* (1975) have been used in several laboratories to estimate infants' absolute hearing thresholds as well as their ability to detect changes in frequency, amplitude, and spectral content (Trehub *et al.* 1980, 1986; Berg and Smith 1983; Sinnot *et al.* 1983; Nozza and Wilson 1984; Olsho 1984; Clarkson *et al.* 1988; see also Schneider and Trehub 1992; Werner 1992). The advantage of these procedures is that they allow for multiple stimulus comparisons within each subject and for establishing thresholds for an individual subject (see Olsho *et al.* 1987). In contrast, procedures that are based on the habituation/dishabituation of a response, such as the high-amplitude sucking procedure, yield only a single data point. They allow for the interpretation of group data but not of individual data. However, the advantage of the high-amplitude sucking procedure (HAS) originally developed by Siqueland and DeLucia (1969) is that it can be used with newborns and very young infants. It has gained widespread usage particularly in studies investigating newborns' and young infants' speech capacities (for example, Jusczyk 1985; Bertoncini *et al.* 1988) and has yielded reliable results (see Fassbender 1993). The newborn is already able to control and vary the strength and rate of his sucking response to a high degree (Sameroff 1967, 1968; Siqueland and DeLucia 1969; Butterfield and Siperstein 1972; Crook 1979). In contrast, infants show reliable, short-latency, conditionable head turns (as needed in VRA methods) only at ages greater than 5 months when the neck muscles are strong enough to support the head and to allow for precise head turns (Chun *et al.* 1960; Moore and Wilson 1978). Information about the auditory sensitivity of infants younger than 5 months comes mainly from studies using the high-amplitude sucking procedure (see Fassbender 1993) and observing auditory evoked brainstem responses (for example, Hecox 1975) and cortically evoked potentials (for example, Hecox 1975; Klein 1984).

Recently, Olsho *et al.* (1987) have introduced an observer-based psychoacoustic procedure that may be applicable to younger infants. This procedure combines features of the forced choice preferential looking technique (Teller 1979) and of VRA (Moore *et al.* 1975). Observers have to decide, on the basis of the infant's general behaviour, whether a signal had occurred on a given trial or not. Observers wear masking headphones or are located in another room and therefore are isolated from the stimuli heard by the infants. When the observer correctly judges from the movements of the infant that a signal has been presented, a visual reinforcer is given to the infant. As this procedure takes any behaviour of the infant into account and the observer receives feedback about his decision, this procedure is thought to be very sensitive in assessing infants' hearing abilities. This procedure seems to be free of the procedural effects identified in visual reinforcement audiometry. Observer-based procedures accept any response that reliably differentiates between two different sounds or between the sound and no-sound presentation. In behavioural observation audiometry even response that occurs in temporal proximity to the sound stimulation is considered as evidence of hearing (Northern and Downs 1991). Recently, preferential looking procedures (Fernald 1985) were employed in infant studies using longer-lasting acoustical stimuli. Essentially, by turning to a light (red lamp placed left and right of the infant), infants start the presentation of sound that lasts until the infant looks away for some period (for example, 2 s). Two different stimuli are presented for a certain number of times randomized in respect to order of presentation and presentation side (left or right). A preference is assumed when the infant listens significantly longer to one stimulus over the other summed over all trials. The experimenter who records the looking/turning behaviour and starts the trials is blind to the location of sound presentation.

2.2   Absolute thresholds

Trehub *et al.* (1980) investigated the absolute frequency thresholds for infants 6, 12, and 18 months of age using VRA. Thresholds were defined as 65 per cent correct head turns and were obtained for octave-band noises with centre frequencies at 200, 400, 1000, 2000, 4000, and 10 000 Hz. Results indicated a decrease in threshold from 200 to 10 000 Hz for all groups. The 6-month-old infants showed a threshold of about 38 dB at

200 Hz, 31 dB at 400 Hz, 23 dB at 1000 Hz, 26 dB at 2000 Hz, 20 dB at 4000 Hz, and about 17 dB at 10 000 Hz. The 12- and 18-month-old infants performed similarly across the frequency range but were about 5–8 dB more sensitive at lower frequencies than were the 6-month-olds. No significant age differences were found at higher frequencies. Adult thresholds were lower by 20 to 28 dB at low frequencies (approximately 15 dB) but converged with those of infants at higher frequencies. At 10 000 Hz there were only small differences between the infant age groups; all showed a threshold of about 20 dB, which is still higher than in adults (about 12 dB).

Testing thresholds at even higher frequencies (19 000 Hz), Schneider *et al.* (1980) found that 24-month-old infants performed similarly to adults, and the younger age groups (6, 12, 18 months) were only about 5 dB less sensitive. However, this convergence in thresholds is due to a larger drop of high-frequency sensitivity for adults than for infants. Whereas the threshold for infants at 10 000 Hz is about 20 dB, it is increased to about 35 dB at 19 000 Hz. Thus the threshold at very high frequencies is higher than at very low frequencies. The human hearing range generally only extends up to 19 000 Hz. Most adults eventually acquire a hearing loss in the high-frequency range due to exposure to noise, the effects of ototoxic damage, and the effects of ageing. The elevated threshold for frequencies at 19 000 Hz may indicate a hearing loss for adults, whereas it may indicate immaturity of the auditory system for infants.

The results of Trehub *et al.* (1980) and Schneider *et al.* (1980) show that developmental changes in auditory frequency sensitivity occur mainly in the low-frequency range after the first 6 months of infancy. It should, however, be kept in mind that differences in thresholds between adults and infants may be partly due to differences in response measures. The percentage of correct responses of infants in the studies by Trehub *et al.* (1980) and Schneider *et al.* (1980) never reached 100 per cent, even at high intensity levels. This fact may be explained by momentary lapses of attention during testing. However, it may also indicate an unreliability of the method leading to an underestimation of the infant's true auditory thresholds. (For a discussion of this issue see Schneider and Trehub (1992).)

Other researchers, however, reported a smaller infant–adult threshold difference. Berg and Smith (1983) presented 250-ms long pure tones with frequencies of 500, 1000, and 8000 Hz to infants 6–18 months of age over headphones or in a free field situation. With headphones, thresholds for the 6-month-olds were about 10 dB higher than for adults at 500 and 2000 Hz but 14 dB higher at 8000 Hz. In comparison to the 6-month-olds, the 10-month-olds with headphones showed slightly lower thresholds at 2000 and 8000 Hz but higher thresholds at 500 Hz.

Their thresholds were about 7 dB above adult ones at 2000 and 8000 Hz and about 15 dB above adult ones at 500 Hz. Thresholds obtained in the open sound field were about 20 dB for the 10-, 14-, and 18-month-old infants across all frequencies. Because adults performed better in the free sound field at 2000 and 8000 Hz, the difference in threshold between infants and adults was about 6 dB at 500 Hz, 12 dB at 2000 Hz, and 10 dB at 8000 Hz. Thresholds with headphones were not obtained for the older age groups because they did not tolerate headphones to the same degree as did the younger ones. A similar sensitivity for 6- and 12-month-old infants was reported by Nozza and Wilson (1984). They found pure-tone thresholds of 20 dB at 1000 Hz and 16 dB at 4000 Hz for 6-month-olds and for the 12-month-olds they found thresholds that were 2 dB lower. Infants' thresholds were larger than those of adults by about 14 dB at 1000 Hz and about 7 dB at 4000 Hz.

Olsho *et al.* (1987) used the observer-based psychoacoustic procedure described above that was thought to be more sensitive to the infants' true thresholds. With this procedure 6-month-old infants evidenced a pure-tone detection threshold of 30 dB at 500 Hz, of about 13 dB at 1000 Hz, and of 12 dB at 4000 Hz. These thresholds are only 8–12 dB above adult thresholds and 10–20 dB lower than those reported by Trehub *et al.* (1980) and Sinnot et al. (1983).

It is not clear what factors contributed to the large discrepancy in results among these studies. Trehub *et al.* (1980) and Sinnot *et al.* (1983) employed a head-turning procedure that may have confounded the infants' abilities to localize sounds with true frequency thresholds. In addition, head-turning procedures require a split of attention between the simultaneously visual and auditory stimuli. Attentional capacities may be less developed in infants than in adults, which may also contribute to the elevated thresholds of infants. When these factors are taken into consideration, as was the case in the study by Olsho *et al.* (1987), infants prove to be much more sensitive than previously thought. Nozza and Wilson (1984) also employed a visually reinforced head-turn procedure and found much lower thresholds than Trehub *et al.* (1980) and Sinnot *et al.* (1983). Despite the discrepancies in the results of the above studies, the available data suggest that young infants are less sensitive to low frequencies than to high frequencies, both in absolute terms and as compared to adults.

2.3 Masked thresholds

Evidence for developmental changes in infants' auditory sensitivity also comes from studies of tonal masking. Masking is of interest because of its relevance to natural auditory phenomena and its potential for explaining the analytical capacities of the developing ear. A target tone, for example, will only be masked when the target and the masker overlap in frequency. A pure tone can be masked by another pure tone when the frequencies of the tones are within the same critical band (see Scharf 1970). A masked tone can be detected only if it increases in intensity within its critical band, by at least 40 per cent, which corresponds to an increase of about 1.5 dB (Scharf 1970). Critical band refers to the range of frequencies in which sound powers are perceptually combined and is generally about one-third of an octave wide. If the critical band, for example, were wider in infants than in adults, one would expect a decreased sensitivity to individual frequency components of a complex tone, such as formants within speech.

Bull *et al.* (1981) tested 6-, 12-, 18-, and 24-month-old infants with an octave-band noise that was set at a centre frequency of 4000 Hz at two noise levels of 42 dB and 60 dB. The results indicate that thresholds were similar for the 12-, 18-, and 24-month-old infants at both background noise levels, but were about 7 to 8 dB higher for the 6-month-old group. Increasing the masker by 18 dB resulted in a raise of the threshold by about 18 dB for all age groups including adults. It can be concluded that the infants and adults reacted similarly to changes in the level of the masker. Results also revealed thresholds for infants that were 16 to 25 dB higher than those for adults at all masking levels. This infant–adult difference in masked-tone detection is similar to the adult–infant difference for absolute-frequency thresholds as reported by Trehub *et al.* (1980).

Further evidence for masking effects in infants was reported by Nozza (1987). He tested 6- and 12-month-old infants with a head-turning procedure using broadband maskers and 1000- and 4000-Hz pure-tone targets. His results corroborate the data obtained by Bull *et al.* (1981) in that infants showed elevated thresholds as compared to adults. However, the slope of the threshold functions was constant for the infants and adults at both frequency targets. Thus, whereas absolute thresholds showed developmental improvement, the relation between signal intensity and the masking noise seems to stay constant during development. It appears that the adult–infant differences are independent of the level of background noise.

Nozza and Wilson (1984) also investigated infants' detection thresholds for tones embedded in noise. They presented 6- and 12-month-old infants with 1000- and 4000-Hz pure tones masked with white noise having a 26-dB spectral level. Thresholds for the 6-month-olds were 50 and 55 dB, respectively, and were 2 dB lower for the 12-month-olds and 8 dB lower for adults.

Olsho (1985), however, using a visually reinforced head-turn procedure in combination with an adaptive psychophysical method, tested 4–8-month-old infants at four probe frequencies (500, 1000, 2000,

4000 Hz). With a simultaneous tonal masking procedure she obtained neither age-related differences in the infants' frequency resolution nor differences between infants and adults in the masked tuning curve widths and slopes. Nevertheless, tuning curves were lower than those of adults, indicating poorer performance.

Nozza *et al.* (1988) investigated binaural release from masking for a speech sound in infants, preschoolers, and adults. The speech sound /ba/ was presented under two interaural-phase conditions (noise and signal in phase; noise and signal 180° out of phase). The syllable had a duration of 300 ms and the masker was a bandpass 300–3000 Hz noise presented at 69 dB SPL (spectrum level 35 dB). Unmasked thresholds obtained in a visual reinforcement head-turn procedure were 29.7, 20.7, and 13 dB for the infants (7 to 8 months), preschoolers, and adults, respectively. The mean binaural masked thresholds for the in-phase condition were 56.5, 54.4, and 50.8 dB for the respective age groups. The release from masking in the out-of-phase condition amounted to 5, 8.3, and 10.8 dB, respectively. However, when the masker intensity was adjusted to account for the adult–infant differences in absolute thresholds (masker set at 49 dB), the binaural masking level difference (BMLD) for adults diminished to 7.9 dB. This BMLD is similar to the one for preschoolers and only about 3 dB below the infants' BMLD. It can be concluded from these results that the BMLDs for speech sounds in infants are only slightly different from those in adults.

In summary, a consistent relation exists across frequencies for both infants and adults—for increases in masking level intensity and threshold increases in the detection of a masked stimulus. Thus, frequency selectivity in infants is proportional to that in adults. Nevertheless, infants' thresholds for detecting a masked target tone are higher than those for adults. This indicates that infants have a slight disadvantage in detecting a target embedded in noise. This is of particular importance because many sounds co-occur in the normal acoustic environment, masking each other. Since this effect is proportional to the elevated absolute thresholds for infants, masking in infants seems to have an effect similar to that in adults.

2.4 Frequency discrimination

The discrimination of complex auditory signals such as speech and tone patterns depends on the ability to resolve small frequency differences. Leventhal and Lipsitt (1964) observed newborns and found no discrimination of pure tones when the tones were changed from 200 to 500 Hz and from 200 to 1000 Hz. Similarly, in Trehub's (1973) study, 1- to 4-month-old infants evidenced no discrimination of frequency shifts from 100 to 200 Hz, 200 to 1000 Hz, and 1000 to 2000 Hz, for square-wave and sine-wave tones. Trehub employed the high-amplitude sucking (HAS) procedure. In contrast, Wormith *et al.* (1975) did find discrimination of a 200- to 500-Hz shift in 1-month-old infants when using the HAS procedure. Trehub used tones that comprised octaves and it is likely that the infants did not react to the change in frequency but rather perceived the similarity between the tones due to the octave relationship. Demany and Armand (1984) confirmed that 3-month-old infants demonstrate octave generalization.

Olsho (1984) determined the frequency difference limens (FDLs), that is, the frequency disparity between two tones that leads to discrimination, for infants aged 5 to 8 months and for adults. In order to assess infants' sensitivity, VRA was employed and combined with an adaptive psychophysical procedure. In her study, Olsho (1984, 1985) trained infants to make a head turn of at least 45° to the right when they detected a change in frequency of a repeating stimulus as compared to a 'background' stimulus that was also repeated constantly. Correct head turns were reinforced. This procedure puts few memory demands on the infant and allows for constant comparison of the target and background stimuli.

FDLs were based on 70 per cent correct head turning and were determined for frequencies ranging from 250 to 8000 Hz. The results indicated that infants required significantly larger frequency differences to achieve discrimination at frequencies below 2000 Hz than did adults (tones were 500 ms in length and presented at 70 dB SPL). At 4000 and 8000 Hz, there were no significant differences; in fact, the infants performed relatively better than the adults. The values of Weber's fraction (ratio of FDL to standard frequency) for infants decreased from approximately 0.038 at 250 Hz to 0.01 at frequencies above 1000 Hz. For adults, Weber's fraction decreased from about 0.02 at 250 Hz to 0.006 at 1000 Hz and then increased to little above 0.01 at 4000 Hz (Olsho 1984).

These results indicate that infants discriminate high frequencies better than low frequencies. In fact, infants performed better than adults at high frequencies. At low frequencies infants' thresholds were twice as high as those of adults; at frequencies greater than 2000 Hz, they did not differ from those of adults. In general, infants seem to be able to reliably detect a frequency change of 2 per cent at low frequencies and of 1 per cent at high frequencies, whereas adults detect changes of 1 per cent or even less.

Less sensitivity was reported in a subsequent study by Olsho *et al.* (1987) using an observer-based psychoacoustic procedure. The results obtained showed that infants detected a frequency change of about 3 per cent at 500 Hz and a change of about 2 per cent at both 1000 and 4000 Hz. The FLDs reported by Olsho (1984) suggested a greater sensitivity for all three frequencies. Thus it is not clear whether the differences obtained here reflect methodological differences between the studies, other effects, or true differences in thresholds.

2.5   Pitch discrimination

Do infants discriminate pitches of complex tones as readily as they discriminate pure tones? This is an important question because a pure tone pitch corresponds to its physical frequency in a one-on-one relationship, which is not the case for complex tones. Complex tones possess a fundamental frequency and a number of overtones with frequencies that are multiple integers of the fundamental one. The pitch of a complex tone corresponds to the fundamental frequency and arises from the overtones. The frequencies of the overtones, as well as their number, harmonic relations, and relative amplitude, also contribute to the timbre of the tone or sound and provide the basis for discrimination among different sound sources. The pitch of a complex tone is perceived even if the fundamental frequency is physically absent. The fundamental frequency has been referred to as residue pitch (Schouten 1940) and virtual pitch (Terhardt 1974).

Bundy *et al.* (1982) attempted to assess the ability to extract pitch from complex tones in 4-month-old infants. They presented infants in a habituation/dishabituation paradigm with a tone sequence comprised of three complex tones with different pitches. In one situation the spectral components of the individual tones varied from trial to trial while leaving the melody unchanged. In another situation the spectral components of the tones remained invariant. The fundamental frequency was not present. Infants did not show recognition of a change in the order of tones after they had habituated to the original version. Since a change in order can be readily detected by adults when the fundamental frequency is extracted from the upper harmonics, the results indicate that infants do not seem to extract pitch from the combination of upper harmonics. However, in the study by Bundy *et al.* (1982), infants also failed to discriminate a change in tone order when the fundamental frequency was physically present. This fact sheds some doubt on the results reported by Bundy *et al.* because under normal circumstances infants readily detect a change in the order of tones like the ones employed in the study (see Trehub 1987).

Clarkson and Clifton (1985) reinvestigated pitch perception of complex tones with 7–8-month-old infants using a visually reinforced conditioned head-turning paradigm. In their study infants successfully discriminated complex tones with several upper harmonics. Tones corresponded to the fundamental frequencies 160, 200, and 240 Hz, but differed in the number and absolute frequencies of the upper harmonics. Infants also showed a categorization of complexes that differed in the number of harmonic overtones while corresponding to the same fundamental frequency. Infants did so regardless of whether the fundamental frequency was absent or present.

These results suggest that infants at 7 months probably already process complex tones in a manner similar to that of adults, that is, by extracting the pitch of complex tones with missing fundamental frequency. However, more research is needed to clarify this issue.

2.6 Timbre discrimination

In addition to pitch and loudness, timbre plays a role in the subjective experience of complex tones. It refers to the spectral composition of a tone and relates to the number, the frequency, and the relative amplitude of the harmonics (Preis 1984). Tone onset effects (such as rise time, unequal rise of partials, and noise) and inharmonic partials, as well as steady-state effects (such as amplitude modulation, vibrato, and pitch instability), contribute to the perception of a certain timbre (Plomp 1970). Timbre is generally defined as that attribute by which the differentiation of two sounds with identical pitch and loudness is possible. For example, it is the difference between a piano and a violin when the same note is played for the same duration and at the same loudness.

Seven-month-old infants are sensitive to timbre differences among tones. Clarkson *et al.* (1988) presented 7–9-months-olds with tones having the same pitch but different harmonics. In one situation the fundamental frequencies were physically present; in another they were missing. Tones had a duration of 500 ms, always had six upper harmonics, and were presented with identical loudness. Clarkson *et al.* (1988) employed a conditioned head-turning paradigm and found that infants discriminated tones that differed only in the spectral envelopes. Discrimination was equally good whether the harmonics of the target tones were higher or lower than the harmonics of the comparison tone. Similar results were obtained for tones with missing fundamentals; fewer subjects, however, met the performance criterion. Clarkson *et al.* suggest that infants use acoustical information about the harmonic content of tones for discrimination. However, it remains unclear whether infants use the entire range of the spectral envelope, that is, all six harmonics, or only one or few upper harmonics for discrimination.

Trehub *et al.* (1990) also reported evidence for the perception of timbre. In their investigation they tested infants 7–8.5 months of age in a head-turn paradigm. Infants first heard exemplars taken from a set of complex tones that had the same specific spectral structure but differed in fundamental frequency (or intensity or duration depending on the experimental condition). Then they heard tones taken from a set of complex tones that differed from the first set only in their spectral structure. The stimuli were tones with a fundamental frequency of 100, 200, 300, or 400 Hz with overtones up to 4000 Hz and were filtered with two triangular bandpass filters having centre frequencies at 270 and 2300 Hz for one set of tones and centre frequencies at 570 and 840 Hz for the other contrasting set of tones. Infants detected the change in spectral structure in all three experimental conditions.

Infants' sensitivity to the spectral structure of tones was also shown in a study assessing perceptual grouping in infancy (Thorpe and Trehub 1989). Infants perceived temporal increments in silent intervals when these silent intervals were located within groups of tones but not when located between groups of tones. One group of tones consisted of three 440-Hz sine tones, and the other group consisted of three 440-Hz sawtooth-wave tones. Thus, infants between 6 and 9 months of age perceived the duration illusion similarly to adults. The results indicate that the infants are sensitive to the spectral content of tones and that a perceptual grouping process on the basis of the spectral information in the acoustic stimulus is operative at this early age.

2.7 Summary

In comparison to adults infants seem to respond to high frequencies better than low frequencies. At frequencies above 4000 Hz, infants perform even better than adults. The improvement for infants from 6 to 24 months, particularly in the low-frequency region, is in agreement with data that shows that auditory sensitivity improves gradually until the age of 10 years, and that low-frequency sensitivity improves to the greatest degree (Elliot and Katz 1980; Yoneshighe and Elliot 1981). Infants detect frequency changes more readily in the low-frequency region than at high frequencies. Their ability to detect frequency changes of 2 and 1 per cent, respectively, seems to be not much different from that of adults. Infants are sensitive to increments in loudness (3 dB) and seem to perceive pitch and timbre in a manner similar to that of adults. Their ability to detect signals embedded in noise is only slightly weakened and yields a constant relation across frequencies as compared to adults. In short, while their absolute thresholds for frequencies below 2000 Hz seem to be somewhat elevated, infants seem to be highly sensitive to changes in ongoing acoustical events across all frequencies.

The age-related improvement and particularly the differential improvement in frequency discrimination could reflect the immaturity of the auditory system and the auditory central nervous structures of the young infant. The structures of the inner ear seem to be mature at birth (Bredberg 1985). Nevertheless, the reduced responsiveness of very young infants may also be due to the greater stiffness of the basilar membrane at young ages, which only decreases later (Ehret and Romand 1981).

Certainly, structures of the auditory system, such as the size and shape of the pinna and the ear canal, the tympanic membrane, and the middle ear cavity, show maturational change during early life (see Miller 1983; Saunders *et al.* 1983; Northern and Downs 1974). Because the adult audibility curve is primarily determined by the properties of the outer and middle ear, and because the resonance characteristics of the outer and middle ear elevate higher frequencies in the young infant than in the adults, it can be expected that the resonance frequency decreases with age. This effect may explain the relatively elevated thresholds at lower frequencies during infancy. Furthermore, some more central structures of the central nervous system such as the inferior colliculi or the auditory cortex are not mature at birth but develop during the first years of life. Maturation of these structures most probably contributes to behavioural changes in auditory perception.

Other factors may play a role as well. High tones, for example, seem to be more alerting and attention-getting than low tones (Dearborn 1910; Haller 1932), which in turn may result in better perception. Training and experience with sound discrimination have recently been shown to affect hearing thresholds for adults but, even when training and experience factors are taken into account, infants' thresholds at low frequencies remain elevated in comparison to those of adults (Olsho *et al.* 1988). At the same time, these results indicate that non-sensory factors do affect infants' performance. Infants have limited attentional, motivational, and memory capacities. Since these capacities are to a certain degree involved in all procedures used with infants, they can affect estimations of true thresholds. Future research that takes these factors into account may demonstrate an even greater infant auditory sensitivity than is currently assumed. Further research is also needed to broaden our knowledge about infants below 6 months of age.

One may question the relevance of devoting such a large part of this chapter to the development of the infant's basic auditory sensitivity, since the main part of the book, as well as the next part of this chapter, deals with the infant's perception of acoustical patterns in language and music. In addition, research on auditory pattern perception in infancy is done in suprathreshold contexts. One reason for this extended treatment of auditory sensitivity is that perception of complex sounds and acoustical patterns is dependent in certain aspects on the sensitivity to subtle changes and variations in the stimulus. For example, in auditory sequential grouping of rapid tone sequences it has been shown for adults that subtle changes in frequency, timbre, and duration of tones as well as in presentation speed alter the perception of tones as being located in one or in two streams (Miller and Heise 1950; Bregman 1990).

When auditory sensitivity is not developed to an adult level, the perception of grouping phenomena, as investigated extensively with adults (for a review see Bregman 1990), may be drastically different or even not present. Complex tones can be decomposed into or composed by a certain set of sine waves. Thus, the perception of complex tones will be affected by the infant's basic auditory sensitivity. It is paramount for the understanding of the development of auditory pattern perception to trace the development of basic auditory sensitivity in absolute terms as well as in respect to adult sensitivity. This knowledge allows the differentiation between developmental changes in auditory pattern perception that are due to developmental aspects of the auditory system and those due to developing cognitive functions. Lecanuet (Chapter 1) describes the development of the auditory system and its sensitivity towards acoustic stimuli during the prenatal period. The first part of this chapter has extended the description of the development of auditory sensitivity to the postnatal period.

3 AUDITORY GROUPING AND SEGREGATION PROCESSES

In contrast to the previous section on auditory sensitivity, which deals with the ability to detect and differentiate sounds and tones, this section deals with auditory grouping and segregation processes, that is, the organization of the acoustic environment into orderly and meaningful configurations. The terms 'auditory grouping' and 'segregation' are used to refer to the perceptual organization that is imposed on incoming information from the auditory senses. They refer to the fact that we perceive an acoustic world of separate objects that are placed in distinct locations within the auditory space relative to us and to one another. Auditory grouping is the organization of sound elements with one another to form coherent wholes. A review of research on adult auditory grouping and segregation processes can be found in Bregman (1990; see also Fassbender 1993).

Research about auditory grouping mechanisms suggests that several Gestalt principles seem to be involved in the perception of acoustic information. The early Gestalt psychologists believed that the principles upon which perceptual organization is based are innate. Evidence from visual perception indicates that the Gestalt principles of good continuation and common fate are indeed already effective in 40-day-old infants (Bower 1965, 1967). Evidence that infants may also group auditory information along principles similar to those used by adults comes from studies on auditory stream segregation in infancy (Demany 1982; Fassbender 1993) and the duration illusion (Thorpe *et al.* 1988; Thorpe and Trehub 1989).

3.1 Auditory stream segregation

Demany (1982) investigated whether the Gestalt factor of spectral similarity serves as a perceptual cue for auditory grouping even in very young infants. He constructed several four-tone sequences in which the frequency proximity among tones differed. Demany employed these tone sequences in a discrimination task in which the original sequence had to be discriminated from its order reversal. The efficiency in discriminating the forward from the backward order of tones rests on the ability to detect a change in the order of a tone sequence. This ability has been demonstrated (Chang and Trehub 1977*a,b*; Trehub *et al.* 1985; Morrongiello 1986). The tone sequences were constructed in such a way that the retrograde order of tones could be discriminated from the original only when all four tones in each sequence were perceptually grouped into a particular melody, that is, into a coherent stream of tones. When, however, the tones one and three in the four-tone sequence were grouped together but apart from the tones two and four on the basis of frequency similarity, two parallel streams each consisting of two alternating tones would be heard. Hearing the tone sequence '1-3-1-3-1...' would not be different from hearing its reverse order '3-1-3-1-3...'. If the infants would group the tones in this manner, the original tone sequence could not be discriminated from the reverse version.

Demany employed three stimulus conditions: in the first (C1), three tones were similar in frequency (330, 370 and 440 Hz) but very different in frequency from the fourth tone (932 Hz); in the second (C2), two pairs of tones in different frequency regions were produced (330 Hz and 370 Hz; 698 Hz and 932 Hz); in the third (C3), two tones had similar frequencies (330 and 370 Hz), one tone had a higher frequency (698 Hz), and the fourth tone had an even higher frequency (2489 Hz). The three conditions were employed to induce perceptual grouping of three tones into one stream (C1 and C3; makes detection of reversal possible) or of two tones into one stream (C2; makes detection of reversal impossible). Demany employed square-wave tones of 100-ms duration that were segregated by 100-ms silent intervals.

Demany found that for adults it was much more difficult to discriminate the original sequence from its retrogradation when sequence C2 was employed than when sequence C1 or sequence C3 were used. This had been predicted.

Demany then tested 44 infants 1.5–3.5 months of age with the same stimulus material in a visually controlled habituation/dishabituation paradigm. By looking at a white light that was positioned 20° left of the midline, the infant initiated a sound presentation that was terminated when the infant looked away. During the first three visual fixations no sound was elicited. During the next 12 fixations he/she received the sound sequence in original order, and during the following fixations the retrograde version of that same sequence. Infants were each assigned to one condition.

The results indicated that only the subjects of groups C1 and C3 reacted significantly to the change in stimulus. The results of the groups C1 and C3 did not differ on this score but both differed significantly from group C2. The infant results parallelled those of the adults and were taken as evidence that infants already at this young age group auditory stimuli according to the Gestalt laws of frequency proximity.

Fassbender (1993) investigated whether the Gestalt principles of 'proximity' and of 'similarity' are available to the young infant as means of perceptually organizing the acoustical environment, and whether auditory grouping takes place along the stimulus attributes frequency, amplitude, and spectral content.

A variation of the HAS procedure was employed. This procedure has been used to study speech perception and general auditory perceptional abilities in infants younger than 6 months. In auditory studies, the HAS procedure involves the repeated presentation of an auditory stimulus contingent on the infant's sucking response in such a way that sucks exceeding a certain amplitude criterion of strength trigger the presentation of acoustic stimuli. The procedure used by Fassbender (1993) was set up such that an infant could achieve continuous stimulation at a sucking rate of 30 sucks per minute with efficient timing of the sucking responses. The possibility for continuous stimulus presentation was introduced to increase the response–stimulus contingency with the relatively long stimuli used in this study. During a preshift phase the same stimulus had been presented until the sucking response declined to a preset habituation criterion. When the criterion had been reached, a new stimulus was presented for several minutes in a postshift phase. When the change in sucking rate from preshift to postshift period was significantly different from the change in sucking rate of a control group that received the same stimulus during the preshift and postshift phase, this was taken as evidence that the subjects in the experimental group recognized the change in the stimulus. The advantages of this procedure are: (1) that it can be used with infants below 6 months of age; (2) that it accounts for infants' different processing capacities; and (3) that it yields many stimulus presentations for the infants to encode the stimulus.

The construction of the stimuli was also based on the fact that infants are highly sensitive to changes in the contour of tone sequences (Trehub *et al.* 1984, 1987). Thus, a change in contour from an ascending tone order to a descending tone order was employed as the difference between preshift and postshift stimuli. Repeating six-tone sequences were employed that had tones with a preselected frequency in the first, third, and fifth positions forming an ascending or a descending order. Tones located at the second, fourth, and sixth positions in the repeating six-tone sequence were randomly selected from a pool of eight chromatic tones each time they occurred.

Preselected-frequency tones were alternated with the random-frequency tones for two reasons: first, to make the perception of the order in the preselected-frequency tones impossible where all tones in the sequence have similar physical attributes; and, second, to make the perception of the order of the preselected-frequency tones possible where the preselected-frequency tones are different from the random-frequency tones in one physical attribute, such as frequency, amplitude, or spectral content. For example, tone sequence S1 consisted of six tones: 'A3-R-C#4-R-E4-R' (R, random tone), whereas the contrasting sequence S1r (r, reverse order) consisted of the six tones: 'E4-R-C#4-R-A3-R'. The second sequence pair (S2 and S2r) was identical to the S1–S1r pair with the exception that all random-frequency tones were increased in frequency by one octave. The third sequence pair (S3 and S3r) was also identical to the S1–S1r pair; however, the amplitude of the random-frequency tones was decreased by 25 per cent (12 dB). Finally, the fourth sequence pair differed from S1–S1r only in that the tones with pre-selected frequency were complex tones with added upper harmonics and the random-frequency tones were sine tones. Thus all sequence pairs in the four conditions were identical except for variations in frequency, amplitude, and spectral content. All tones were 100 ms in length and were separated by pauses of 100 ms length. The study involved five stimulus conditions—one control group and four experimental groups. In the control condition, the infants received one of the eight different tone sequences during the preshift period and the same one during the postshift period. Sixty 58–165-day-old infants (mean 103.95; SD = 24.74) of both sexes (male, 39; female, 21) were tested.

The results show that the average sucking rate of all groups increased from baseline (BAS1) to the third minute before stimulus shift (PRE1) and habituated during the last minutes of preshift period (PRE2). It was further observed that the sucking rate of the experimental groups, frequency-variation (S2), amplitude-variation (S3), and spectral-variation (S4) increased after the shift in stimulus. This is not the case for the control group, which showed continued habituation. The sucking rate during the postshift period of the basic-sequence group (S1) also stayed below the PRE2 level, indicating that there was no response recovery after stimulus shift in this condition.

Fassbender (1993) concluded from these results that infants 2–5½ months of age already organize rapid tone sequences perceptually on the basis of the Gestalt principles of proximity and similarity among sequence elements. Grouping on the basis of these Gestalt principles occurred for the stimulus attributes of frequency, amplitude, and spectral content.

3.2 Duration illusion

Information about auditory grouping in infancy also comes from studies investigating the duration illusion (Thorpe *et al.* 1988; Thorpe and Trehub 1989). The term 'duration illusion' refers to the phenomenon that identical silent intervals are generally perceived as longer when they occur between groups of sounds than when they occur within groups of sounds. Perceptual grouping affects the subjective perception of sound duration (Woodrow 1909). Perceptual grouping is influenced by differences in stimulus attributes, such as the duration, frequency, and amplitude, among stimulus components. But even uniform tones or clicks are perceptually grouped or chunked in certain ways (Fraisse 1982). This change can be readily detected when silent intervals are introduced or extended within such perceptual groups. Changes in silent intervals between groups are generally not detected (see Fitzgibbons *et al.* 1974). This phenomenon has been used to study perceptual organization in adults (Fitzgibbons *et al.* 1974) and children (Thorpe *et al.* 1988).

Thorpe *et al.* (1988) employed the auditory duration illusion to study the effect of frequency similarity on perceptual grouping among tones. Infants between 6 and 9 months of age heard six-tone sequences that consisted of three tones of 440 Hz followed by three tones of 659 Hz. All tones were 200-ms sine tones. Contrasting sequences had a prolonged silent interval (lengthened by 75, 100, 125, or 200 ms) either between groups (third to fourth tone) or within groups (fourth to fifth tone). Infants were tested with a visually reinforced head-turn technique. The infants detected all increments at all locations with the exception of the 75-ms increase at the between-group-location. But the results did not yield significant differences in the ability to detect pause increments between the within-group locations and between-group locations.

Thorpe and Trehub (1989) reasoned that the frequency difference between the tone groups (440 to 659 Hz) may not have been large enough to give rise to the duration illusion. Therefore, they investigated the duration illusion using a larger frequency difference (282 to 1470 Hz) between tone groups. Between-group and within-group pauses were lengthened by 80 or 100 ms. In contrast to the previous study (Thorpe *et al.* 1988), the infants detected both increments in the within-group condition but not the pause increments in the between-group condition. A comparison of the performance for the two locations, however, was significant only in the 100-ms increase condition. The duration illusion seems to work for infants as it does for adults, but larger frequency differences between tone groups are necessary. These results indicate that infants 6 to 9 months of age perceptually group tones in auditory sequences on the basis of frequency similarity between the tones.

Thorpe and Trehub (1989) also investigated whether the duration illusion would arise when waveform or intensity differences were introduced between tone groups. In the waveform condition the stimuli consisted of three 440-Hz sawtooth tones followed by three 440-Hz sine tones. As in the previous conditions, tones and silent intervals between tones were 200 ms in length. Again, the standard tone sequence was contrasted for discrimination in a visually reinforced head-turn technique with a sequence in which a silent interval was prolonged. The prolonged interval was positioned either in a within-group location or in a between-group location. Infants of 6–9 months of age detected the increased silent intervals (increase by 80 and 100 ms) in the within-group location but not in the between-group location. A comparison of the performance for locations revealed significant differences for both conditions of increase. The results show that the duration illusion can be observed when groups of tones differ in their waveform, for example, their spectral content.

In another experiment Thorpe and Trehub (1989) made the first three 1000-Hz sine tones of a six-tone sequence louder (25 dB) than the last three tones. Again, the silent intervals were increased by 80 ms in within-group and between-group conditions. Infants 7 to 11 months of age discriminated the within-group silent interval increases but not the between-group ones. A comparison of performance between locations showed no differences. It seems that the intensity difference among the tone groups was not used as an auditory cue to perceptually group the tones.

The studies employing the duration illusion show that infants of 6 to 11 months of age detected increases in silent intervals when they occurred within a group of similar tones. Infants did not detect such increases when these occurred between groups that differed in frequency, waveform, and amplitude. An exception was the 100-ms increment with small frequency disparity between groups which was detected. Significant differences of the performances between the within- and between-group locations, however, were found only for the waveform condition with both 80 and 100-ms increments, and the frequency condition with large frequency differences and 100-ms increments. Infants seem to experience the duration illusion under these conditions. Location differences were not observed for the intensity condition, small-frequency condition, and for the large-frequency condition when the increment was 80 ms.

4 IMPLICATIONS FOR PATTERN PERCEPTION IN
SPEECH AND MUSIC

Acoustic messages seldom occur in a quiet environment. In order to attain a clear representation of a certain acoustic message so that higher mental processes can work on it, the relevant speech stream must be separated from competing and interfering 'noises' and other speech streams. During the first months of life, auditory cues that signal location seem to undergo major developmental shifts and may not be available to the very young infants to the same degree as to adults. Nevertheless, young infants are very sensitive to temporal changes of sound attributes such as frequency, amplitude, frequency spectrum, and harmonicity as has been described in the first part of this chapter. In addition, infants seem to be able to organize the auditory space on the basis of temporal coherence of these attributes. The studies on auditory grouping and perception of the duration illusion introduced in the second part of the chapter have shown that auditory grouping mechanisms are functional very early in infancy. Therefore, one may ask which role these mechanisms play in the perception of music and speech, and in language acquisition and music acculturation besides the fact that they are important for structuring the acoustic space into coherent sound sources.

In speech perception, infants not only need to structure the acoustic space in respect to sound sources and speakers but they need to structure the speech stream itself. In learning a language they need to detect which parts and units of the speech stream carry or correspond to a certain meaning they experience (for example, soothing by the mother). They also have to learn what constitute the basic acoustic units of speech and how they are combined to indicate meanings. In order to do this infants must be able to segment the speech stream into appropriate units for further processing. The questions then are: what is an appropriate unit in speech for infants and what parameters constitute such units?

Hirsh-Pasek *et al.* (1987) assessed whether or not clauses are perceptual units for infants. Research with adults has shown that clause boundaries are clearly marked by prosodic changes such as rise and fall in fundamental frequency and lengthening of the syllable preceding the clause boundary (Klatt 1975; Stern *et al.* 1983). Seven- to ten-month-old infants were assessed using a head-turning procedure for their preferences while listening to a mother speaking to her 19-month-old daughter. Infants listened to speech that was segmented at major clause boundaries or within clauses by the inclusion of short pauses. The reasoning behind this is that pauses inserted within a clause, a perceptual unit, or an auditory group would be better detected than pauses of identical duration when placed between clauses, perceptual units, or auditory groups. A clear preference for speech with pauses inserted at clause boundaries over speech with pauses inserted within clauses was found.

Kemler Nelson *et al.* (1989) replicated the results about infants' sensitivity to clause units in child-directed speech. They also assessed whether or not infants of 7 to 10 months of age would be sensitive to the clause units in adult-directed speech, but did not find a preference for between-clause-segmented over within-clause-segmented speech.

For phrases it has been shown as well that phrase boundaries are often marked by changes in prosody such as a drop in fundamental frequency and a lengthening of vowels in the final word of a phrase (Klatt 1975; Cooper and Sorensen 1977). In a number of experiments Jusczyk *et al.* (1992) examined infant's sensitivity to acoustic correlates of phrasal units in their native English language and assessed in particular the role of intonation contour. Infants of 6 to 10 months of age were assessed using a preference procedure (Jusczyk *et al.* 1992). Jusczyk *et al.* found that 9-month-old infants preferred to listen to speech samples segmented at major phrase boundaries. This preference remained even when the stimuli were low-pass filtered in order to eliminate cues to the linguistic content while leaving the prosodic information intact. On the other hand 6-month-old infants showed no significant preference for speech that was segmented at major phrase boundaries. Jusczyk *et al.* (1992) explained this result by the fact that by 9 months the infants have a greater familiarity with the prosodic structure of the language and that the detection of speech segments related to phrase units may depend on experience with a specific language. Jusczyk *et al.* (1992) used stimuli that were taken from a conversation between a mother and her 2-year-old child. Since mothers adjust their language to the perceptual language capabilities of the infant, the kind of motherese spoken to a 6-month-old infant and a 2-year-old child is likely to be different, the latter being much more like adult-directed speech. It is clear that a 9-month-old infant has more experience of this kind of speech than a 6-month-old infant. The question remains, whether or not the 6-month-old infants would be as sensitive to prosodic markers of phrase units when 6-month-old-directed speech would be used.

The studies of Hirsh-Pasek *et al.* (1987), Jusczyk *et al.* (1992), and Kemler Nelson *et al.* (1989) show that infants already parse the speech stream in units like clauses and phrases which are important syntactic units. The results show as well that infants perform this segmentation on the basis of prosodic information. Prosody in turn is the most prominent aspect in child-directed speech.

Motherese or 'baby talk', that is, infant-directed speech by parents and adults, plays an important role in early language acquisition and social interaction (see M. Papoušek, Chapter 4; Papoušek 1994; Papoušek and Papoušek 1987). Papoušek reports that motherese entails modifications to adult-directed speech such as segmentation, repetitiveness, syntactic simplicity, slow tempo, and, most markedly, simplified patterns of expressive melodic contours. Since these aspects of motherese and, in particular, the prosodic or melodic ones can be observed in different native languages and different cultures (Grieser and Kuhl 1988; Fernald *et al*. 1989), it is assumed that motherese exhibits universal prosodic features that are not only brought about by cultural tradition and education but also by genetic predispositions (Papoušek 1987; Trehub 1990). It seems that, through a kind of intuitive parental didactic, parents increase the salience of those aspects of speech that indicate appropriate segments in the ongoing speech stream, such as clauses, phrases, and words, and which reflect the hierarchical syntactical organization of the language. At the same time, motherese is an adjustment to, and reflects the perceptual capacities of, the newborn infant and draws upon the infant's intra-uterine experience. The intra-uterine experience seems to be a sensitization to specific aspects of speech, namely, prosody or melodic line. The newborn has extensive experience with the mother's voice and language (see Lecanuet, Chapter 1). Even though it is adult-directed speech that the fetus has experience of, she or he hears predominantly the prosodic information of the maternal speech. Most other acoustical information is filtered and absorbed during its transmission from air to fluid at the abdominal wall and is masked by the intra-uterine sound environment (Versyp 1985; see Lecanuet, Chapter 1). The prenatal experience shows up after birth in that newborns prefer their mother's voice (DeCasper and Fifer 1980) and prefer stories (DeCasper and Spence 1986) or music (Panneton 1985) that they have heard for some time before birth. Most importantly, they show a strong preference for the prosody in mothers' speech (Fernald 1985; Fernald and Kuhl 1987, Mehler *et al*. 1988).

It is not clear yet whether or not this early postnatal sensitivity for the prosodic features in speech is itself based on a genetic predisposition or on prenatal experience. Some authors assume a predisposition for the perception of prosodic contours (Fernald 1984; Jusczyk and Bertoncini 1988). However, it may as well be a predisposition for the perception of melodic contour in general be it in speech or music. Such a predisposition could be based on Gestalt perception. The Gestalt psychologists assumed that the incoming perceptual information is analysed and grouped into configurations on the basis of simple principles early in the perceptual process (Wertheimer 1923). The early Gestalt psychologists believed that these principles upon which perceptional organization is based are innate (Köhler 1929; Koffka 1935). Research on auditory grouping has shown that infants structure tonal sequences on the basis of frequency similarity as well as on similarity of amplitude and spectral content (Demany 1982; Thorpe *et al.* 1988; Thorpe and Trehub 1989; Fassbender 1993) which gives support to this assumption.

If this assumption were true, infants would not only be sensitive to speech units such as clauses, phrases, and words but they would also be sensitive to structures in music such as musical phrases. Both, music and speech, are hierarchically organized into units that vary in their duration (Lerdahl and Jackendorff 1983). Speech can be divided into clauses, clauses into phrases, phrases into words, and words into syllables. Similarly, a musical piece can be divided into sections, sections into smaller musical phrases, and phrases into melodic and rhythmic figures that are themselves constituted by individual tones. In speech segmentation it has been shown that changes in prosody as well as lengthening of words mark the borders of segments. Since prosody in speech corresponds to melodic line in music it can be expected to play an important role in the segmentation of music as well. Actually, it has been shown that changes in melodic line, lengthening of tone durations, contrasts in pitch range and dynamics, as well as tonal and harmonic stress all contribute to the perceptual segmentation of music (Palmer and Krumhansl 1987*a*, *b*; Clark and Krumhansl 1990).

Krumhansl and Jusczyk (1990), using a visual preference procedure (head turning), investigated whether infants 4½ and 6 months of age would be sensitive to phrase structure in music. Infants listened to excerpts of Mozart minuets in which pauses were included between and within phrases that had been determined by the experimenter's intuition and were checked against adult listeners' perceptions of phrase structure. Infants of both age groups listened significantly longer to those versions of the minuets that contained pauses at phrase boundaries than to those containing pauses within the phrases. The musical cues that would signal phrase boundaries were a drop in pitch height, an increase in pitch duration at the end of the phrase, and octave simultaneities. From the results it seems that infants are sensitive to these parameters and use them for perceptual segmentation of the music in a manner similar to their procedure in speech perception. Other research has demonstrated infants' sensitivity to melodic contour (Trehub 1987), octave equivalence (Demany and Armand 1984), and auditory grouping on the basis of frequency similarity, amplitude similarity, and spectral similarity (Demany 1982; Thorpe *et al.* 1988; Thorpe and Trehub 1989; Fassbender 1993).

Jusczyk and Krumhansl (1993) extended the above findings. They employed the same design of inserting pauses between or within musical phrases of Mozart minuets, thus creating naturally and unnaturally segmented stimuli. Infants were about 4½ months of age. In a series of experiments they first replicated Krumhansl and Jusczyk's (1990) results showing that infants were really reacting to the phrase boundaries and not to the beginnings and endings of the minuet stimuli as could have been the case by their previous choice of stimuli. A second experiment showed that infants had no preference for music with pauses inserted at phrase boundaries over the original musical passages. In a third experiment infants listened to naturally segmented music and to this music played in reversed tone order. It was reasoned that playing the music in reverse order keeps the complexity of the melodic contour, harmonic intervals, and the individual pitches but changes the directionality of melodic contour and tone duration. Since infants showed a preference for naturally segmented music over music played in reversed order, this is taken as evidence that the directionality of changes, that is a drop in pitch height and a lengthening of tones occurring before phrase boundaries is important for segmenting the music and not merely the existence of a discontinuity in these variables. This interpretation was supported by the fact that in the fourth experiment infants had no preference when both within- and between-phrase segmented music was played in reverse order. In the final experiment infants compared the original music and the original music played in reverse order. No preference for either condition was found which had not been expected on the basis of the previous results, particularly since experiments 3 and 4 clearly indicated that the directionality of change in intonation contour and tone duration is the important marker for a phrase boundary and not only a change as such. Even though it is not clear how the results should be interpreted, they seem to indicate that infants segment the stream of musical tones in units that correspond to musical phrases. It seems that they do this on the basis of acoustical information that generally occurs at phrase boundaries such as change in melodic contour, lengthening of tone duration, and change in harmonies.

In summary, it seems that infants parse ongoing acoustical stimuli, be they speech or music, on the basis of information that marks important syntactical units. The acoustical environment in the uterus and the post-natally experienced motherese provide frames to signal and teach the infant the important markers necessary to segment and structure speech and music. At the same time it seems that the infant brings with him or her important predispositions to perceive and learn these markers. The infant is highly sensitive to melodic and temporal variations in speech and music from early on, and it seems that this sensitivity is based in part on the ability to group and segment auditory information on the basis of Gestalt principles. In the beginning, perceptions of speech and music seems to arise from the same basis, but they may take different developmental courses when meaning becomes attached to specific acoustical information in the social interaction of intuitive parenting.

REFERENCES

Bartoshuk, A. K. (1962). Human neonatal cardiac acceleration to sound: habituation and dishabituation. *Perceptual Motor Skills*, **15**, 15–27.

Berg, W. K. and Berg, K. M. (1979). Psychophysiological development in infancy: state, sensory function and attention. In *Handbook of infant development* (ed. J. Osofsky), pp. 283–343. Wiley, New York.

Berg, W. K. and Smith, M. C. (1983). Behavioral thresholds for tones during infancy. *Journal of Experimental Child Psychology*, **35**, 409–25.

Bertoncini, J., Bijeljac-Babic, R., Jusczyk, P. W., Kennedy, L. J., and Mehler, J. (1988). An investigation of young infants' perceptual representations of speech sounds. *Journal of Experimental Psychology: General*, **117**, 21–33.

Bower, T. G. R. (1965). The determinants of perceptual unity in infancy. *Psychonomic Science*, **3**, 323–4.

Bower, T. G. R. (1967). Phenomenal identity and form perception in an infant. *Perception and Psychophysics*, **2**, 74–6.

Brackbill, Y. (1970). Acoustic variation and arousal level in infants. *Psychophysiology*, **6**, 517–26.

Bredberg, G. (1985). The anatomy of the developing ear. In *Auditory development in infancy* (ed. S. E. Trehub and B. Schneider), pp. 3–20. Plenum Press, New York.

Bregman, A. S. (1990). *Auditory scene analysis: The perceptual organization of sound*. MIT Press, Cambridge, Massachusetts.

Bronshtein, A. I., Antonova, T. G., Kamenetskaya, A. G., Luppova, N. N., and Sytova, V. A. (1958). On the development of the functions of analysers in infants and some animals at the early stage of ontogenesis. In *Office of Technical Services Report* no. 60-61066 (Ed.). [Translation obtainable from the United States Department of Commerce, Office of Technical Services (pp. 106–16).] Academiya Nauk, Moscow.

Bull, D., Schneider, B. A., and Trehub, S. E. (1981). The masking of octave-band noise by broad-spectrum noise: A comparison of infant and adult thresholds. *Perception and Psychophysics*, **30**, 101–6.

Bundy, R. S., Colombo, J., and Singer, J. (1982). Pitch perception in young infants. *Developmental Psychology*, **18**, 10–14.

Butterfield, E. C. and Siperstein, G. N. (1972) Influence of contingent auditory stimulation upon non-nutritional suckle. In *Oral sensation and perception: the mouth of the infant* (ed. J. Bosma), pp. 103–19. C. C. Thomas, Springfield, Illinois.

Chang, H. W. and Trehub, S. E. (1977a). Auditory processing of relational information by young infants. *Journal of Experimental Child Psychology*, **24**, 324–31.

Chang, H. W. and Trehub, S. E. (1977b). Infants' perception of temporal grouping in auditory patterns. *Child Development*, **48**, 1666–70.

Chun, R. W. M., Pawsat, R., and Forster, F. M. (1960). Sound localization in infancy. *Journal of Nervous and Mental Disease*, **130**, 472–6.

Clark, E. F. and Krumhansl, C. L. (1990). Perceiving musical time. *Music Perception*, **7**, 213–52.

Clarkson, M. G. and Clifton, R. K. (1985). Infant pitch perception: evidence for responding to pitch categories and the missing fundamental. *Journal of the Acoustical Society of America*, **77**, 1521–8.

Clarkson, M. G., Clifton, R. K., and Perris, E. E. (1988). Infant timbre perception: discrimination of spectral envelopes. *Perception and Psychophysics*, **43**, 15–20.

Clifton, R. K. (1992). The development of spatial hearing in human infants. In *Developmental psychoacoustics* (ed. L. A. Werner and E. W. Rubel), pp. 135–57. Psychological Association, Washington, DC.

Clifton, R. K., Morrongiello, B. A., Kulig, J. W., and Dowd, J. M. (1981). Newborn's orientation toward sound: possible implications for cortical development. *Child Development*, **53**, 833–8.

Clifton, R. K., Morrongiello, B. A., and Dowd, J. M. (1984). A developmental look at an auditory illusion: the precedence effect. *Developmental Psychobiology*, **17**, 519–36.

Cooper, W. and Sorensen, J. (1977). Fundamental frequency contours at syntactic boundaries. *Journal of the Acoustical Society of America*, **62**, 683–92.

Crook, C. K. (1979). The organization and control of infant sucking. In *Advances in child development and behavior*, Vol. 14 (ed. H. W. Reese and L. P. Lipsitt), pp. 209–52. Academic Press, New York.

Dearborn, G. V. N. (1910). *Moto-sensory development: observations of the first three years of a child*. Warwick & York, Baltimore, Maryland.

DeCasper, A. J. and Fifer, W. P. (1980). Of human bonding: newborns prefer their mother's voice. *Science*, **208**, 1174–6.

DeCasper, A. J. and Spence, M. J. (1986). Newborns prefer a familiar story over an unfamiliar one. *Infant Behavior and Development*, **9**, 133–50.

Demany, L. (1982). Auditory stream segregation in infancy. *Infant Behavior and Development*, **5**, 261–76.

Demany, L. and Armand, F. (1984). The perceptual reality of tone chroma in early infancy. *Journal of the Acoustical Society of America*, **76**, 57–66.

Ehret, G. and Romand, R. (1981). Postnatal development of absolute auditory thresholds in kittens. *Journal of Comparative Physiological Psychology*, **95**, 304–11.

Eimas, P. D. (1974). Auditory and linguistic processing of cues for place of articulation by infants. *Perception and Psychophysics*, **16**, 513–21.

Eisenberg, R. B. (1976). *Auditory competence in early life*. University Park Press, Baltimore.

Elliot, L. L. and Katz, D. R. (1980). Children's pure tone detection. *Journal of the Acoustical Society of America*, **67**, 343–4.

Fassbender, C. (1993). *Auditory grouping and segregation processes in infancy*. Kaste Verlag, Norderstedt.

Fernald, A. (1984). The perceptual and affective salience of mothers' speech to infants. In *The origins and growth of communication* (ed. L. Feagans, D. Garvey, and R. Golinkoff), pp. 5–29. Ablex, Norwood, New Jersey.

Fernald, A. (1985). Four-month-old infants prefer to listen to motherese. *Infant Behavior and Development*, **8**, 181–95.

Fernald, A. and Kuhl, P. (1987). Acoustic determinants of infant preference for motherese speech. *Infant Behavior and Development*, **10**, 279–93.

Fernald, A., Taeschner, T., Dunn, J., Papousek, M., Boysson-Bardies, B., and Fukui, I. (1989). A cross language study of prosodic modifications in mother's and father's speech to preverbal infants. *Journal of Child Language*, **16**, 977–1001.

Fitzgibbons, P. J., Pollatsek, A., and Thomas, I. B. (1974). Detection of temporal gaps within and between perceptual tonal groups. *Perception and Psychophysics*, **16**, 522–8.

Fraisse, P. (1982). Rhythm and tempo. In *The psychology of music* (ed. D. Deutsch), pp. 149–80. Academic Press, New York.

Grieser, D. L. and Kuhl, P. K. (1988). Maternal speech to infants in a tonal language: support for universal prosodic features in motherese. *Developmental Psychology*, **24**, 14–20.

Haller, M. (1932). The reactions of infants to changes in the intensity and pitch of pure tones. *Journal of Genetic Psychology*, **40**, 162–80.

Hecox, K. (1975). Electrophysiological correlates of human auditory development. In *Infant perception* (ed. L. B. Cohen and P. Salapatek), pp. 151–91. Academic Press, New York.

Hirsh-Pasek, K., Kemler Nelson, D. G., Jusczyk, P. W., Druss, K. W. C. B., and Kennedy, L. (1987). Clauses are perceptual units for young infants. *Cognition*, **26**, 269–86.

Jusczyk, P. W. (1985). The high-amplitude sucking technique as a methodological tool in speech perception research. In *Measurement of audition and vision in the first year of life* (ed. G. Gottlieb and N. A. Krasnegor), pp. 195–222. Ablex, Norwood, New Jersey.

Jusczyk, P. W. and Bertoncini, J. (1988). Viewing the development of speech perception as an innately guided learning process. *Language and Speech*, **31**, 217–37.

Jusczyk, P. W. and Krumhansl, C. L. (1993). Pitch and rhythmic patterns affecting infant's sensitivity to musical phrase structure. *Journal of Experimental Psychology: Human Perception and Performance*, **19**, 627–40.

Jusczyk, P. W., Hirsch-Pasek, K., Kemler Nelson, D. G., Kennedy, L. J., Woodward, A., and Piwoz, J. (1992). Perception of acoustic correlates of major phrasal units by young infants. *Cognitive Psychology*, **24**, 252–93.

Kaye, H. (1966). The effects of feeding and tonal stimulation on non-nutritive sucking in the human neonate. *Journal of Experimental Child Psychology*, **3**, 131–45.

Kaye, H. and Levin, G. R. (1963). Two attempts to demonstrate tonal suppression of nonnutritive sucking in the neonate. *Perceptual and Motor Skills*, **17**, 521–2.

Kemler Nelson, D. G., Hirsh-Pasek, K., Jusczyk, P. W., and Cassidy, K. W. (1989). How the prosodic cues in motherese might assist language learning. *Journal of Child Language*, **16**, 55–68.

Klatt, D. H. (1975). Vowel lengthening is syntactically determined in connected discourse. *Journal of Phonetics*, **3**, 129–40.

Klein, A. J. (1984). Frequency and age-dependent auditory evoked potential thresholds in infants. *Hearing Research*, **16**, 291–7.

Kïhler, W. (1929). *Gestalt psychology*. Horace Liveright, New York.

Koffka, K. (1935). *Principles of Gestalt psychology*. Harcourt & Brace, New York.

Krumhansl, C. L. and Jusczyk, P. W. (1990). Infant's perception of phrase structure in music. *Psychological Science*, **1**, 70–3.

Lerdahl, F. and Jackendorff, R. (1983). *A generative theory of tonal music*. MIT Press, Cambridge, Massachusetts.

Leventhal, A. and Lipsitt, L. P. (1964). Adaptation, pitch discrimination and sound localization in the neonate. *Child Development*, **35**, 759–67.

Mehler, J., Jusczyk, P., Lambertz, G., Halsted, N., Bertoncini, J., and Amiel Tison, C. (1988). A precursor of language acquisition in young infants. *Cognition*, **29**, 143–78.

Miller, A. R. (1983). *Auditory physiology*. Academic Press, New York.

Miller, C. L. and Byrne, J. M. (1983). Psychophysiologic and behavioral response to auditory stimuli in the newborn. *Infant Behavior and Development*, **6**, 369–89.

Miller, G. A. and Heise, G. A. (1950). The trill threshold. *Journal of the Acoustical Society of America*, **2**, 637–8.

Moore, J. M. and Wilson, W. (1978). Visual reinforcement audiometry (VRA) with infants. In *Early diagnosis of hearing loss* (ed. S. E. Gerber and G. T. Mencher), pp. 177–213. Grune and Stratton, New York.

Moore, J. M., Thompson, G., and Thompson, M. (1975). Auditory localization of infants as a function of reinforcement conditions. *Journal of Speech and Hearing Disorders*, **40**, 29–34.

Morrongiello, B. A. (1986). Infant's perception of multiple-group auditory patterns. *Infant Behavior and Development*, **9**, 307–19.

Morrongiello, B. A. and Rocca, P. T. (1987a). Infants' localization of sounds in the horizontal plane: effects of auditory and visual cues. *Child Development*, **58**, 918–27.

Morrongiello, B. A. and Rocca, P. T. (1987b). Infant's localization of sounds in the median vertical lane: estimates of minimum audible angle. *Journal of Experimental Child Psychology*, **43**, 181–93.

Muir, D., Abraham, W., Forbes, B., and Harris, L. (1979). The ontogenesis of an auditory localization response from birth to four months of age. *Canadian Journal of Psychology*, **33**, 320–33.

Nordmark, J. O. (1978). Frequency and periodicity analysis. In *Handbook of perception: hearing* (ed. E. C. Carterette and M. P. Friedman), pp. 243–82. Academic Press, New York.

Northern, J. L. and Downs, M. P. (1974). *Hearing in children*. Williams & Wilkins, Baltimore, Maryland.

Northern, J. L. and Downs, M. P. (1991). *Hearing in children* (4th edn). Williams & Wilkins, Baltimore, Maryland.

Nozza, R. J. (1987). The binaural masking level difference in infants and adults: developmental change in binaural hearing. *Infant Behavior and Development*, **10**, 105–10.

Nozza, R. J. and Wilson, W. R. (1984). Masked and unmasked pure-tone thresholds of infants and adults: development of auditory frequency selectivity and sensitivity. *Journal of Speech and Hearing Research*, **27**, 613–22.

Nozza, R. J., Wagner, E. F., and Crandell, M. A. (1988). Binaural release from masking for a speech sound in infants, preschoolers, and adults. *Journal of Speech and Hearing Research*, **31**, 212–18.

Olsho, L. W. (1984). Infant frequency discrimination. *Infant Behavior and Development*, **7**, 27–35.

Olsho, L. W. (1985). Infant auditory perception: tonal masking. *Infant Behavior and Development*, **8**, 371–84.

Olsho, L. W., Koch, E. G., Halpin, C. F., and Carter, E. A. (1987). An observer-based psychoacoustic procedure for use with young infants. *Developmental Psychology*, **23**, 627–40.

Olsho, L. W., Koch, E. G., Carter, E. A., Halpin, C. F., and Spetner, N. B. (1988). Pure-tone sensitivity of human infants. *Journal of the Acoustical Society of America*, **84**, 1316–24.

Palmer, C. and Krumhansl, C. L. (1987a). Independent temporal and pitch structures in determination of musical phrases. *Journal of Experimental Psychology: Human Perception and Performance*, **13**, 116–26.

Palmer, C. and Krumhansl, C. L. (1987b). Pitch and temporal contributions to musical phrase perception: effects of harmony, performance timing, and familiarity. *Perception and Psychophysics*, **41**, 505–18.

Panneton, R. K. (1985). Prenatal experience with melodies: effect on postnatal auditory preferences in newborns. Unpublished D. Phil. thesis. University of North Carolina at Greensboro.

Papoušek, H. and Papoušek, M. (1987). Early ontogeny of human social interaction: its biological roots and social dimensions. In *Human ethology* (ed. M. von Cranach, K. Foppa, W. Lepenies, and D. Ploog), pp. 456–78. Cambridge University Press, London.

Papoušek, M. (1987). Melodies in motherese in tonal and nontonal languages: Mandarin Chinese, Caucasian American, and German. Presentation at the Ninth Biennial Meeting of the International Society for the Study of Behavioral Development, Tokyo. Japan, July 1987.

Papoušek, M. (1994). *Vom ersten Schrei zum ersten Wort: anfänge der Sprachentwicklung in der vorsprachlichen Kommunikation*. Verlag Hans Huber, Berne.

Plomp, R. (1970). Timbre as a multidimensional attribute of complex tones. In *Frequency analysis and periodicity detection in hearing* (ed. R. Plomp and G. F. Smoorenburg), pp. 397–411. Sijthoff, Leiden.

Preis, A. (1984). An attempt to describe the parameter determining the timbre of steady-state harmonic complex tones. *Acoustica*, **55**, 1–13.

Sameroff, A. J. (1967). Nonnutritive sucking in newborns under visual and auditory stimulation. *Child Development*, **38**, 443–52.

Sameroff, A. J. (1968). The components of sucking in the human newborn. *Journal of Experimental Child Psychology*, **6**, 607–23.

Saunders, J. C., Kaltenbach, J. A., and Relkin, E. M. (1983). The structural and functional development of the outer and middle ear. In *Development of auditory and vestibular systems* (ed. R. Romand), pp. 3–22. Academic Press, New York.

Scharf, B. (1970). Critical bands. In *Foundations of modern auditory theory*, Vol. 1 (ed. J. V. Tobis), pp. 159–202. Academic Press, New York.

Schneider, B. A. and Trehub, S. E. (1985). Infants auditory psychophysics: an overview. In *Measurement of audition and vision in the first year of life: a methodological overview* (ed. G. Gottlieb and N. A. Krasnegor), pp. 119–26. Ablex, Norwood, NJ.

Schneider, B. A. and Trehub, S. E. (1992). Sources of developmental change in auditory sensitivity. In *Developmental psychoacoustics* (ed. L. A. Werner and E. W. Rubel), pp. 3–46. American Psychological Association, Washington, DC.

Schneider, B. A., Trehub, S. E,. and Bull, D. (1980). High-frequency sensitivity in infants. *Science*, **207**, 1003–4.

Schouten, J. F. (1940). The perception of pitch. *Philips Technical Review*, **5**, 286–94.

Sinnot, J. M., Pisoni, D. B., and Aslin, R. M. (1983). A comparison of pure tone auditory thresholds in human infants and adults. *Infant Behavior and Development*, **6**, 3–17.

Siqueland, E. R. and DeLucia, C. A. (1969). Visual reinforcement of non-nutritive sucking in human infants. *Science*, **165**, 1144–6.

Stern, D., Spieker, S., Barnett, R., and MacKain, K. (1983). The prosody of maternal speech: infant age and context related change. *Journal of Child Language*, **10**, 1–15.

Suzuki, T., Kamijo, Y., and Kiuchi, S. (1964). Auditory tests of newborn infants. *Annals of Otology*, **73**, 914–23.

Teller, D. Y. (1979). The forced-choice preferential looking procedure: a psychophysical technique for use with human infants. *Infant Behavior and Development*, **2**, 135–53.

Terhardt, E. (1974). Pitch, consonance, and harmony. *Journal of the Acoustical Society of America*, **55**, 1061–9.

Thorpe, L. A. and Trehub, S. E. (1989). Duration illusion and auditory grouping in infancy. *Developmental Psychology*, **25**, 122–7.

Thorpe, L. A., Trehub, S. E., Morrongiello, B. A., and Bull, D. (1988). Perceptual grouping by infants and preschool children. *Developmental Psychology*, **24**, 484–91.

Trehub, S. E. (1973). Infants' sensitivity to vowel and tonal contrasts. *Developmental Psychology*, **9**, 91–6.

Trehub, S. E. (1987). Infant's perception of musical patterns. *Perception and Psychophysics*, **41**, 635–41.

Trehub, S. E. (1990). The perception of musical patterns by human infants: the provision of similar patterns by their parents. In *Comparative perception*, Vol. 1. *Basic mechanisms* (ed. M. A. Berkley and W. C. Stebbins), pp. 429–59. Wiley, New York.

Trehub, S. E., Schneider, B. A., and Endman, M. (1980). Developmental changes in infants' sensitivity to octave-band noises. *Journal of Experimental Child Psychology*, **29**, 283–93.

Trehub, S. E., Bull, D., and Thorpe, L. A. (1984). Infant's perception of melodies: the role of melodic contour. *Child Development*, **55**, 821–30.

Trehub, S. E., Thorpe, L. A., and Morrongiello, B. A. (1985). Infants' perception of melodies: changes in a single tone. *Infant Behavior and Development*, **8**, 213–23.

Trehub, S. E., Bull, D., Schneider, B. A., and Morrongiello, B. A. (1986). PESTI: a procedure for estimating individual thresholds in infant listeners. *Infant Behavior and Development*, **9**, 107–18.

Trehub, S. E., Thorpe, L. A., and Morrongiello, B. A. (1987). Organizational processes in infants' perception of auditory patterns. *Child Development*, **58**, 741–9.

Trehub, S. E., Endman, M. W., and Thorpe, L. A. (1990). Infant's perception of timbre: classification of complex tones by spectral structure. *Journal of Experimental Child Psychology*, **49**, 300–13.

Turkewitz, G., Moreau, T., Birch, H. G., and Davis, L. (1971). Relationships among responses in the human newborn: the non-association and non-equivalence among different indicators of responsiveness. *Psychophysiology*, **7**, 233–47.

Versyp, F. (1985). Transmission intra-amniotique des sons et des voix humains. Unpublished MD thesis. University of Lille, France.

Wedenberg, E. (1956). Auditory tests on newborn infants. *Acta Otolaryngologica*, **46**, 446–61.

Werner, L. A. (1992). Interpreting developmental psychoacoustics. In *Developmental psychoacoustics* (ed. L. A. Werner and E. W. Rubel), pp. 47–88. American Psychological Association, Washington, DC.

Wertheimer, M. (1923). Untersuchung zur Lehre von der Gestalt II. *Psychologische Forschung*, **4**, 301–50.

Woodrow, H. (1909). A quantitative study of rhythm. *Archives of Psychology*, **14**, 1–68.

Wormith, S. J., Pankhurst, D., and Moffit, A. R. (1975). Frequency discrimination by young infants. *Child Development*, **46**, 272–5.

Yoneshighe, Y. and Elliot, L. L. (1981). Pure-tone sensitivity and ear canal pressure at threshold in children and adults. *Journal of the Acoustical Society of America*, **70**, 1272–6.

4

Intuitive parenting: a hidden source of musical stimulation in infancy

Mechthild Papoušek

1 INTRODUCTION

Inspired by ingenious pioneers such as Kodály, Orff, or Suzuki, preschool music education has spread across many countries over the past decade and has progressively been encountered by children as young as 3- or even 2-years-old. Formal music education based on various musicological approaches has proved effective in the majority of children independently of a special gift for music and has also proved supportive for other domains of psychological development. However, formal music education, whether traditional or innovative, has left unexplored the period of infancy and the toddler age group.

A similar gap is apparent in scientific approaches to musical development. Yet, two converging lines of research have recently stimulated the interest of both psychologists and musicologists in the earliest stages of musical development, namely, the growing evidence of early predispositions for musical perception in human infants, on the one hand, and, on the other, extensive research on early sources of musical stimulation in infants' caregiving environment, particularly in infant-directed speech and infant-directed singing.

1.1 Predispositions for music in human infants

Infants and toddlers seem to be well prepared for musical experience. Although their movements are not yet co-ordinated enough to allow infants to handle a musical instrument, their ability to perceive and process fundamental musical qualities is evident even prior to birth. Moreover, infants are born with a vocal tract that provides a powerful and increasingly functional musical instrument before it becomes capable of producing speech sounds. Infants soon reveal a strong intrinsic motivation for vocal practising or vocal play, together with special capacities for vocal imitation.

Auditory competencies for differentiating and processing fundamental features and global patterns of musical stimulation have been shown to develop strikingly early. Infants in the first postpartum months are able to detect and discriminate small differences in frequency, amplitude, and the harmonic spectrum (see the review by Fassbender in Chapter 3). They are able to process time-related information and to differentiate sounds in terms of duration, pause length, tempo, and relative timing in rhythmic sequences (see the review by Pouthas in Chapter 5). Early functioning of auditory grouping processes allows infants to structure their auditory environment into coherent global patterns from distinctive sound sources, and they do so on the basis of the sound attributes of frequency, amplitude, and spectral information (Fassbender 1993; Chapter 3). Infants are also capable of sensorimotor and intersensory processing of temporal information and of integrating information across auditory, visual, and proprioceptive modalities (Meltzoff and Borton 1979; Spelke 1979; Pouthas, Chapter 5).

Some of these early perceptual capacities have been demonstrated to function even 3–4 months prior to birth (see the review by Lecanuet in Chapter 1). Prenatal exposure to and familiarization with salient auditory stimuli most probably accounts for the newborn's auditory preference for the mother's voice (DeCasper and Fifer 1980), for a familiarized melody (Panneton 1985), for the prosody (that is, melody, rhythm, and dynamics) of a familiarized spoken text (DeCasper and Spence 1986), and for the mother's language (Mehler *et al.* 1988). Current evidence on infants' predispositions for musical stimulation has consequently inspired a shift in research to the natural sources of musical experiences in infants' caregiving environment.

1.2 Predispositions for music education in parents

Although infants' predispositions for music have long escaped the attention of scientists and music teachers, they have not remained unnoticed by parents and other caregivers who, typically, surround infants with a wealth of lively musical stimulation. Caregivers' singing, rocking, or dancing may challenge infants' attention and integrative processes, and may function as early forms of musical fostering. Unfortunately, in present industrialized societies, parental tendencies to sing and dance have decreased in many families, probably due to a surplus of reproduced background music, or due to dramatic changes in contemporary style. Only one hidden source of early musical stimulation has remained relatively unchanged and protected against artificial manipulation, namely, the intrinsic, non-consciously determined music of infant-directed speech.

Our own interest in the origins of musical competence grew from our detection of rich sources of musical stimulation in preverbal vocal communication between parents and infants (Papoušek and Papoušek 1981). In spite of a wide gap between parents and infants in communicative and integrative competencies, behavioural microanalyses of parent–infant interactions revealed common ground for three aspects of early musical experience.

(1) From early on, parents and infants share a 'prelinguistic alphabet' or code in the form of musical elements that both infant-directed speech and infant vocal sounds have in common. In fact, musical elements, such as pitch and melody, temporal patterns and rhythm, loudness and accent, and timbre and harmony, are the most salient features of both partners' vocal utterances, and soon become the earliest means of reciprocal communication, preverbal vocal imitation, and playful vocal interchanges.

(2) The presence of a common elementary musical code is supplemented by a striking correspondence and complementarity between infants' early perceptual competence and the infants' auditory input as present in the social caregiving environment. Parents and other caregivers demonstrate intuitive propensities both for speaking to newborn infants as reported by Rheingold and Adams (1980), and for providing what may be called the earliest forms of music education. They adjust their vocal, visual, facial, and tactile stimulations in ways that correspond to infants' perceptual and integrative capacities, respect infants' preferences and constraints, and thus facilitate and didactically support infants' early musical competence.

(3) The vocal domain alone does not capture the full richness of early musical experience. From the beginning, vocal production and perception of musical elements are embedded in multimodal patterns of preverbal communication, including tactile, kinaesthetic, and vestibular forms of stimulation (Sullivan and Horowitz 1983*b*). Again, the most salient features of multimodal stimulation are consistent with the most relevant incentives for early musical development, namely, modulations in rhythm and dynamics in kinetic, proprioceptive, and vestibular forms of stimulation. In turn, the parents' multimodal patterns of stimulation complement infants' early capacities for transmodal or amodal perception and integration (Spelke 1979).

1.3 Musical elements in preverbal communication: the Papoušeks' approach to the earliest stages of musical stimulation

Identification of musical elements in preverbal communication stimulated us to formulate descriptive and analytic methods for studying the structure, functions, and meanings of musical elements in preverbal parent–infant dialogues (Papoušek and Papoušek 1981; Papoušek 1994*a*). The methods included musical transcription as well as sonagraphic and digital acoustic analyses of fundamental frequency, amplitude, time, and harmonic spectrum (Fig. 4.1). Examination of these data opened empirical access to three closely interrelated facets of preverbal communication: emotional signalling; precursors to speech; and playful creative activity in spontaneous singing. We soon became aware that the preverbal origins of musical skills cannot easily be differentiated from

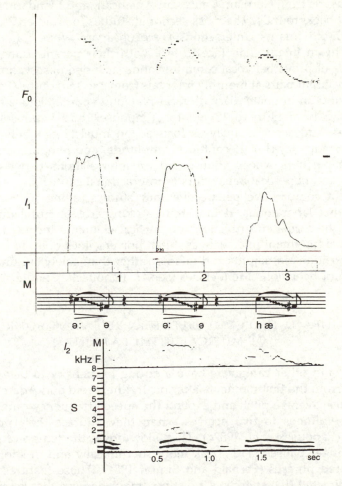

Fig. 4.1 Combined methods of auditory and acoustic analyses. Sequence of euphonic cooing sounds from a 2-month-old infant. From top to bottom: F_0, fundamental frequency contours; I_1, intensity contours; T, temporal structure; M, musical transcription and phonetic transcription; I_2 and S, intensity and spectrogram from sonagraphy, respectively.

the prelinguistic stages of speech acquisition and from the basic alphabet of emotional communication (Papoušek 1989).

This report is based on a series of studies including not only naturalistic observations in both cross-sectional and longitudinal studies, but also experimental approaches in playback studies (Papoušek *et al.* 1987*a*, 1991; M. Papoušek and Papoušek 1991). Spontaneous vocal communication was observed, videorecorded, and audiorecorded in free-play contexts of parent–infant interactions in the laboratory. For comparative analyses across parental gender and culture, we studied some 80 parent–infant dyads from German, Caucasian American, and Mandarin Chinese cultural backgrounds. The cross-sectional studies focused on 2-, 3-, and 4-month-old infants. Interactions were observed while infants were seated in an infant chair face to face with their parent. Longitudinal analyses of preverbal vocal communication included observations in 18 mother–infant pairs at monthly intervals from 2 to 15 months (Papoušek 1994*a*) and an intimate diary of vocal play and spontaneous singing in one child from birth to 18 months (Papoušek and Papoušek 1981). Auditory and acoustic analyses focused on musical elements (fundamental frequency (F_0), F_0 contours, amplitude, and temporal structure) in both partners' vocalizations, and on interrelations between vocal sounds and non-vocal behaviours in interactional contexts.

From a comparative perspective, our studies, along with research from other laboratories, demonstrate striking cross-cultural universalities in the forms and functions of musical elements included in preverbal parent–infant interchanges. Such universalities point to biological predispositions in parents and infants rather than solely cultural transmission of behavioural tendencies (see H. Papoušek, Chapter 2).

2   INFANT-DIRECTED SPEECH: A RELEVANT SOURCE OF MUSICAL STIMULATION

Parents and other caregivers have a strong propensity to talk to their infants from the first moments after birth (Rheingold and Adams 1980). They raise average pitch and expand the speech frequency ranges from seven semitones to two octaves when they address their preverbal infants (Papoušek *et al.* 1987*a*). They slow down the tempo of speech, make longer pauses, and speak more rhythmically and in short, well-segmented phrases (Fernald and Simon 1984). These features qualify infant-directed (ID) speech as a distinct linguistic form that is known in the literature as motherese, 'Ammensprache', or baby talk. The overall rise in pitch helps infants to identify and track auditory stimulation directed to them in the context of background noises. Caregivers also modify articulatory, phonological, and syntactic aspects of speech, but these linguistic adjustments become prominent only when infants are addressed who already have begun to speak (Snow 1972; Ferguson 1977).

During the first year, the melodic contours of ID utterances represent the most salient features of ID speech. Melodic contours are expanded to seven semitones per utterance on the average, and they form simple unidirectional contours (rising, falling, or flat) or bidirectional contours (bell-shaped or ∪-shaped) in two-thirds of utterances (Papoušek *et al.* 1985). Caregivers tend to use a limited set of five to six distinctive melodic prototypes (Fig. 4.2). The prototypical contours are frequently repeated and, in spite of changing verbal contents, are highly similar across repetitions without becoming stereotypic.

In most cases, the melodic contours of ID speech do not resemble sung melodies with discernible notes; rather, they represent smooth, continuously gliding pitch contours. Caregivers preferably use one-syllable utterances, often without much linguistic information, such as interjections, calls, and imitative sounds. They tend to prolong the vowel segments in these utterances and utilize them for extensive melodic modulations. As pointed out by Fernald (1984) and Trehub (1990), the acoustic features of melodic contours in ID speech strikingly fulfil the basic principles of Gestalt perception, namely, coherence (based on proximity and similarity), figure–ground contrast, prototypicality, and

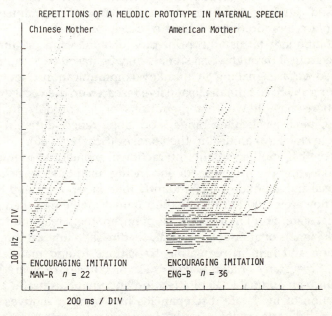

Fig. 4.2 Prototypical rising contours from a Mandarin Chinese (MAN) and an American (ENG) mother. Repetitive F_0 contours of maternal utterances were extracted from 3-min dialogues with their 2-month-old infants.

common fate (see Fassbender, Chapter 3). These qualities facilitate perceptual processing of melodic units in speech (Trehub *et al.* 1984). Moreover, caregivers tend to use melodic contours found in preceding infant sounds; thus they fulfil crucial prerequisites for efficient familiarization, learning, and conceptualization (Papoušek and Papoušek 1984).

2.1   Functional significance of infant-directed melodies in speech

2.1.1   *Modulation of arousal and attention*

In spite of numerous repetitions of prototypical contours, ID speech does not seem to sound monotonous or boring. Like endless variations on a small set of themes or motives in music, sequential contours are constantly varied in ways that are reminiscent of three principles in music: build-up of arousal and tension; release of arousal and tension; and playful elaboration on a high level of arousal. The human voice offers a rich source for varying melodies in terms of tempo and rhythm, duration and pausing, absolute pitch, pitch excursions and intervals, overall loudness and accent, and quality of voice. While transcribing sequences of repetitive ID contours into musical notes, we were often tempted to use musicological connotations, such as transposition to another key, augmentation or inversion of melody, ornamentation with trills or grace notes, and dynamic descriptions such as crescendo/diminuendo, rallentando/accelerando, legato/staccato, dolce, or agitato.

In evolutionary terms, the principles of enhancing or diminishing affective arousal through vocal signals may be traced back to the advent of graded vocal signalling in monkey communication (Newman and Goedeking 1992). In humans, extensive research on the vocal expression of emotions has shown that gradations of F_0 contours in terms of duration, pitch level, pitch range, and slope reflect different levels of psychophysiological arousal in the speaker (Scherer 1986).

In preverbal mother–infant interactions, moment-to-moment variations following the principles of enhancing, maintaining, or diminishing arousal and attention are abundantly found (Papoušek and Papoušek 1987). They are finely attuned to the infants' momentary behavioural–emotional state. From moment to moment, mothers respond to infants' feedback signals of attention, arousal, readiness to interact, boredom or exhaustion and help in regulating transitions to and maintenance of either optimal states of alert wakefulness or states of recovery in restful sleep. Once an optimal level of attention and joyful arousal is achieved, introduction of moderate discrepancies into familiar motives helps to maintain that state as long as the infant can tolerate it (McCall and Kagan 1967). In other words, when mothers respond to infant signals of tension, hyperarousal, or exhaustion with soothing–calming interventions, they tend to reduce the rate and intensity of stimulation: the melodies become significantly longer, flatter, and lower in range and level of pitch (Fig. 4.3) (Papoušek *et al.* 1991). When mothers respond to infant cues of passivity and inattentiveness with alerting interventions, they non-consciously increase the rate and intensity of stimulation: the melodies become shorter, steeper, and higher in level and range of fundamental frequency.

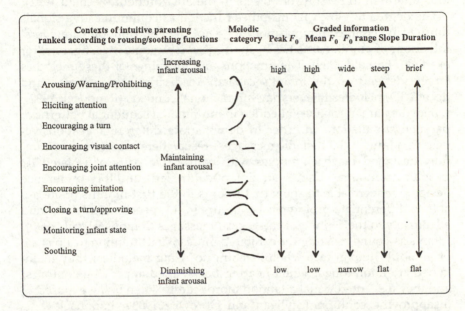

Fig. 4.3 Graded and categorical information in melodies of ID speech: relation of melodic form to arousing/soothing functions of intuitive parenting.

These findings suggest that ID melodies are intimately related to basic regulatory processes of affective arousal and attention. They represent relevant means that allow parents to modulate behavioural–emotional states in infants during preverbal interactions (Papoušek 1994*b*).

2.1.2 *Categorical messages related to caregivers' intuitive didactic guidance*

As well as the graded information described above, ID melodic contours also carry categorical information (Papoušek *et al.* 1991). Interesting form–function relations were found when individual categories of ID melodic contours were analysed in relation to common interactional frames of intuitive parental caregiving. Parents tend to use rising melodies for eliciting or enhancing arousal and attention and/or for giving the infant a turn in dialogue; they use falling melodies for soothing a hyperaroused infant, or for ending a turn-taking sequence. Extended bell-shaped contours prevail when mothers reinforce or approve preceding infant behaviours. Conversely, bell-shaped contours become sharp, brief, and staccato-like when mothers want to disrupt some unfavourable activity or express disapproval or warning. Cuckoo calls are mostly heard when mothers call for visual attention to their face, whereas high-pitched, steeply falling melodies are used to establish joint attention to persons or objects in the environment (Fernald 1992).

The degree to which ID melodies function as communicative signals during preverbal communication does not depend only on caregivers' intentions or emotions, as has been suggested by some investigators (for example, Fernald 1989). The functions and meanings of these melodies largely depend on the infant's capacity to discriminate, process, and decode ID melodies in everyday interactional contexts (Papoušek 1992), where they are normally embedded in multimodal sequential patterns of parental stimulation. In order to demonstrate differential responsiveness in infants to ID melodic messages, researchers are in need of carefully designed playback studies with contrastive pairs of isolated ID melodic contours. Using an infant-controlled auditory-preference design, we were able to show that infants in the first months of life are able to differentiate prototypical contours in ID speech, and to respond adequately to their inherent categorical messages (Papoušek *et al.* 1990). Infants as young as 4 months exhibited more visual attention to a picture of an adult human face when listening to rising melodies; they maintained attention longer when hearing bell-shaped approving contours; and they disrupted visual attention more readily when being exposed to disapproving contours (Sullivan and Horowitz 1983*a*; Papoušek *et al.* 1990; Fernald 1992). At the same time, infants responded with positive affect more often to approving than to disapproving contours, and more often with negative affect to disapproving than to approving contours (Fernald 1992).

Current evidence suggests three mechanisms that may contribute to infants' precocious capacities to decode the meaning of ID melodies: (1) infants may bring to the task some innate programme; (2) on the parents' part, the basic melodies of ID speech may be endowed with intrinsic qualities or functional meanings that immediately affect infant behavioural–emotional states in a manner similar to the arousing, soothing, or blessing effects of music (Fernald 1984); (3) the regular association between melodic contour and relevant caregiving frames may assign ID melodies the role of caregiving messages and thus facilitate infant learning in the everyday contexts of parent–infant interactions (Papoušek 1994*b*).

To summarize, parents intuitively use melodic contours in their speech as a basic communicative code of preverbal communication. In concert with gradations in frequency, amplitude, or timing, categorical cues in the shape of ID melodies seem to function as the first messages that guide the infant in regulating states of arousal, attention, and affect. These cues may help infants in learning how to control visual, facial, and vocal behaviours in preverbal dialogues.

Interestingly, the same form–function relations exist universally in mother–infant dialogues across cultures and language groups. This is the case even in cultures as distant in tradition and linguistic structure as Western German or Caucasian American cultures, which use stress languages, and Far Eastern Asian cultures, which use tone languages (H. Papoušek and Papoušek 1991). Stress and tone languages differ significantly in their functional uses of F_0 patterns. Yet, when addressing their preverbal infants, Mandarin Chinese mothers use very similar contour types in comparable caregiving contexts to those used by German- or English-speaking mothers; most notably, Mandarin-speaking mothers even sometimes violate linguistic tone rules in their production of ID melodies (Papoušek *et al.* 1991). These data in particular point to a primacy of non-linguistic uses of melodic contours in ID speech, and suggest that the functions and meanings of melodic shapes originate from biological rather than cultural roots.

2.1.3 *Models for infants' vocal learning*

Prototypical melodic contours in ID speech closely match and model those features that infants first learn to control in their presyllabic cooing and exploratory vocalizations: prolongation of phonation; euphonic vowel-like resonance; and pitch modulation (Oller 1980). But, according to traditional views on the development of imitative capacities in infants, true vocal imitation, that is, imitation of novel sounds, is not expected to occur prior to the last trimester of the first year of life (Piaget 1962).

Interestingly, parents themselves have strong propensities to imitate infants' non-crying vocalizations in the first interactions after birth. Caregivers' matching and modelling of sounds from the infant's vocal repertoire have been known for a long time as potent means of stimulating infants to vocalize (Piaget 1962). By utilizing this strategy, parents soon become engaged with their infants in episodes of reciprocal vocal play and vocal matching (Papoušek *et al.* 1987*b*; Papoušek and Papoušek 1989). Careful auditory and acoustic analyses of preverbal vocal communication at 2, 3, 5, and 7 months demonstrate that 34–53 per cent of infant vocal sounds are part of reciprocal matching sequences, framed by mothers' modelling and/or matching utterances. On all age levels, matching in absolute pitch clearly dominates in both mother–infant and infant–mother sequences, but increasingly involves other musical

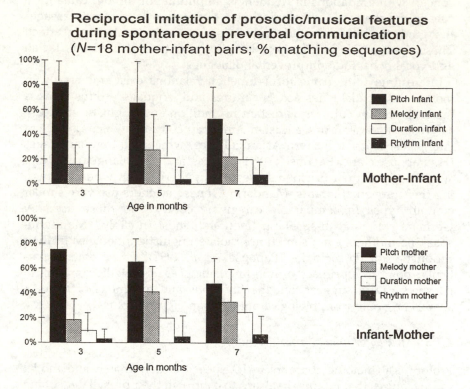

Fig. 4.4 Reciprocal vocal imitation of musical elements during spontaneous preverbal communication. Matches in pitch, melody, duration, and rhythm are given as percentages of total matching sequences, separately for mother–infant and infant–mother sequences. *N* = 18 mother–infant pairs.

elements as well, such as melodic contour, duration, and rhythm (Fig. 4.4). From the beginning, reciprocal matching of speech sounds, vowel-like resonance in particular, is occasionally included in matching sequences as well and gradually gains in frequency and complexity (Papoušek and Papoušek 1989; Masataka 1992; Papoušek 1994*a*).

However, from interactional analyses alone, it is impossible to determine who imitates whom, and whether and to what degree infants are capable of imitating musical elements in the frame of naturalistic parent–infant interactions. Recent research on infant imitation in well-controlled experimental studies has shown that infants below 5 months of age are capable of imitating absolute pitch (Kessen *et al.* 1979), pitch contours (Kuhl and Meltzoff 1982), and vowel-like harmonic resonance (Legerstee 1990). More research is needed to establish whether or not young infants are able to imitate musical features in focused experimental approaches and whether they use such capacities when being exposed to the complexity of naturalistic social interactions. Nevertheless, their preverbal vocal productions tend to be surrounded or framed by matching parental utterances. The parent's tendency to create imitative vocal frames or formats provides the infant with everyday opportunities to compare and detect similarities between the auditory feedback from his/her own vocal sounds and preceding as well as subsequent parental utterances. Guided by parents' intuitive didactic framing (M. Papoušek and Papoušek 1991), infants get an early chance to learn and practise how to control and eventually imitate musical and speech-like sound features. According to Snow (1989), the mothers' tendency to match and model infant sounds during preverbal infancy is significantly correlated with the infants' tendency to utilize imitation as a useful strategy for lexical acquisition. Similarly, Papoušek (1994*a*) has demonstrated that a high proportion of reciprocal vocal matching and maternal imitation during mother–infant interactions before 6 months of age predicts the rate of infant lexical imitation at 15 months of age.

2.1.4 Linguistic functions

From the beginning of life, melodies in ID speech also serve to mediate and model linguistic information to some extent (Cooper 1993). They segment the flow of speech into linguistically meaningful units (Stern *et al.* 1982) and highlight phonological information and new words by placing them on the accented peaks of melodic contours (Fernald and Mazzie 1991). Infants' primary selective attention to melodic contours may pave the way for detecting relevant phonological information of the mother tongue (Jusczyk and Bertoncini 1988). Infants as young as 1 and 4 months old are able to discriminate syllabic information in polysyllabic sequences ([malana] versus [marana]), if highlighted and stressed by raised pitch, intensity, and duration as typical for ID speech (Karzon 1985). In the first half-year of life, infants are sensitive to and prefer the natural phrasing of spoken language over a speech sample with randomly placed pauses (Kemler-Nelson *et al.* 1989). Infants primarily respond to linguistically universal features of phrasing: between 4 and 6 months, they become sensitive to the specific prosodic phrasing of mother tongue; around 9 months, they begin to process phonological information in subunits of prosodic phrases (Jusczyk and Bertoncini 1988). Similarly, 6-month-old infants have been shown to be perceptually aware of 'good' phrasing in music (Krumhansl and Jusczyk 1990). They selectively listen for longer periods of time to well-phrased music than to poorly phrased music.

3 BEYOND MELODIC CONTOURS: RHYTHM AND DYNAMICS

Responses to music do not depend on melody alone but also to a large degree on rhythm and dynamics. Four-month-old infants' preference for ID speech over adult-directed speech seems to be exclusively accounted for by the salience of melodic contours rather than by temporal or dynamic structure alone (Fernald and Kuhl 1987). These experimental findings may not fully apply in the naturalistic contexts of preverbal communication. During mother–infant interactions, maternal melodic contours are closely interrelated with mothers' kinetic behaviour patterns. Regular synchronization of vocal and kinetic patterns provides the infant with multimodal sensory information including tactile (stroking, patting, tapping, poking), kinaesthetic (moving infants' hands or feet), and visual information (head nodding, head shaking) (Sullivan and Horowitz 1983*b*). Microanalytical comparisons of vocal and kinetic motor behaviours in mothers' communicative repertoires have revealed striking correspondence in terms of temporal patterns, phrasing, and intensity contours, pointing to synchronization of vocal and motor behaviours (Stern *et al.* 1977; Stern 1984). Consequently, the temporal and dynamic aspects of ID melodies are often transmitted through other than the auditory modality alone.

Parents also tend to synchronize their rhythmic activities and to fine-tune the dynamics of behaviours to the timing and intensity of infant behaviours. Variations in tempo, rhythm, and amplitude thus become closely interrelated with the patterns of infants' own motor and vocal activities and respective proprioceptive feedback.

Parents' multimodal stimulation is tailored to infants' early competence for perceiving information through different senses as co-ordinated wholes. According to Bower (1977), very young infants first perceive information obtained by looking, by listening, and by touching as amodal and are sensitive to synchrony rather than to perceptual differences in modalities. Although research in other than visual and auditory modalities is still very difficult, due to methodological obstacles, sensory integration has been experimentally shown in tactile and visual modalities (Meltzoff and Borton 1979), and between visual and auditory modalities (Spelke 1979; Kuhl and Meltzoff 1984).

On the basis of Gibson's studies (1979), Stern (1984) also speculated that the dynamics of a stimulus, as given by its temporal structure and intensity contour, may be equivalent across modalities and may function as a common denominator for transmodal integration of multimodal stimulation.

Rhythmic–dynamic stimulation appears to be abundant during fetal life. Prenatal exposure to rhythmic stimulation includes the variable rhythms of maternal heartbeat and breathing, maternal walking, and the rhythms of maternal speech. Some authors have speculated on early forms of imprinting to maternal heartbeat (Salk 1962) and on newborns' motor entrainment to the rhythm of maternal speech (Condon and Sander 1974). However, these speculations have remained controversial and data relevant to them have been inconclusive. Careful experimental studies have demonstrated that young infants are sensitive to temporal information, such as stimulus duration, pausing, and rhythmic patterns, and that they are able to entrain their own behaviour to some temporal cues in environmental stimulation (see the review by Pouthas in Chapter 5).

3.1 Early rhythmic stimulation

During early infancy, an abundance of rhythmic–dynamic stimulation in caregiving environments is related to several salient and universal components of intuitive parenting. Mothers of 17 3-month-olds were shown to use an average of 50 per cent of face-to-face interaction time for display of rhythmically organized non-vocal stimulations (Koester *et al.* 1989). Rhythmic patterns included the tactile mode (stroking, tapping/ patting, and tickling), the kinaesthetic mode (shaking the infant's feet or hands), the vestibular mode (rocking), and the visual mode (head nodding and shaking). The data clearly showed that the periodicities of rhythmic stimulation did not depend on a common '*Zeitgeber*'. Differences in beat were determined by momentary states of arousal and attention on the infant's side, and by the weight and velocity of movement of respective body parts on the maternal side.

Four classes of periodicities were observed: a slow rhythm of head nodding (0.51 beats per second on the average); an intermediate rhythm of head shaking (1.28 beats/s); and two clusters of faster tempos, one including tactile stroking, kinaesthetic and vestibular stimulation (1.72 beats/s), and one including the more playful rapid behaviours of tapping, tickling, and tongue play (2.64 beats/s). Co-occurrences of non-vocal with vocal rhythmic patterns were not systematically analysed in the study. However, independent analyses of periodicities in mothers' vocal stimulation revealed interesting parallels (Papoušek, unpublished data). For instance, head nodding was often synchronized with prosodic stress in maternal utterances, and the tempo of head nodding paralleled the rate of vocal utterances. Similarly, head shaking seemed to be synchronized with the German wording of disapproving utterances such as 'nein nein' ('no no'). The beats of rocking and stroking corresponded most closely to the tempo of maternal singing, and the beats of tapping and tickling corresponded most closely to mothers' tempo of articulation (that is, number of syllables per second).

3.2   The musical structure of interactional games

A particularly rich source of rhythmic stimulation is involved in the typical interactional games, both traditional, and idiosyncratic (M. Papoušek and Papoušek 1991). Around 5 months, that is, shortly before the onset of regular rhythmic syllables in infants, mothers tend to replace part of their ID melodic prototypes by another category of musical stimulation, which in a way models the next vocal milestone to come, canonical repetitive babbling. Mothers stimulate with sequences of repetitive syllables characterized by regular rhythmic segmentation of phonation and superimposed melodies (Papoušek 1994a); these regularities are reminiscent of sung melodies with discernible notes rather than of spoken language.

The mothers' new strategy precedes and accompanies the onset of regular rhythmic motor activities in infants, such as hand banging or regular rhythmic kicking (Thelen 1981). Moreover, it heralds a significant progress, in the infants' nervous systems enabling the production of speech-like canonical syllables in regular rhythmic sequences. As shown in cross-linguistic analyses, canonical syllables such as [dadada] or [mamammam] are likely to be common to all living languages of the world (Locke 1990), representing universal minimal rhythmic units of spoken languages (Oller and Eilers 1992). Moreover, the minimal rhythmic units in the vocalizations of infants are often grouped into higher-order units or utterances which in turn tend to be embedded within prelinguistic phrases (Lynch *et al.* in press) and are structured similarly to the ways in which adults structure their phrases in speech. Interestingly, mothers tend to include both minimal rhythmic units and phrasing when engaging the infant in interactional games.

Early interactional games such as the typical tickling games are characterized by relatively simple and predictable interactional sequences or 'phrases' including multimodal forms of maternal stimulation and infant responses. Depending on infant signals of interest, pleasure, and interactional readiness, the sequences are repeated, enhanced, or playfully varied and diversified to maintain the infant's attention and pleasurable arousal on a potentially optimal level (Papoušek *et al.* 1987b). Microanalytical studies of these interactional games have revealed interactional sequences that are common to a wide range of traditional and idiosyncratic games in different cultures and thus seem to be universal. The salience of musical elements in games is evident in their participation in three functional parts characterizing interactional sequences:

(1) a fast-beat rising melody performed in a crescendo and accelerando mode during the attention-eliciting, arousing part; (2) a tension-eliciting pause followed by the culmination of sequence and a peak in melody and dynamics; and (3) a falling melody performed in a diminuendo and rallentando mode during the part of mutual relaxation (M. Papoušek and Papoušek 1991). The vocal part is typically accompanied by synchronous tactile and/or kinaesthetic stimulation. First results of cross-modal analyses of interactional games indicate not only synchronies but also interesting equivalencies in vocal and tactile forms of stimulation that distinguish arousing from soothing forms of stimulation. In the case of arousing stimulation, rising melodies tend to accompany poking tactile stimulation with finger tips moving upwards on the infant's body or limbs. In cases of soothing stimulation, falling melodies in turn tend to accompany smooth tactile stimulation with open palms moving downwards on the infant's body (M. Papoušek, unpublished data).

Another salient source of musical stimulation in early infancy is present in infant-directed singing as discussed in detail by H. Papoušek (Chapter 2) and in joint singing as described below. ID singing seems to be a universal part of human caregiving (Unyk *et al.* 1992; Trehub *et al.* 1993). Structural similarities between nursery songs and melodic care-giving messages in ID speech point to functional similarities as well, for instance, in modulating infant states of affective arousal and attention. Typically, ID singing becomes incorporated in either playful (Figs 4.6 and 4.7) or soothing caregiver–infant interactions (Papoušek and Papoušek 1981).

The amount and forms of rhythmic–dynamic stimulation in infants' everyday life also depend on sociocultural and ecological factors and culture-specific caregiving practices. For instance, sleeping together and continuous carrying in close body contact provide a wealth of rhythmic stimulation, rhythms caused by the mother's respiratory movements, by walking, by daily working routines, and by dancing in social groups. Exposing infants to the rhythmic vibrations of a running car or washing machine in Western industrialized societies—although effective in soothing an excessively crying infant—is certainly a poor substitute for the natural rhythms affecting infants in our evolutionary past.

4 PRECURSORS OF SINGING IN INFANTS' PREVERBAL VOCAL DEVELOPMENT

Recent accounts of prelinguistic stages of vocal development from a number of laboratories (Oller 1980; Stark 1980; Holmgren *et al.* 1986; Koopmans-van Beinum and van der Stelt 1986; Papoušek 1994*a*) converge on a differentiation of six stages of vocal production: phonation

(0–1 months); melodic modulation and primitive articulation in cooing (2–3 months); exploratory vocal play (4–6 months); repetitive babbling (7–11 months); variegated babbling and early words (9–13 months); and the one-word stage (12–18 months).

Precursors of spontaneous singing may be indiscriminable from precursors of early speech. Preverbal communication may represent a common ontogenetic avenue along which two highly structured and exclusively human capacities develop: (1) speech, enabling verbal communication and thinking; and (2) singing, enabling creative activities in vocal music. Both capacities are also intimately related to functions of affective vocal signalling and communication.

Our first attempts to analyse development of infant control over musical elements suggested that common precursors may be traced back to the earliest non-crying vocalizations, also called quasi-resonant sounds or fundamental voicing (Papoušek and Papoušek 1981). Infants first learn how to control and co-ordinate breathing and phonation. In the cooing stage, they begin to modulate pitch contours and to control harmonic resonance in euphonic vowel-like sounds.

The cooing stage is followed by a stage of vocal expansion (Stark 1980) or exploratory play (Lewis 1936; Papoušek and Papoušek 1981). Infants alternately produce squealing and growling sounds, screams and whispers, brief staccato-like noises, and drawn-out vowel-like sounds with extensive frequency modulation, which occasionally expand across one or two octaves. Infants keep discovering new means (for example, saliva, finger play with tongue or lips) of enriching their vocal repertoire and making it sound more interesting, such as in blowing bubbles or raspberry sounds.

In this stage, infants expand their vocal repertoire and seem to playfully explore the sound-making potentials of the lower and upper vocal tract in close relation to its anatomical and neuromotor maturation. Infants seem to be highly motivated to practise vocal sounds as if to learn how to control pitch registers and timbre, loudness, temporal features, and frequency modulation of vocal sounds in the context of the more speech-specific articulatory properties of the vocal tract.

4.1 Creative play with vocal sounds

The stage of vocal play is particularly interesting in relation to early musical competence because of its intrinsic creativity. Vocal play has mostly been attributed to infant monologues (Weir 1962; Papoušek and Papoušek 1981; Kuczaj 1983), in which infants seem to use their voice as a favourite, inexhaustible toy available even in the parent's absence. The impression of playful creative exploration arises from observations of infants' persistent motivation to reproduce sounds discovered by chance, and to repeat and modify their vocal products with overt signs of effort, eagerness, and joy.

As part of intuitive parenting, parents tend to participate in vocal play. They echo the sounds discovered by the infant, provide models for creative modifications, and sometimes compete with the infant for the most elaborate variations. The parents' own vocal repetitions typically include graded or sudden variations in pitch, tempo, rhythm, or loudness. Variations of ID melodies enhance or mitigate preceding utterances, make them pleasantly discrepant, or transpose them into unexpected contexts (Papoušek and Papoušek 1981). Vocal play reaches a first peak towards the end of the first half year, but keeps accompanying subsequent stages of vocal development and early lexical acquisition and eventually continues into spontaneous singing and into learning of conventional songs (Papoušek and Papoušek 1981; Kelley and Sutton-Smith 1987).

4.2 From common roots to diverging specializations

The stage of canonical babbling may be characterized by a much more restricted vocal repertoire than the preceding stage of vocal expansion due to the emergence and transitory prevalence of rhythmic syllabic sequences. Because of its distinct beginning and linguistic significance, canonical babbling is generally recognized as an important vocal milestone for speech acquisition. Canonical syllables induce new patterns of intuitive didactic caregiving that more specifically pave the way for language proper (Papoušek 1994a).

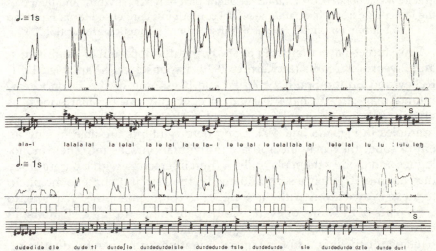

Fig. 4.5 Spontaneous singing of musical phrases at 16 months. Playful variations on a theme. (a) Sequence of large-interval leaps from a high to a low register. (b) Sequence of rising melodic contours with an accentuated final note: raised pitch following a pause of variable length.

At the same time, however, canonical babbling involves production of regular-beat rhythms with superimposed melodies, short musical patterns or phrases that soon become the core units for a new level of vocal practising and play in the second expansion stage, also called the stage of variegated babbling. At this stage, the repertoire of vocal play may expand to new dimensions of specific musical creativity and familiarization with conventional forms of music, particularly in singing and dancing. Syllabic sequences are sung in short well-structured melodies in which familiar musical elements are creatively combined into new patterns with distinct rhythm and accent. Such phrases are typically repeated as a whole and varied in at least one interesting musical dimension (see examples in Fig. 4.5(a), (b)).

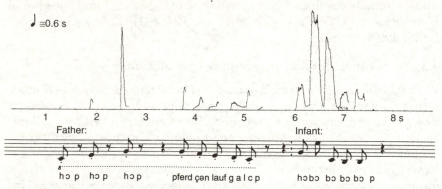

Fig. 4.6 Joint singing in father–infant interactions at 12 months. The infant's imitation ('hobobobobop') mimics a salient part of lyrics, rhythm, and tempo of the father's final syllables, and the global contour in a condensed form. From top to bottom: amplitude; musical transcription; phonetic transcription.

Few studies have attempted to study the development of singing in 1- and 2-year-old infants (McKernon 1979; Papoušek and Papoušek 1981; Kelley and Sutton-Smith 1987). At the beginning of the second year, infants may already have learned to conceptualize familiar songs, as global contours or in salient parts of melody, rhythm, or lyrics (see examples in Figs 4.6 and 4.7). Long before infants are able to sing an entire song, they may incorporate individual phrases into their monologues and modify them playfully. When interacting with a parent, they may attempt to join in a song initiated by the parent, to tune to the pitch, to move in synchrony with the song, or to complement the final note, to echo parts of the tune, or even to anticipate the next phrase. Parents, in turn, tend to encourage joint singing by slowing down the tempo or by pausing for the infant to tune in, by imitating, or by playful duetting.

Kelley and Sutton-Smith (1987) analysed musical production in three infants aged from 0 to 24 months. These infants grew up in widely differing environments, one from parents with professional training in

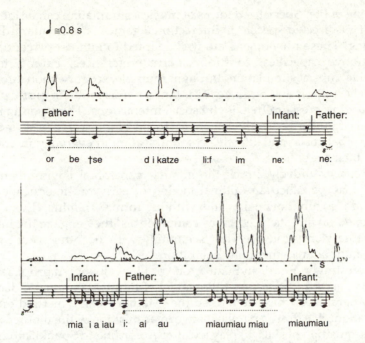

Fig. 4.7 Intuitive didactics in father's singing to his 13-month-old infant. ('a b c, die Katze lief im Schnee; i ei au, miau miau miau'.) The father begins the first part of the song slowing down the tempo and pausing for the infant to complement the final note; he confirms the infant's correct pitch by imitation and pauses again; the infant then takes the initiative and, by anticipating her favourite last phrase of the song, prompts the father to continue; the father sings to the end, which the infant echoes on pitch.

music and a musically oriented background, the other two from musically and non-musically oriented households respectively. These studies suggest that elementary forms of musical production in infants are to be found strikingly early in all infants, but the amount of music productivity, and its accuracy and richness, depend to a large degree on the musical environment. According to the authors, the parents' own singing seemed to be an important determinant of infants' musical competence. However, the individual differences in music orientation of the three caregiving environments also point to genetic differences in musical competence which the infants may have shared with their parents.

5 CONCLUDING REMARKS

Human infants around the world grow up in social caregiving environments that provide salient sources of musical stimulation from the beginning of life. Specialized forms of musical stimulation can be identified in infant-directed speech, in interactional games, and in infant-directed singing. These phenomena are well adapted to infants' perceptual and integrative capacities, constraints, and preferences. Parents tend to provide music stimulation through multiple sensory modalities and actively support and facilitate the infant's participation in music production during pressure-free, joyful social interactions. Thus, young infants become familiarized with elementary forms of music as a basic means of non-verbal social and affective communication in everyday interactions with their parents.

Parents intuitively enrich the infants' perceptual environment with what may be called an optimal model for early music education. But they do so unknowingly, and without formal training. Even if uninformed on infants' precocious competences, they engage the infant in elementary musical activities, seemingly with no other goal in mind than mutual enjoyment and relaxation.

Interestingly, Shin'ichi Suzuki, one of the well known propagators of early music education, used the model of intuitive parental didactics in his programme which he termed the 'Mother tongue method of music education'. He drew a parallel between acquisition of the mother tongue and acquisition of skills to play a violin. According to Suzuki, all children have natural predispositions for both speech and music, and should learn music early and as naturally as they learn how to speak. They should first play an instrument and then read music as they first speak and only later learn writing. Parents should participate with encouragement, emotional engagement, and support. Under the parents' guidance, daily musical activities should include regular listening to well-performed rehearsals of the music, learning through delayed imitation, frequent practising of partial skills until they become automated, and innumerable repetitions of basic familiar pieces. For the infancy period, however, it may be advisable not to disturb the earliest forms of intuitive musical stimulation by rationally guided artificial manipulations and formal educational interventions, but to keep them concealed as a precious part of early parent–infant relationships.

REFERENCES

Bower, T. G. R. (1977). *A primer of infant development*. Freeman, San Francisco.
Condon, W. S. and Sander, L. W. (1974). Synchrony demonstrated between movements of the neonate and adult speech. *Child Development*, **45**, 456–52.
Cooper, R. P. (1993). The effect of prosody on young infants' speech perception. In *Advances in infancy research*, Vol. 8 (ed. C. Rovee-Collier and L. P. Lipsitt), pp. 137–67. Ablex, Norwood, New Jersey.

DeCasper, A. J. and Fifer, W. P. (1980). Of human bonding: newborns prefer their mothers' voices. *Science*, **208**, 1174–6.

DeCasper, A. J. and Spence, M. J. (1986). Newborns prefer a familiar story over an unfamiliar one. *Infant Behavior and Development*, **9**, 133–50.

Fassbender, C. (1993). *Auditory grouping and segregation processes in infancy*. Kaste Verlag, Norderstedt.

Ferguson, C. A. (1977). Baby talk as a simplified register. In *Talking to children: language input and acquisition* (ed. C. E. Snow and C. A. Ferguson), pp. 206–35. Cambrige University Press, Cambridge.

Fernald, A. (1984). The perceptual and affective salience of mothers' speech to infants. In *The origins and growth of communication* (ed. L. Feagans, D. Garvey, and R. Golinkoff), pp. 5–29. Ablex, Norwood, New Jersey.

Fernald, A. (1989). Intonation and communicative intent in mothers' speech to infants: is the melody the message? *Child Development*, **60**, 1497–510.

Fernald, A. (1992). Meaningful melodies in mothers' speech to infants. In *Nonverbal vocal communication: comparative and developmental approaches* (ed. H. Papoušek, U. Jürgens, and M. Papoušek), pp. 262–82. Cambridge University Press, Cambridge.

Fernald, A. and Kuhl, P. K. (1987). Acoustic determinants of infant preference for motherese speech. *Infant Behavior and Development*, **10**, 279–93.

Fernald, A. and Mazzie, C. (1991). Prosody and focus in speech to infants and adults. *Developmental Psychology*, **27**, 209–21.

Fernald, A. and Simon, T. (1984). Expanded intonation contours in mothers' speech to new-borns. *Developmental Psychology*, **20**, 104–13.

Gibson, E. J. (1979). *The ecological approach to visual perception*. Houghton Mifflin, Boston.

Holmgren, K., Lindblom, B., Aurelius, G., Jalling, B., and Zetterström, R. (1986). On the phonetics of infant vocalization. In *Precursors of early speech*, Wenner-Gren International Symposium Series, Vol. 44 (ed. B. Lindblom and R. Zetterström), pp. 51–63. Stockton Press, New York.

Jusczyk, P. W. and Bertoncini, J. (1988). Viewing the development of speech perception as an innately guided learning process. *Language and Speech*, **31**, 217–37.

Karzon, R. G. (1985). Discrimination of polysyllabic sequences by one- to four-month-old infants. *Journal of Experimental Child Psychology*, **39**, 326–42.

Kelley, L. and Sutton-Smith, B. (1987). A study of infant musical productivity. In *Music and development* (ed. J. C. Peery, I. W. Peery, and T. W. Draper), pp. 35–53. Springer, New York.

Kemler-Nelson, D. G., Hirsh-Pasek, K., Jusczyk, P., and Wright Cassidy, K. (1989). How the prosodic cues in motherese might assist language learning. *Journal of Child Language*, **16**, 55–68.

Kessen, W., Levine, J., and Wendrich, K. (1979). The imitation of pitch in infants. *Infant Behavior and Development*, **2**, 93–9.

Koester, L. S., Papoušek, H., and Papoušek, M. (1989). Patterns of rhythmic stimulation by mothers with three-month-olds: a cross-modal comparison. *International Journal of Behavioural Development*, **12**, 143–54.

Koopmans-van Beinum, F. J. and van der Stelt, J. M. (1986). Early stages in the development of speech movements. In *Precursors of early speech*, Wenner-Gren

International Symposium Series, Vol. 44 (ed. B. Lindblom and R. Zetterström), pp. 37–50. Stockton, New York.

Krumhansl, C. L. and Jusczyk, P. W. C. (1990). Infants' perception of phrase structure in music. *Psychological Science*, **1**, 70–3.

Kuczaj II, S. A. (1983). *Crib speech and language play*. Springer, Tokyo.

Kuhl, P. K. and Meltzoff, A. N. (1982). The bimodal perception of speech in infancy. *Science*, **218**, 1138–41.

Kuhl, P. K. and Meltzoff, A. N. (1984). The intermodal representation of speech in infants. *Infant Behavior and Development*, **7**, 361–81.

Legerstee, M. (1990). Infants use multimodal information to imitate speech sounds. *Infant Behavior and Development*, **13**, 343–54.

Lewis, M. M. (1936). *Infant speech. A study of the beginning of language*. Harcourt Brace, New York.

Locke, J. L. (1990). Structure and stimulation in the ontogeny of spoken language. *Developmental Psychobiology*, **23**, 621–43.

Lynch, M. P., Oller, D. K., Steffens, M. L., and Buder, E. H. (in press). Phrasing in prelinguistic vocalizations. *Developmental Psychobiology* (in press).

McCall, R. and Kagan, J. (1967). Attention in the infant: effects of complexity, contour, perimeter, and familiarity. *Child Development*, **39**, 939–52.

McKernon, P. E. (1979). The development of first songs in young children. In *Early symbolization. New directions for child development*, Vol. 3 (ed. H. Gardner and D. Wolf). Jossey-Bass, San Francisco.

Masataka, N. (1992). Early ontogeny of vocal behavior in Japanese infants in response to maternal speech. *Child Development*, **63**, 1177–86.

Mehler, J., Jusczyk, P., Lambertz, G., Halsted, N., Bertoncini, J., and Amiel Tison, C. (1988). A precursor of language acquisition in young infants. *Cognition*, **29**, 143–78.

Meltzoff, A. N. and Borton, R. W. (1979). Intermodal matching by human neonates. *Nature*, **282**, 403–4.

Newman, J. D. and Goedeking, P. (1992). Noncategorical vocal communication in primates: the example of common marmoset phee calls. In *Nonverbal vocal communication: comparative and developmental approaches* (ed. H. Papoušek, U. Jürgens, and M. Papoušek), pp. 87–101. Cambridge University Press, Cambridge.

Oller, D. K. (1980). The emergence of the sounds of speech in infancy. In *Child phonology: production*, Vol. 1 (ed. G. H. Yeni-Komshian, J. F. Kavanagh, and C. A. Ferguson), pp. 93–112. Academic Press, New York.

Oller, D. K. and Eilers, R. E. (1992). Development of vocal signalling in human infants: toward a methodology for cross-species vocalization comparisons. In *Nonverbal vocal communication: comparative and developmental approaches* (ed. H. Papoušek, U. Jürgens, and M. Papoušek), pp. 174–91. Cambridge University Press, Cambridge.

Panneton, R. K. (1985). Prenatal experience with melodies: effect on postnatal auditory preference in human newborns. Unpublished D. Phil. thesis. University of North Carolina at Greensboro.

Papoušek, H. and Papoušek, M. (1984). Learning and cognition in the everyday life of human infants. In *Advances in the study of behavior*, Vol. 14 (ed. J. S. Rosenblatt, C. Beer, M.-C. Busnel, and P. J. B. Slater), pp. 127–63. Academic, New York.

Papoušek, H. and Papoušek, M. (1987). Intuitive parenting: a dialectic counter-part to the infant's integrative competence. In *Handbook of infant development* (2nd edn) (ed. J. D. Osofsky), pp. 669–720. Wiley, New York.

Papoušek, H. and Papoušek, M. (1991). Innate and cultural guidance of infants' integrative competencies: China, the United States, and Germany. In *Cultural approaches to parenting* (ed. M. H. Bornstein), pp. 23–44. Lawrence Erlbaum, Hillsdale, New Jersey.

Papoušek, M. (1989). Determinants of responsiveness to infant vocal expression of emotional state. *Infant Behavior and Development*, **12**, 505–22.

Papoušek, M. (1992). Early ontogeny of vocal communication in parent–infant interactions. In *Nonverbal vocal communication: comparative and developmental aspects* (ed. H. Papoušek, U. Jürgens, and M. Papoušek), pp. 230–61. Cambridge University Press, Cambridge.

Papoušek, M. (1994a). *Vom ersten Schrei zum ersten Wort. Anfänge der Sprachent-wicklung in der vorsprachilichen Kommunikation*. Huber, Berne.

Papoušek, M. (1994b). Melodies in caregivers' speech: a species-specific guid-ance toward language. *Early Development and Parenting*, **3**(1), 5–17. [Special Issue 'Intuitive parenting: comparative and clinical approaches'.]

Papoušek, M. and Papoušek, H. (1981). Musical elements in the infant's vocaliz-ations: their significance for communication, cognition and creativity. In *Advances in infancy research*, Vol. 1 (ed. L. P. Lipsitt), pp. 163–224. Ablex, Norwood, New Jersey.

Papoušek, M. and Papoušek, H. (1989). Forms and functions of vocal matching in precanonical mother–infant interactions. *First Language*, **9**, 137–58. [Special Issue 'Precursors to speech'.]

Papoušek, M. and Papoušek, H. (1991). Preverbal vocal communication from zero to one: preparing the ground for language acquisition. In *Perspectives on infant development: contributions from German-speaking countries* (ed. M. E. Lamb and H. Keller), pp. 299–328. Erlbaum, Hillsdale, New Jersey.

Papoušek, M., Papoušek, H., and Bornstein, M. H. (1985). The naturalistic vocal environment of young infants: on the significance of homogeneity and variability in parental speech. In *Social perception in infants* (ed. T. Field and N. Fox), pp. 269–97. Ablex, Norwood, New Jersey.

Papoušek, M., Papoušek, H., and Haekel, M. (1987a). Didactic adjustments in fathers' and mothers' speech to their three-month-old infants. *Journal of Psycholinguistic Research*, **16**, 491–516.

Papoušek, M., Papoušek, H., and Harris, B. J. (1987b). The emergence of play in parent–infant interactions. In *Curiosity, imagination, and play. On the develop-ment of spontaneous cognitive and motivational processes* (ed. D. Görlitz and J. F. Wohlwill), pp. 214–46. Erlbaum, Hillsdale, New Jersey.

Papoušek, M., Bornstein, M. H., Nuzzo, C., Papoušek, H., and Symmes, D. (1990). Infant responses to prototypical melodic contours in parental speech. *Infant Behavior and Development*, **13**, 539–45.

Papoušek, M., Papoušek, H., and Symmes, D. (1991). The meanings of melodies in motherese in tone and stress languages. *Infant Behavior and Development*, **14**, 415–40.

Piaget, J. (1962). *Play, dreams, and imitation in childhood*. Norton, New York.

Rheingold, H. L. and Adams, J. L. (1980). The significance of speech to new-borns. *Developmental Psychology*, **16**, 397–403.

Salk, L. (1962). Mother's heartbeat as an imprinting stimulus. *Transactions of the New York Academy of Science*, **24**, 753–63.

Scherer, K. R. (1986). Vocal affect expression: a review and a model for future research. *Psychological Bulletin*, **99**, 143–65.

Snow, C. E. (1972). Mothers' speech to children learning language. *Child Development*, **43**, 549–65.

Snow, C. E. (1989). Imitativeness: a trait or a skill? In *The many faces of imitation in language learning* (ed. G. Speidel and K. Nelson), pp. 73–90. Springer, Heidelberg.

Spelke, E. S. (1979). Perceiving bimodally specified events. *Journal of Experimental Child Psychology*, **15**, 626–36.

Stark, R. E. (1980). Stages of speech development in the first year of life. In *Child phonology: production*, Vol. 1 (ed. G. H. Yeni-Komshian, J. F. Kavanagh, and C. A. Ferguson), pp. 73–92. Academic Press, New York.

Stern, D. N. (1984). Affect attunement. In *Frontiers of infant psychiatry*, Vol. 2 (ed. J. D. Call, E. Galenson, and R. L. Tyson), pp. 3–14. Basic Books, New York.

Stern, D. N., Beebe, B., Jaffe, J., and Bennet, S. L. (1977). The infant's stimulus world during social interaction: a study of caregiver behaviours with particular reference to repetition and timing. In *Studies in mother–infant interaction* (ed. H. R. Schaffer), pp. 177–202. Academic Press, London.

Stern, D. N., Spieker, S., and MacKain, K. (1982). Intonation contours as signals in maternal speech to prelinguistic infants. *Developmental Psychology*, **18**, 727–35.

Sullivan, J. W. and Horowitz, F. D. (1983*a*). The effects of intonation on infant attention: the role of the rising intonation contour. *Child Language*, **10**, 521–34.

Sullivan, J. W. and Horowitz, F. D. (1983*b*). Infant intermodal perception and maternal multimodal stimulation: implications for language development. In *Advances in infancy research*, Vol. 2 (ed. L. P. Lipsitt and C. K. Rovee-Collier), pp. 183–239. Ablex, Norwood, New Jersey.

Thelen, E. (1981). Rhythmical behavior in infancy: an ethological perspective. *Developmental Psychology*, **17**, 237–57.

Trehub, S. E. (1990). The perception of musical patterns by human infants: the provision of similar patterns by their parents. In *Comparative perception: basic mechanisms*, Vol. 1 (ed. M. A. Berkley and W. C. Stebbins), pp. 429–59. Wiley, New York.

Trehub, S. E., Bull, D., and Thorpe, L. A. (1984). Infants' perception of melodies: the role of melodic contour. *Child Development*, **55**, 821–30.

Trehub, S. E., Unyk, A. M., and Trainor, L. J. (1993). Maternal singing in cross-cultural perspective. *Infant Behavior and Development*, **16**, 285–95.

Unyk, A. M., Trehub, S. E., Trainor, L. J., and Schellenberg, E. G. (1992). Lullabies and simplicity: a cross-cultural perspective. *Psychology of Music*, **20**, 15–28.

Weir, R. H. (1962). *Language in the crib*. Mouton, The Hague.

PART III

Time and Childhood

5

The development of the perception of time and temporal regulation of action in infants and children

Viviane Pouthas

Music is commonly said to be the art of time. It is clear that the development of musical competence is partly related to the development of temporal competence: perception of duration and rhythms on the one hand and temporal regulation of actions on the other hand. The first section of this chapter reviews studies relating to the early development of temporal competence, while the second section is concerned with its evolution during childhood.

1 TIME AND RHYTHMS IN INFANTS

Both the environment and the behaviour of the infant possess a temporal organization. The ability to process time-related information and the ability to structure his or her own action within time (that is, the capacity to act at the 'right time') are, as we will see later, essential to the development of the infant's motor skills, perceptual and cognitive abilities, capacity to learn languages, and, finally, development of his or her affective behaviour. We assume (Pouthas 1990) that the temporal regulations acquired during early childhood may act as a basis for future, more complex temporal learning.

The first year of life is that of sensorimotor development. We must therefore examine when and how temporal skills develop in infants, from both a motor and perceptual point of view. We will then close the first section by examining how these skills enable infants to interact efficiently with their parents and caretakers. We will deliberately focus on a few key experiments and observations that are of special interest in their methodology and results.

1.1   Motor rhythms and temporal regulations of behaviour

The infant is born into a temporally organized world. Furthermore, he or she is endowed with a host of biological rhythms and motor rhythms whose range of frequency is very wide as it varies from several hours (sleep–wake rhythmicity, feeding rhythms, etc.) to a few hundred milliseconds (heart rate, sucking, etc.). These rhythms are similar in that they are systems where periods of activity or tension (wake, movement, attention) alternate with periods of rest or relaxation (sleep, quiet, inattention). Here, we will only consider rhythms whose frequencies are close to musical tempi.

1.1.1   *Rhythmical stereotypes: the kicking example*

During the first year of the infant's life, rhythmical stereotypes such as rhythmic movements of the head, arms, chest, and legs are frequently observed. As Thelen (1981) points out, 'the quantity and diversity of rhythmically repetitive movements are so great that the infant appears to be following the dictum: if you move, move in rhythm'. Such rhythmic behaviour is generally believed to play a major role in the early motor development of the infant. Wolff (1967) suggests that early rhythmic behaviours are controlled by endogenous microrhythms, which are the forerunners of the internal time bases that regulate motor co-ordination in older children and adults. The ability to perform a complex motor act depends, in fact, on the capacity to choose appropriate motor routines and on the practice of regulating the duration between two given routines.

Thelen describes in detail the rhythmic movement of the legs, known as kicking. Such behaviour can be observed from birth (even in premature infants) but it is at around 6 months of age that it is most frequent. At that age, the kick is made up of a rapid flexion (200–300 ms) followed by a slightly longer extension (300–600 ms) and a pause at the end. According to Thelen, such rhythmic movements of the legs are the expression of a central motor programme that is later used when learning how to walk. The speed and rhythm of both locomotion and kicking are dependent on the duration of the pause (stance phase in the former and kick interval in the latter). If the infant increases the length of the pause, the rhythm of the kicking will decrease, similarly to the way our walking pace slows down if we prolong the stance phase. An example of a modification of the kicking rhythm through learning and exercise was indirectly provided by the Rovee-Collier team (for reviews, see Rovee-Collier and Gekoski 1979; Rovee-Collier 1993) whilst experimenting on infant memory. Babies learned to kick in order to make a mobile move. The faster they kicked, the faster it moved. The frequency of the kicks was compared over different time intervals and used as an indicator of memorization for infants.

1.1.2 *Temporal regulation of non-nutritive sucking activity*

Experiments conducted by DeCasper and Sigafoos (1983) and Provasi (1988) showed that infants are capable of modifying the temporal parameters of non-nutritive sucking activity. This activity consists of an alternation of bursts of sucking (pressure on the nipple at a frequency of 2 or 3 per second) and pauses (or interburst intervals, IBI) of a length of 3 to 15 seconds (see Fig. 5.1(a)). In order to test the babies' capacity to acquire temporal regulation of the sucking activity, DeCasper and Sigafoos (1983) and Provasi (1988) first recorded the duration of the pauses between bursts of spontaneous sucking activity (baseline phase). Then, during the reinforcement phase, a pleasant auditory stimulation (such as recordings of the mother's voice, of intra-uterine heartbeat, or of music) was made contingent on shortening or lengthening of the duration of pauses (see Fig. 5.1(b) for more details about the procedure). The results showed that 3-day-old babies can easily learn to diminish the duration of these pauses, but find it very difficult to learn to lengthen

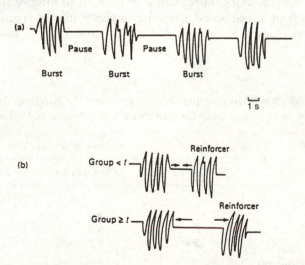

Fig. 5.1 (a) An example of a 3-day-old infant's non-nutritive sucking behaviour (redrawn from a polygraph recording). (b) Schema of the experimental procedure. *t* represents the reinforcement criterion imposed during the reinforcement phase. In group '<*t*' a sucking burst produced the pleasant auditory stimulation only if it followed an interburst interval (IBI) that was less than the 30th percentile of the baseline intervals. In group '>*t*' a sucking burst produced the auditory event only if the preceding IBI was greater than the 70th percentile of the baseline intervals (DeCasper and Sigafoos 1983; Provasi 1988).

them. Several explanatory hypotheses may be put forward to account for these results. It may be that the lengthening of the pauses beyond a certain threshold results in the loss of the rhythmic quality of the activity and finally cessation. This was confirmed by the fact that, the longer the spontaneous pause was in the first phase, the more difficult it was for the baby to increase the pause during the second phase. Furthermore, it has been shown that very young infants find it difficult to inhibit their actions (Hulsebus 1973).

Ashton (1976) suggests that the infant becomes less dependent on his or her endogenous rhythms as he or she progressively learns to integrate them with those of the environment. To test this hypothesis, Provasi (1988) compared the performances of newborns and 2-month-old babies using the same experimental procedure as above. The older infants learned to lengthen the pauses between bursts of sucking, whereas the newborns seemed to be unable to do so. However, this ability was not observable at the beginning of the experiment. The lengthening of the pauses only became significant with practice, as can be seen in Table 5.1. Indeed, the infants needed many more trials to learn to lengthen the pauses than they did to learn to shorten them.

Thus the results obtained through these experiments support the claim that very young children are able to learn to modify the temporal organization of a pre-wired rhythmic activity that is regulated by an endogenous clock.

Table 5.1 Median interburst intervals (IBIs) during the baseline, the beginning, and the end of testing session for newborns and 2 month-old infants

Condition[a]	Median IBI(s)		
	Baseline	22 first pauses	22 last pauses
Newborns			
<t	5.0	3.9	4.0
>t	5.1	5.3	5.4
Control	5.2	5.2	5.4
2-month-old infants			
<t	5.1	4.3	3.7
>t	5.1	4.9	6.1
Control	5.0	4.8	5.2

[a] In group '<t' a sucking burst produced the pleasant auditory stimulation only if it followed an interburst interval (IBI) that was less than the 30th percentile of the baseline intervals. In group '>t' a sucking burst produced the auditory event only if the preceding IBI was greater than the 70th percentile of the baseline intervals.

1.1.3 Temporal learning

Young infants are also capable of regulating their actions along arbitrary periodicities that do not correspond to biological oscillations. Thus, Rivière (1992) and Darcheville *et al.* (1993) ingeniously showed that 4-month-old-babies are able to postpone a response until the time when a reward is available (in this case, the response consisted in pressing on a tactile screen to see a cartoon video). The procedure used was a fixed-interval schedule (FI) where an interesting event could only be triggered several seconds after the previous rewarded response had elapsed. The results are especially striking in that the length of the pauses, that is, the interval during which no response was given, was accurately adjusted to the delay for each child (see Table 5.2), showing the quality of the acquired temporal regulation.

Table 5.2 Post-reinforcement pause as a function of interval duration

Subjects	Post-reinforcement pause (s) for fixed-interval (FI) duration (s) of					
	10	20	30	40	60	80
S1	13.5	26.4	32.5	42.7	63.8	89.4
S2	15.9	28.8	35.1	49.2	64.4	87.3
S3	11.1	21.8	33.4	42.3	63.7	83.7
S4	16.7	26.9	34.5	43.5	67.8	82.7
S5	17.2	31.8	39.2	48.7	65.2	83.7
S6	12.4	23.2	32.1	41.9	62.7	83.1
S7	12.1	21.7	31.9	43.2	63.5	82.8
S8	13.7	26.6	37.1	47.5	67.2	88.3

1.2 The perception and processing of temporal information

Many experiments have shown that very young infants are able to perceive the duration of auditory and visual stimuli as well as the duration of the intervals between these stimuli. Most of these studies deal with auditory stimuli, that is to say, the anticipation of the actual occurrence of sounds, the detection of length differences in various linguistic sounds, and the discrimination between an array of rhythmic auditory sequences. We will only be dealing with a few of these studies (for a more comprehensive review, see Fassbender, Chapter 3). We will also give a few examples relating to the visual perception of infants and, as the events which make up the young infant's world stem from several sensory modalities, we will conclude with studies relating to the inter-sensory processing of temporal parameters of stimulation.

1.2.1   *Do infants anticipate temporally predictable events?*

To answer this question, researchers often measure and analyse variations in heart rate. Thus Stamps (1977) presented two groups of 30- to 80-hour-old babies with a succession of 2-s sounds. The sound was repeated at 20-s intervals for the first group (experimental group) and was repeated at random intervals of between 10 s and 20 s for the second group (control group). It was therefore possible to anticipate the sound in the first group but not in the latter. The variation in heart rate was analysed. The results were as follows.

1. During the first 10 s of the interval, the response to the stimuli was an acceleration in both groups. However, the return to the baseline rate occurred much faster in the experimental group than in the control group.

2. During the last 10 s of the interval, no deceleration was recorded, contrary to what was observed in the case of stimuli anticipation in adults (Coles and Duncan-Johnson 1975; Bohlin and Kjellberg 1979).

3. When the stimulus was omitted, there was a deceleration in the heart rate of experimental subjects. This deceleration may be the sign of an orienting response, as if the infants were waiting for the sound to happen again. Similarly, in Clifton's (1974) experiment a large heart-rate deceleration appeared in response to the absence of the stimulus during extinction in the conditioning group and not in the control group. The

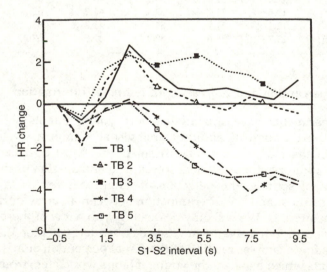

Fig. 5.2 Infant heart rate (HR) change over the S1–S2 interval for trial blocks 1–5. (From Donohue and Berg (1991), with permission.)

author interpreted this deceleration as an orienting response to the absence of an expected event.

From the Clifton (1974) and the Stamps (1977) studies we are led to the conclusion that the newborn is capable of adapting to the temporal regularity of events and can react to an interruption of this regularity.

Later on in his or her development, the infant is not only able to react to the omission of a temporally predictable event but can also anticipate this event, as was shown by the recent studies on 7-month-old infants by Donohue and Berg (1991). In this case, a white noise S1 was made audible for 15 s. After 10 s of that time had elapsed, a second stimuli S2 (a musical toy and light) occurred for a duration of 2 s. There were 20 trials (five blocks of four trials). As can be seen in Fig. 5.2, the heart rate slowly decelerated by the fourth block of trials, thus confirming the fact that the infants had learned to anticipate the second stimuli (S2).

1.2.2 Temporal discrimination abilities in the auditory modality

The data obtained from studies on infants' capacity to discriminate linguistic sounds indicate that infants are able to detect very small differences in time lapses. Thus, the studies made by Eilers and collaborators (1984) showed that babies between the ages of 5 and 11 months are able to detect the difference in the length of a vowel 'A' in words with one (mad), two (samad), or three (masamad) syllables. For example, infants were repeatedly presented with the two-syllable stimulus in which the second 'A' vowel lasted 300 ms (habituation procedure). During the test trials, the duration of the same vowel 'A' was of 400 ms duration. The infants looked at an illuminated target for a longer period than the one observed during the last habituation trials. This reaction to a novel event shows the infant's capacity to differentiate between events of 400 and 300 ms, that is, to perceive a difference of duration of as little as 100 ms.

A number of studies have focused on the development of perception and the ability to discriminate among auditory rhythmic sequences in infants. Two such studies are reported here.

The first study In a rhythmical sequence, such as the one depicted in Fig. 5.3 (R1), an adult will not perceive a series of isolated sounds but a repetition of the same group of three sounds. The two short intervals between the three sounds (respectively, 97 and 291 ms) are part of an integrated auditory sequence. The long interval (582 ms) that links one group of sounds to the next is considered as a pause. This is, in fact, what allows us to differentiate and link sequences to one another. Is this ability, which appears so natural in adults, innate or does it develop with age? In other words, does a very young infant perceive a series of

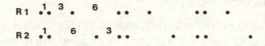

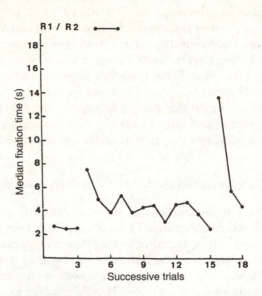

Fig. 5.3 Top of the figure: sound sequences. Numbers indicate the duration of the intervals between sounds in comparison with a 97-ms time unit. Bottom of the figure: median fixation time during successive trials. (Redrawn from Demany (1979), experiment 1.)

isolated sounds or a rhythmic sequence? Demany's experiments (1979) were aimed at resolving this issue.

In one of these experiments, a 2½-month-old infant initiated a rhythmic sequence (say R1) by turning his head to look at a small bright light. This rhythmic sequence continued as long as the subject continued to stare at the light. When the infant looked away, the rhythmic sequence would be halted at the end of the given group. A new trial would then be initiated if the infant looked at the luminous target again. For each trial, the amount of time spent staring at the light was assessed. After a block of 15 trials with the same sequence, a new rhythmic sequence (say R2) was introduced. Both sequences were made up of sounds, separated by the same time intervals (97, 291, 582 ms) but the order of the intervals was permuted between the sequences R1 and R2. The duration of the period spent staring at the light decreased progressively during the first 15 trials (habituation) but strongly increased when the sequence changed (Fig. 5.3). This reaction to novelty is the clue that the

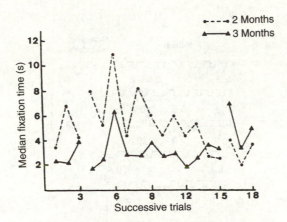

Fig. 5.4 (Top) Sound sequences. The duration of intervals between the sounds was 150 ms and the duration of the intervals between the groups of sounds was 300 ms. (Bottom) Median fixation time during successive trials. (Redrawn from Demany (1979), experiment 2.)

infant is able to detect a change, and more specifically to discriminate one rhythmic sequence from another. Thus the infant does not perceive sounds as a series of isolated events.

In the sequences used in this experiment, there was a long interval (582 ms) that can be considered as a pause. What would happen if the rhythmic groups were repeated without pauses (as in the case of sequences A and B in Fig. 5.4)? In order to differentiate these two sequences, it was necessary to grasp the order of the groups, that is, to join these groups in a repetitive configuration of six sounds. The experiment was conducted in a similar manner to the one described above, with 2½- and 5-month-old infants. The results showed that only the older infants were able to differentiate between the two rhythmic sequences. It must be noted that the sequences A and B only differed by the order of the groups of sounds (1,2,3, for A and 1,3,2, for B), and were therefore very difficult to differentiate, even for an adult who would be aware of these differences. It would seem that, at 5 months of age, the ability to temporally structure auditory events is already well developed.

The second study A study conducted by Morrongiello (1984) is also of special interest as it deals with the discrimination of rhythmic sequences by the infants but differentiates between: (1) the perception of absolute time (the duration of events and the silences between these events); and (2) the perception of relative time (that is, the position within time of a

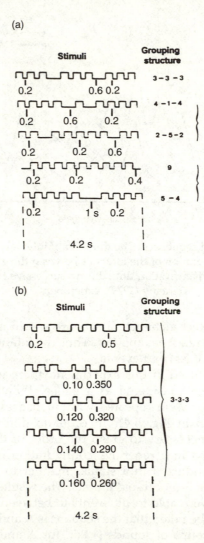

Fig. 5.5 Schematic diagram of the sound patterns: (a) used in experiment 1; (b) used in experiment 2. (Redrawn from Morrongiello (1984).)

given auditory event in relation to all the other events within the sequence). The sequences were made up of bursts of white noise. Indeed, according to the author, discriminations can occur on the basis of a variation of intensity or frequency rather than duration when tones are involved. The procedure used was a conditioning procedure operating on a go/no-go basis. First, a base sequence was repeatedly played to the infant. Then, he or she was taught to turn his or her head when a change from the base sequence occurred. This was achieved by guiding the infant's head and reinforcing this response by a visual stimulus (a small toy monkey or a small toy dog). The auditory sequences used in the first experiment are shown in Fig. 5.5(a); the base sequence lasted for 4.2 s and was composed of three groups of three white-noise stimuli of 200 ms and two intervals of 600 ms. All the infants (6- and 12-month-olds) turned their head when the 3–3–3 sequence was changed to a 9 or a 5–4 sequence, thus indicating their awareness of the change. However, only the 12-month-old babies differentiated the 3–3–3 sequences from the 4–1–4 or 2–5–2 sequences. These results suggest that there is an evolution in the perception of relative time in infants between the ages of 6 and 12 months and also indicate that both 6- and 12-month-old infants are sensitive to changes in terms of absolute time. Nevertheless, it was necessary to check whether, in the case of the younger infants, this sensitivity was not merely due to a change in the number of groups.

A second experiment was therefore set up where the number of groups was kept constant but where the duration of the events and intervals was varied (see Fig. 5.5(b)). All the infants of 6 and 12 months could differentiate the sequences, that is to say, could detect differences in duration from 40 to 150 ms. These results confirm the fact that, from 6 months of age, children are sensitive to changes in information in terms of absolute time. The author argues that, unlike other researchers (Chang and Trehub 1977; Demany 1979), the lack of discrimination found in terms of relative time was due to the fact that white noise was used as auditory stimulation instead of tones and that the sequences involved were longer and more complex.

1.2.3 *Temporal discrimination abilities in the visual modality*

We will only give a brief overview of the studies made in this field (for a review, see Lewkowicz 1989), as they are less pertinent to the development of musical competence than those made in the auditory modality.

There are two forms of studies dealing with temporal discrimination in the visual modality. The first kind uses a static stimulus: lights or squares on a chessboard that blink at various frequencies (Allen *et al.* 1977; Marcell 1979; Lewkowicz 1985). It emerges from these studies that a developmental change occurs. Four-month-old infants discriminate

Rate (Hz)	On time (ms)	Off time (ms)	Duty cycle (%)	
8	50	75	40	
4	50	200	20	
2	50	450	10	
8	62.5	62.5	50	
4	125	125	50	
2	250	250	50	

←——— 1 s ———→

Fig. 5.6 Schematic representation of the temporal distribution of stimuli. (From Lewkowicz (1985).)

using non-temporal information such as quantity, whereas children of 6 months of age differentiate on the basis of temporal information *per se*. For example, 4-month-old babies can discriminate 8, 4, and 2 Hz frequencies when the *on* duration of the visual stimulus is maintained at a constant level (50 ms) and the *off* duration varies with the frequency (75 ms for an 8-Hz frequency, 200 ms for a 4-Hz frequency, and 450 ms for a 2-Hz frequency). However, they cannot differentiate among the three frequencies when the *on* and *off* durations are of equal length (respectively 62.5, 125 and 250 ms) (see Fig. 5.6).

The second type of study concerns dynamic temporal information (movement and speed). Infants live in a world where objects move. The

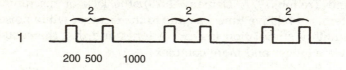

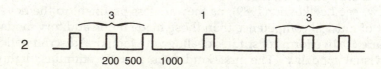

Fig. 5.7 Schematic representation of the temporal distribution of stimuli. (From Mendelson (1986).)

type of movement is important to the perception and differentiation of these objects one from another. Indeed, an object can have a smooth, regular movement or an abrupt one. This motion can be fast or slow.

Mendelson (1986) wanted to determine whether 4-month-old babies can discriminate various rhythmic sequences of motion. He therefore showed infants of that age a film where a hand opened and closed following the rhythms (1 or 2) shown in Figure 5.7. The hand movement lasted 200 ms. The interval between each movement was 500 ms. The interval between each group of movements was 1000 ms. The results showed that the infants who were familiarized with one of the two rhythms watched for a longer period of time when a new rhythm was introduced (reaction to novelty), whereas the habituation was prolonged (progressive decrease of the time of observation) when the rhythmic sequence was left unchanged.

1.2.4 *Intersensory processing of temporal information*

As we have just seen, infants are capable of discerning temporal auditory patterns from the age of 2½ months (Demany *et al.* 1977; Demany 1979). This ability progressively improves during the first year of life (Chang and Trehub 1977; Morrongiello 1984). Infants can also differentiate various visual patterns on the basis of a change in temporal parameters: frequencies of a flashing light (Allen *et al.* 1977; Marcell 1979; Lewkowicz 1985) or rhythmic movements (Mendelson 1986). During the last decades, it has also been shown that the various sensory modalities are co-ordinated at a very early stage in life (Hatwell 1993). However, very few studies have tried to determine whether there is an intermodal function that relies on the temporal characteristics of stimuli.

Spelke (1979) showed 4-month-old infants a film where two dolls were jumping at different tempi. The film was accompanied by a rhythmic sound sequence with a tempo corresponding to the tempo of one of the jumping dolls. The infants exhibited a visual preference for the doll whose jumping motion was linked to the auditory sequence. These results provide evidence that infants can associate what they see with what they hear when the auditory and visual stimuli are linked. However, these results do not show that infants transfer temporal information (in this case the tempo) from one sensory modality to another.

In 1982, Mendelson and Ferland familiarized 4-month-old children with a syllable (auditory modality) that was played following two different rhythms: a regular one (II II II II) and an irregular one (III I III I). Then, they showed a film where a puppet opened its mouth, either following the auditory rhythm to which the infants had been accustomed in the auditory modality or a new rhythm. The temporal structure of these two rhythms was the same as the one used by Mendelson (1986) (see Fig. 5.7). The authors predicted that the infants would look at something new for a longer period of time, that is to say, the visual rhythm that was different to the auditory rhythm to which they had been accustomed. The results supported the prediction: those infants who had been accustomed to the regular auditory rhythm were more interested in the visual stimulus with an irregular rhythm and vice versa. This reaction to novelty can be interpreted as the ability to differentiate between the rhythm of the doll's mouth movements and the rhythm of the auditory sequence which the children had memorized. These results therefore suggest that young infants are able to abstract the temporal information from a stimulus presented in one modality and indeed can memorize and compare it to the temporal information that they have abstracted from a stimulus in a second modality. Nevertheless, as the authors remark, such transfers are probably more easily accomplished when the experimental situation is close to a natural one (in this case syllables and puppets miming speech).

1.2.5 *Temporal information in early interactions and 'dialogues'*

We have seen that rhythms are omnipresent and develop in the earliest stages of childhood. We have also examined the development of the ability to process time-related information in external events. The ability to process this information and to learn to control one's own rhythm paves the way for the young human child towards more differentiated temporal behaviour.

Early social interactions and, in particular, game playing and 'dialogue' with parents are preferential situations of learning. The numerous studies of the Papoušeks (Papoušek and Papoušek 1987, among others) have provided evidence that parents adjust stimulations to their infant's perceptual capacities and, thus, intuitively facilitate speech acquisition and support other early competences such as the musical one (see Chapters 2 and 4 by H. and M. Papoušek, respectively). During interactions infants can learn to synchronize their own rhythms with those of their environment. Interactions also offer an opportunity for the infants to develop their ability to perceive order and duration, as shown by the two following experiments.

1. Arco (1983) and Arco and McCluskey (1981) asked parents to play with their infants (of 3 to 5 months of age) at three different rhythms: the normal one; a slower one; and a faster one. This experiment showed that the infants were sensitive to these changes in rhythm and reacted differently to them. When the rhythm was normal or accelerated, the positive facial expressions, smiles, looks, vocalizations, and actions synchronized with their parents were far greater than when the rhythm was slow. Indeed, in the case of the slow rhythm, the infants showed

signs of wanting to end the interaction: they no longer looked at their partner and turned away.

2. Jasnow and Feldstein (1986) observed dyads (a mother and her 9-month-old baby) and recorded their interactions during a game with a puppet. This set-up gave a 'standard format' to the interaction and encouraged the vocal exchange between the mother and the child. These recordings showed that the alternating vocalizations were far more frequent than the simultaneous ones. The length of pauses between phrases of one member of the dyad and the length of time between each member's vocalization was the same for both the mother and the child (on average 800 ms). Both child and mother therefore waited for an equal amount of time to have elapsed before taking his or her speaking turn. Preverbal children are as capable of respecting a silence as their linguistically competent mothers, even if the latter direct this interaction by increasing or decreasing the length of the alternation pauses according to the length of the infant's previous pause. This repeated experience of the temporal structure of 'dialogue' is surely a major contributing factor to the development of the ability to perceive order and duration.

2 ENACTED TIME AND REPRESENTED TIME IN CHILDREN

In Section 1 we examined the various temporal abilities of infants. We saw that these abilities consist in knowing when to act and react at the 'right time' and being able to perceive and process the temporal structure of the events and stimulus that make up an infant's environment. In the second part of this work, we will be looking at how children act within time when they become able of 'reasoning' about representations (Imberty, Chapter 8). The studies to which we will refer will seem of a more eclectic nature than the ones at which we have been looking until now. Indeed, there is still a long way to go before a synthetic view of the development of the children's temporal knowledge is reached.

We will first report studies on the development of the representation of the order of temporal events, then on the emergence of cognitive regulations of actions when the concept of time as a measurable quantity emerges in children. We will close this chapter by presenting the few studies in the literature on timing that are related to the development of the perception and reproduction of auditory rhythms in children.

2.1 The development of representations of the temporal structure of events

Recent studies (O'Connell and Gerard 1985; Bauer and Mandler 1989, 1992) have made a significant contribution ot understanding the representation of the temporal order of events by young children (between the ages of 1 and 3 years). It is very difficult to question children so young, given their limited linguistic abilities. The researchers therefore developed a clever imitation technique that was perfectly suited to children of that age. This technique involved 'miming' a sequence of actions in front of a child (for example, putting a teddy bear in a bathtub, washing it, and then drying it) and then asking the child to reproduce that same sequence, either immediately or at a later date (the delay being of up to 6 weeks). In order to reproduce it, the child had to watch the actions taking place, code the information on the order in which these actions occurred, and, when asked, retrieve that information from memory.

The results showed that, by the end of their second and even first year of life, children are able to reproduce or remember the order of sequences where the various elements bore causal relationships with one another[1] and as long as they have been mimed in the *canonical order*.

By 28 months, they can then correctly reproduce sequences which have been presented with an *inverse order*. It is only at the end of their third year of life, when infants have become able to represent order in an abstract manner, that they reproduce correctly sequences of an *arbitrary nature* (without causal relations between actions)[2] or mimed in a *random order*.

Linguistic research has also provided data on the representation of temporal order. There have been studies on the comprehension and production of terms to describe temporal relations such as before and after (Friedman and Seely 1976; French and Nelson 1981; Carni and French 1984) and on the categorization of events past, present, and future (Harner 1981; Weist 1989). For example, Carni and French (1984) showed that, from the age of 3 years, children are able to form a mental representation of 'before and after' relationships, but only in a context with which they are familiar. In other words, they can represent temporal relations that they have already experienced. Similarly, Harner (1981) showed that 4-year-olds use the appropriate past and present tenses to describe events preceding or just following the instant in which they are speaking (toys with which they have already played as opposed to toys with which they are going to play).

A recent study by Friedman (1990) complements this line of research. It showed that young infants are not only able to include information about temporal order in their representations but also information relating to the length of the events. There again, the correct evaluations

---

[1] These sequences are either familiar to the child (for example, the bath of the teddy bear) or novel for him/her (for example, making a rattle out of two nesting cups and a ball and then shaking the resulting object).

[2] For example, attaching two cars together, laying them on a track, and then placing the doll inside.

first pertain to everyday events such as drinking a glass of milk or watching a cartoon. It is only at a later stage that this ability can be observed in a wider context.

2.2 Temporal regulations of action: from conditioned regulation to cognitive regulation

The objective of our research group over the past 10 years has been to determine how actions come to be controlled by progressively acquired and mastered abstract representation of time. When we first started to study this question, there was very little data available on the development of temporal regulations of behaviour and the process of duration estimation in children aged between 18 months and 6 years. Both theoretical and methodological reasons could explain this lack of knowledge. The studies of Fraisse (1957) and Piaget (1937, 1946) suggested that knowledge of time was specifically human and was acquired at a relatively late stage of ontogenesis. Thus Fraisse (1979) stated: 'Man, like every other living organism, is subject to time. However, he has the privilege of learning to situate himself within time and learns to know time during his development.' Furthermore, according to Piaget (1937), practical time (time during the sensorimotor period) is a specialized time relating to every action, so that there exist as many temporal series as there are schemes of actions. However, still according to Piaget, there is no unique time linking all these schemes and series together. Even if a child, during an action, knows how to use and predict a string of events, he or she must then reconstruct notions of order and duration. This reconstruction of previously 'enacted' notions presupposes a real and new learning process. The lack of data concerning children between the ages of 1½ and 6 years also stems from methodological difficulties. Piaget (1946, p. 271) wrote, 'One should distinguish a period, between the ages of approximately 1½ and 4 years, where all forms of questioning are still impossible.' It is also for theoretical and methodological reasons that psychophysical studies relative to the perception and estimation of duration used children aged 6 years or more. Authors were trying to show the emergence in young children of temporal judgements analogous to those used by adults. The psychological methods involved were therefore much too complex and difficult to apply in the case of younger children.

As we saw previously, recent researchers on the early stages of the development of temporal order representations have tried to create a method that is appropriate for very young infants. They have thus chosen an imitation technique. As far as we are concerned, the procedures for time conditioning supplied by operant methodology seem to be a useful tool for interrogating young children on their temporal behaviour and analysing its evolution during their cognitive development. Indeed, it is a non-verbal method that can also be applied to older children with more advanced linguistic abilities. We have chosen the DRL schedule[3] as it brings together two components: a waiting period and a discrimination of duration. According to early twentieth-century philosophers and psychologists (Guyau 1890; Janet 1928), complex forms of adaptation to time, where processes of a symbolic and conceptual nature intervene, derive from waiting behaviours.

2.2.1   *Evolution with age of time-conditioned behaviours*

Between the ages of 18 and 24 months a regulation of the rate of the operant response first appears. Learning to postpone responses is made easier by the development of concurrent motor behaviours.[4] However, the regulation acquired through these motor activities remains imprecise. The 'waiting periods' are often too long. Between the ages of 4 and 7 years, various kinds of performances coexist. Certain 4½-year-olds are unable to refrain from responding; their interresponse intervals are very short. On the other hand, some children are very capable of providing accurate estimates of the waiting delay. In this case they often manifest rhythmic movements of fingers, hands, or feet, which might be assimilated to forerunners of counting abilities. All 7-year-olds learn to space their responses in time. Some wait for a longer period than is necessary, as if they are taking a 'security margin', whereas others estimate very precisely the delay required.

Children do not consistently use counting as a means of timing the period of waiting between two successive responses (Pouthas and Jacquet 1987). We have shown (Pouthas 1985) that it is only from the age of 11 years that children systematically use counting of a 'stopwatch' nature (for example, 1 per second).

2.2.2   *The emergence of cognitive regulations of action*

The data that we have just summarized show, on the one hand, that certain relatively complex temporal learning, such as postponing an action and estimating the necessary delay before executing it, can be observed from very early childhood. On the other hand, these same data show that such acquired temporal regulations of behaviour only

---

[3] In this schedule, a response is reinforced only if a preset delay has elapsed between that response and the previous one. An anticipated response sets the delay back to zero thus forcing the subject to wait for a certain lapse of time to occur between two successive responses.

[4] One child follows a long path in the experimental room; another turns over a large plastic cube used as a seat; a third leans to one side then to the other side of the table on which the response device has been arranged.

rely on a complex concept of time (such as the idea that time is a quantifiable entity that can be measured) at a relatively late stage of ontogenesis. These results are indeed coherent with those obtained using other theoretical and methodological viewpoints.

However, we have supposed that the situations that we were using did not allow for the children, especially those between the ages of 4 and 6 years, to rely on newly acquired, but not yet mastered, knowledge. We therefore created new situations in order to find out more about the role of the development of the children's ability to represent time in learning how to regulate their action in time. These situations were meant to encourage the children to use their newly acquired knowledge that would otherwise have remained latent. We used the same operant methods, but we gave different types of instructions—verbal, demonstration, or external clocks—to the children. These instructions were thought to direct their attention to the temporal characteristics of the task.

Thus, we trained 4½-year-olds to learn to space out their responses within time using the same situation as the one we had used to obtain our first results, that is, a DRL of 5 seconds, which required them to space their responses by at least 5 seconds. In this case, however, a visual and auditory metronome was present during training (it produced a beep and a flash every 800 ms, hence between 6 and 7 beats for a 5-s delay). We assumed that this device could induce a motor rhythm, that is to say, a tap with the hand or the foot synchronized to the metronome's rhythm. In other words, the metronome could facilitate the emergence of a 'behavioural clock', the importance of which has been shown by the performances of certain 4½-year-olds who did not benefit from such a device (cf. the example of rhythmic finger or feet movements that enabled them to adjust themselves very precisely to a waiting delay). The first four training sessions were made using the metronome. The last two were without it. The results show that the subjects were efficient by the end of the fourth session. They were as efficient as the children who had been told to wait before each press on the button and far more efficient than those who had received no information on the

Table 5.3 Percentage of reinforced interresponse times (IRTs) at the beginning and at the end of DRL 5-s training in 4½ year-old children

Session	IRTs (%) under experimental conditions of		
	Minimal instructions	Verbal instructions	External clock
1	38	66	36
4	35	71	60

temporal constraints involved before starting the experiment (Table 5.3). One must note that there was a real learning: the children gradually started to use the metronome. Furthermore, the acquired temporal regulation was kept. When the metronome was removed, the performances remained at the same level: 60 per cent of reinforced interresponse times (IRTs) at the fourth session with the metronome and 5.5 per cent of reinforced IRTs at the second session after the removal of the metronome.

Another experiment was aimed at determining the importance of verbal instructions and demonstration. In this case, the children no longer had to space out two successive responses by at least 5 s but had to make the response last for at least 4 s and no longer than 6 s (temporal differentiation of response duration). We therefore examined the performances of children aged 4½, 6, and 7 years in the following situations: (1) a *minimal verbal instruction* was given to make a laughing clown appear (feedback to a correct answer); (2) an *informative verbal instruction* was given to make the press last for a certain length of time; (3) the researcher *demonstrated* three times the correct response.

The greatest number of correct answers came from those children who had benefited from an informative verbal instructions or from a demon-

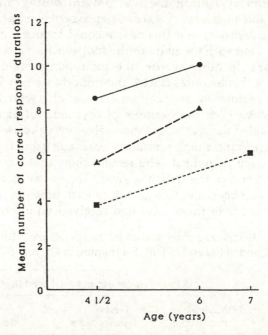

Fig. 5.8 Mean number of correct response durations as a function of age and instruction type. Dots, instructions by demonstration; triangles, verbal instructions; squares, minimal instructions. (Redrawn from Lejeune *et al.* (1992).)

stration (see Fig. 5.8). Furthermore, a significant correlation can be observed in 6-year-olds between the number of successful attempts and the number of verbalizations qualified as 'temporal'. This shows that they are able to describe the temporal constraints involved in a task and can also explain the rule that they are following to perform this task. This result may seem obvious for those children who received an informative verbal instruction, but it is perhaps less so for those who had just received a demonstration. We can therefore conclude that both kinds of instructions helped the elaboration of time-related rules by children under the age of 7 years. This correlates, as in older children, to an adapted temporal behaviour.

The results from the above two studies suggest that, through appropriate means or instructions, it is possible for a child to use knowledge that is generally thought to be acquired or mastered at a much later stage of ontogenesis. The young child might encounter difficulties in utilizing recently acquired knowledge and/or in generalizing this knowledge to all the situations that the child has to face.

2.3 Time as a quantifiable dimension and learning to measure time

A parallel can be drawn between our line of reasoning and that used by Levin and Wilkening (1989) in their studies on the development of the concept of time as a quantifiable dimension. Indeed, they argue that Piaget's conclusions, that children under 10 years do not conceive of time as a measurable quantity, have received wide acceptance simply because such young children experience difficulties in implementing their abilities to quantify time in the particular tasks they are requested to perform. Using counting to measure time implies conceiving of time as a quantifiable dimension. Even though this dimension is continuous, it can be measured by discrete units, notably numbers. It is therefore generally accepted that, before the age of 10 years, children do not systematically employ counting to measure time.[5]

However, the fact that children do not spontaneously count to perform the tasks they are assigned does not imply that they do not realize that time can be measured by numbers. At any rate, when children are placed in a more natural environment, they certainly utilize counting. One only has to look at children playing a game of hide and seek.

Levin and Wilkening (1989) therefore tried to reveal a temporal reasoning dependent on quantifiable bases and a utilization of counting. In the study, which we will briefly describe, they tried to encourage young children to count by placing a metronome in front of them. This metronome had a rhythm of 1 beat/s that therefore enabled a constant rate of

---

[5] The first results we obtained, using an operant methodology, confirmed this assertion (Pouthas 1985).

counting. The task of a group of 5-, 6- and 7-year-olds was to reproduce the total period of time for which a lamp was illuminated. This light was lit twice for, successively, 2, 4, or 6 seconds. There was an interval between the two illuminations. Half the children involved were in possession of a metronome. Results show that the presence of the metronome (that is, a rhythmic segmentation of the intervals) made it easier for the 5- and 6-year-olds to develop a counting strategy. They could count from 1 each time the lamp was lit and add up these two numbers or count the total length of time by stopping during the interval between two successive lightings. This second strategy was the one most used by the 5- and 6-year-olds whilst the first was mainly used by the 7-year-olds. Furthermore, the children that used a counting method proved more precise and more consistent in their evaluations of duration. Finally, those 5-year-olds that did not use a counting technique used other 'measuring strategies': rhythmic movements of the hand; repetition of the same sound; singing a little rhyme. Such strategies were similar to the ones we observed during our experiments on temporal regulations of action (see above).

These results indicate that children of 5 years or more are able to conceive of the idea of measuring time. Furthermore, this measuring can be achieved through counting. However, these results also show the importance of the choice of situations in enabling the temporal abilities of children to come forward and in controlling the emergence and development of time-related knowledge.

2.4 Synchronization of perceived and produced sequences

To end the second part of our chapter, we will be considering the problem of motor and perceptual rhythms in children. It is something of a challenge. Indeed, many works have been produced on the newborns' ability to distinguish perceptual rhythms and their capacity to modify the temporal structure of motor rhythms. However, such data is very sparse for young children. Furthermore, many studies deal with synchronization tasks (tasks where a subject must follow an external sequence, generally auditory, by tapping his hands or feet) in adults. However, ontogenetic research on this subject is practically non-existent or quite old, at least in the literature concerning the developmental psychology of time. Nevertheless, synchronization tasks are of interest in that they allow us to study how subjects encode a duration, in other words, how they form a model of the interval that separates the stimuli to which the subjects must synchronize their action (physical or verbal). It also enables us to see how the subjects maintain this rhythm and thus to see how, from a motor viewpoint, they reproduce the perceptual rhythm.

Such studies on adults show that they are able to synchronize their taps to auditory sequences where the interstimulus intervals are between 200 and 4800 ms. Maximum precision is obtained for interstimulus intervals situated between 400 and 800 ms. These values correspond to musical tempi of 80 to 120 crotchets (quarter notes) per minute and are close to 'spontaneous' motor and perceptual tempi. Indeed, when the subjects are asked to adjust a rhythm of regular sounds to the tempo that, to them, seem most natural, the intervals are situated between 500 and 750 ms. Furthermore, similar results are obtained when subjects are asked to 'tap' (a Morse key for example) at their preferred speed and the time interval between two successive taps is measured.

Adults are able to synchronize a motor action to an external rhythm. Their synchronization performances are characterized, even in the case of musicians, by a 'systematic error', that is to say, an anticipation of the tap over the sound (or negative asynchrony). The value of this anticipation depends on the external rhythm. It is minimal (20 to 50 ms on average) for interstimulus intervals located between 400 and 800 ms (those of the preferred tempi). The value of the anticipation also varies with the subject's training. Several hypotheses have been developed to explain this phenomenon. Many of the current studies are trying to verify the hypothesis put forward by Radil *et al.* (1993) and Prinz (1993). They assume that the feedback resulting from the action operates as a 'landmark' for a 'good' synchronization with the sound. The anticipation would therefore result from the difference in the neural speed transmission of the sensory processing of the sound and the speed of the motor feedback corresponding to the tap.

One may ask whether, like adults, young children have a systematic anticipation of motor action over sound. The small amount of data that has been available up till now did not allow us to easily answer this question. However, some studies on synchronization in children (Auxiette 1992; Gérard and Auxiette 1992) have begun to provide some experimental evidence. These studies deal with the synchronization abilities of 5-year-olds as compared to adults. The subjects had to accompany a sequence of 'beeps' by pressing a button. Two rhythms were tested: a fast rhythm with interbeep intervals of 435 ms; and a slow rhythm with 600-ms interbeep intervals (138 beeps/min in the first case and 100 beeps/min in the second). The results show that the majority of the taps were 'synchronized' for both the children and adults (not more than 150 ms anticipated or 'posticipated' over the sound). Furthermore, an anticipation of the 'press' was also noted for a majority of children. Nevertheless, the children showed less accuracy in their taps. Their anticipated and 'posticipated' taps were more distant from the stimulus than for the adults. According to the authors, there are three main factors that explain these shifts: (1) a less efficient encoding of durations; (2) a less accurate control of the temporal parameters of their action; (3) a tolerance with a higher threshold before deciding to readjust.

The way is now open to new studies that will be aimed at determining the role of these factors on the evolution of rhythmic performances during childhood. The results of these studies will not radically change our knowledge of the ontogenesis of temporal competences, but will give us a more general view of it. In rhythms, indeed, time is *perceived and enacted simultaneously*.

REFERENCES

Allen, T. W., Walker, K., Symonds, L., and Marcell, M. (1977). Intrasensory and intersensory perception of temporal sequences during infancy. *Developmental Psychology*, **13**, 225–9.

Arco, C. M. (1983). Infant reactions to natural and manipulated temporal patterns of paternal communication. *Infant Behavior and Development*, **6**, 391–9.

Arco, C. M. and McCluskey, K. A. (1981). A change of pace: an investigation of the salience of maternal temporal style in mother–infant play. *Child Development*, **52**, 941–9.

Ashton, R. (1976). Aspects in child development. *Child Development*, **47**, 622–6.

Auxiette, C. (1992). Coordination et synchronisation de deux séquences sonores perçues et produites: processus perceptifs, moteurs et cognitifs. Unpublished D. Psychol. thesis. University René Descartes of Paris.

Bauer, P. J. and Mandler, J. M. (1989). One thing follows another: effects of temporal structure on 1- to 2-year olds' recall of events. *Developmental Psychology*, **25**, 197–206.

Bauer, P. J. and Mandler, J. M. (1992). Putting the horse before the cart: the use of temporal order in recall of events by one-year-old children. *Developmental Psychology*, **28**, 441–52.

Bohlin, G. and Kjellberg, A. (1979). Orienting activity in two-stimulus paradigms as reflected in heart rate. In *The orienting response in humans* (ed. H. D. Kimmel, E. H. Von Holst, and J. E. Orlebeke), pp. 169–95. Erlbaum, Hillsdale, New Jersey.

Carni, E. and French, L. A. (1984). The acquisition of before and after reconsidered: what develops? *Journal of Experimental Child Psychology*, **37**, 394–403.

Chang, H. and Trehub, S. E. (1977). Infants' perception of temporal grouping in auditory patterns. *Child Development*, **48**, 1666–70.

Clifton, R. K. (1974). Heart rate conditioning in the newborn infant. *Journal of Experimental Child Psychology*, **18**, 9–21.

Coles, M. G. H. and Duncan-Johnson, C. C. (1975). Cardiac activity and information processing: the effects of stimulus significance, detection, and response requirements. *Human Perception and Performance*, **1**, 418–28.

Darcheville, J. C., Rivière, V., and Wearden, J. H. (1993). Fixed-interval performance and self-control in infants. *Journal of the Experimental Analysis of Behavior*, **60**, 239–54.

DeCasper, A. J. and Sigafoos, A. D. (1983). The intrauterine heartbeat: a potent reinforcer for newborns. *Infant Behavior and Development*, **6**, 12–25.

Demany, L. (1979). L'appréhension perceptive des structures temporelles chez le nourrisson. In *Du temps biologique au temps psychologique*, Symposium de l'APSLF (Poitiers, 1977), pp. 217–27. Presses Universitaires de France, Paris.

Demany, L., McKenzie, B., and Vurpillot, E. (1977). Rhythm perception in early infancy. *Nature*, **266**, 718–19.

Donohue, R. L. and Berg, W. K. (1991). Infant heart rate responses to temporally predictable and unpredictable events. *Developmental Psychology*, **27**, 59–66.

Eilers, R. E., Bull, D. H., Oller, D. K., and Lewis, D. (1984). The discrimination of vowel duration by infants. *Journal of the Acoustical Society of America*, **75**, 1213–18.

Fraisse, P. (1957). *Psychologie du Temps*. Presses Universitaires de France, Paris.

Fraisse, P. (1979). Avant-propos. In *Du temps biologique au temps psychologique*, Symposium de l'APSLF (Poitiers, 1977), p. 7. Presses Universitaires de France, Paris.

French, L. A. and Nelson, K. (1981). Temporal knowledge expressed in pre-schooler's descriptions of familiar activities. *Papers and Reports on Child Language Development*, **20**, 61–9.

Friedman, W. J. (1990). Children's representation of the pattern of daily activities. *Child Development*, **61**, 1399–412.

Friedman, W. J. and Seely, P. B. (1976). The child's acquisition of spatial and temporal word meanings. *Child Development*, **47**, 1103–8.

Gérard, C. and Auxiette, C. (1992). The processing of musical prosody by musical and nonmusical children. *Musical Perception*, **10**, 93–126.

Guyau, J-M. (1890). *La genèse de l'idée de temps*. Félix Alcan, Paris. [English translation under the title The origin of the idea of time. In *Guyau and the idea of time* (1988). (ed. J. A. Michon, V. Pouthas, and J. Jackson), pp. 93–159. North Holland, Amsterdam.]

Harner, L. (1981). Children talk about the time and aspect of actions. *Child Development*, **52**, 498–506.

Hatwell, Y. (1993). Nature et développement des coordinations intermodales chez le nourrisson. In *Les comportements du bébé: expression de son savoir* (ed. V. Pouthas and F. Jouen), pp. 183–5. Mardaga, Liège.

Hulsebus, R. C. (1973). Operant conditioning of infant behavior: a review. In *Advances in child development and behavior*, Vol. 8 (ed. H. W. Reese), pp. 112–57. Academic Press, New York.

Janet, P. (1928). *L'évolution de la mémoire et de la notion de temps*. Chahine, Paris.

Jasnow, M. and Feldstein, S. (1986). Adult-like temporal characteristics of mother–infant vocal interactions. *Child Development*, **57**, 754–61.

Lejeune, H., Pouthas, V., and El Ahmadi, A. (1992). Temporal differentiation of response duration in 4½ and 6-year-olds: role of verbal instructions versus demonstration. *Cahiers de Psychologie Cognitive-European Bulletin of Cognitive Psychology*, **12**, 315–32.

Levin, I. and Wilkening, F. (1989). Measuring time via counting: the development of children's conceptions of time as a quantifiable dimension. In *Time and human cognition: a life span perspective* (ed. I. Levin and D. Zakay), pp. 119–43. Elsevier, North Holland, Amsterdam.

Lewkowicz, D. J. (1985). Developmental changes in infant's response to temporal frequency. *Developmental Psychology*, **21**, 858–65.

Lewkowicz, D. J. (1989). The role of temporal factors in infant behavior and development. In *Time and human cognition: a life span perspective* (ed. I. Levin and D. Zakay), pp. 9–58. Elsevier, North Holland, Amsterdam.

Marcell, M. M. (1979). Auditory and visual discrimination of rhythmic sequences by 1½ and 3½ month-old infants. *Dissertational Abstracts International*, **39**, 5615–16.

Mendelson, M. J. (1986). Perception of the temporal pattern of motion in infancy. *Infant Behavior and Development*, **9**, 231–43.

Mendelson, M. J. and Ferland, M. B. (1982). Auditory-visual transfer in four-month-old infants. *Child Development*, **53**, 1022–7.

Morrongiello, B. A. (1984). Auditory temporal pattern perception in 6- and 12-month infants. *Developmental Psychology*, **20**, 441–8.

O'Connell, B. G. and Gerard, A. B. (1985). Scripts and scraps: the development of sequential understanding. *Child Development*, **56**, 671–81.

Papoušek, H. and Papoušek, M. (1987). Intuitive parenting: a dialectic counterpart to the infant's integrative competence. In *Handbook of infant development* (2nd edn) (ed. J. D. Osofsky), pp. 669–720. Wiley, New York.

Piaget, J. (1937). *La construction du réel*. Delachaux & Niestlé, Neuchâtel.

Piaget, J. (1946). *Le développement de la notion de temps*. Presses Universitaires de France, Paris.

Pouthas, V. (1985). Timing behaviour in young children: a developmental approach to conditioned spaced responding. In *Time, mind and behaviour* (ed. J. Michon and J. Jackson), pp. 100–9. Springer Verlag, Heidelberg.

Pouthas, V. (1990). Temporal regulation of behaviour in humans: a developmental approach. In *Behaviour analysis in theory and practice: contributions and controversies* (ed. D. E. Blackman and H. Lejeune), pp. 33–52. Lawrence Erlbaum Associates, Hove.

Pouthas, V. and Jacquet, A. Y. (1987). A developmental study of timing behavior in 4½ and 7-year-old children. *Journal of Experimental Child Psychology*, **43**, 282–99.

Prinz, W. (1993). Distal focusing in action control. In *Fourth Rhythm Workshop: rhythm perception and production* (ed. C. Auxiette, C. Drake, and C. Gérard), pp. 65–73. Les Editions de la ville de Bourges, France.

Provasi, J. (1988). Capacités et apprentissages de régulations temporelles chez le nourrisson dans l'activité de succion. Unpublished D. Psychol. thesis. University René Descartes of Paris.

Radil, T., Mates, J., Maras, L., Bohdanecky, Z., Indra, M., and Pöppel, E. (1993). Cognitive-motor aspects of following rhythmic tonal sequences. In *Fourth Rhythm Workshop: rhythm perception and production* (ed. C. Auxiette, C. Drake, and C. Gérard), pp. 49–59. Les Editions de la ville de Bourges, France.

Rivière, V. (1992). Ontogenèse de la régulation temporelle et impulsivité. Unpublished D. Psychol. thesis. University of Lille.

Rovee-Collier, C. (1993). La mémoire du nourrisson. In *Les comportements du bébé: expression de son savoir* (ed. V. Pouthas and F. Jouen), pp. 127–45. Mardaga, Liège.

Rovee-Collier, C. and Gekoski, M. J. (1979). The economics of infancy: a review of conjugate reinforcement. In *Advances in child development and research*, Vol. 19 (ed. H. W. Reese and L. P. Lipsitt), pp. 195–255. Academic Press, New York.

Spelke, E. S. (1979). Perceiving bimodally specified events in infancy. *Developmental Psychology*, **15**, 626–36.

Stamps, L. E. (1977). Temporal conditioning of heart rate responses in newborn infants. *Developmental Psychology*, **13**, 624–9.

Thelen, E. (1981). Rhythmical behavior in infancy: an ethological perspective. *Developmental Psychology*, **17**, 237–57.

Weist, R. M. (1989). Time concepts in language and thought: filling the piagetian void from two to five years. In *Time and human cognition: a life span perspective* (ed. I. Levin and D. Zakay), pp. 63–114. Elsevier–North Holland, Amsterdam.

Wolff, P. H. (1967). The role of biological rhythms in early psychological development. *Bulletin of the Menninger Clinic*, **31**, 197–218.

PART IV

School Age

6

The development of artistic and musical competence

David Hargreaves

1 INTRODUCTION

The study of musical development has grown dramatically in recent years, and this has occurred within a number of disciplines including psychology, cognitive science, education, sociology, and anthropology, not to mention music and musicology themselves. These multidisciplinary perspectives have led to 'musical development' and 'musical competence' being defined in various ways, and at varying levels of discourse, so it might be helpful at the outset to establish some of the guiding concerns which have shaped this chapter. It is largely based upon psychological research findings, largely but by no means exclusively in children, and these are used to construct a fairly 'broad-brush', descriptive account of the development of musical competence, with a focus on the phenomena of *singing, graphic representation of music, melodic perception*, and *composition*.

This description must be seen in the context of certain guiding principles, perhaps the most important of which is that the psychological study of musical development necessarily needs to take account of the social, cultural, and, in particular, the educational context in which it occurs. This view has become central to a good deal of research in developmental psychology as a whole: children's cognitive development, for example, is increasingly being studied in its social context. The child's interaction with others, particularly peers, parents, and teachers, now forms an integral part of the description and explanation of development (see, for example, Light *et al*. 1991). I am not alone in having been concerned for some time about the need for bridge-building between research on musical development and classroom practice in music education (see, for example, Hargreaves 1986); this chapter represents yet another attempt to tackle this difficult question.

The chapter falls into two broad parts, the first of which elaborates upon the theoretical and practical issues raised above in terms of four questions. We begin with a brief account of a theory of musical competence that is concerned with the ways in which different cultural groups make sense of the music they hear rather than with the development of musical competence at the individual level; although most of the chapter is concerned with individual psychological developments, the social and cultural context is intrinsically bound up with these. This theory also provides the background for a tentative classification of pedagogical methods in music education in terms of two dimensions, namely 'control–autonomy' and 'generalist–specialist'. The distinction between 'generalist' and 'specialist' approaches to music education also leads directly to the second question of concern, namely, the explanation of normative as distinct from expert development in music.

The research reported in this chapter largely adopts the former approach in dealing with the 'natural' development of musical competence irrespective of specific musical training, and the third and fourth questions arise from this perspective. The third is the vexed question of the existence of stages in artistic and musical development, and the fourth is the extent to which this should be seen within the context of artistic development as a whole. There are some strongly divergent views on this last question, as we shall see, but my own view, which is partly conveyed by the title of this chapter, is that it is indeed helpful to deal with musical development in the context of parallel developments in other art forms.

The second part of the chapter is an abbreviated and revised version of a normative account of artistic development, based on five developmental phases, which was proposed a few years ago (Hargreaves and Galton 1992). Here we look in detail at the research on musical developments only, although illustrations are drawn from other art forms where these are helpful.

2 THEORETICAL AND PRACTICAL ISSUES

2.1 The social and educational context of musical competence

Stefani (1987, p. 7) has proposed a theory of musical competence that interprets the term as 'the ability to produce sense through music', which is itself defined as 'every social practice or individual experience concerning sounds which we are accustomed to group under this name'. It follows from this that what constitutes music in one society may not necessarily do so in another, and our definition of musical competence correspondingly needs to be able to take into account the cultural, artistic, and educational traditions of particular societies.

Stefani's notion of musical competence derives from semiotic and linguistic theory: 'the ability to produce sense through music' is intended to encompass a variety of approaches within different disciplines. These include what might be called the study of individual musicality, as shown in the predominantly psychological contributions to this volume; of musical techniques, which are possessed and intuitively understood by performers, and which can also be the subject of empirical study; of what might be called musical culture, that is, the historical and stylistic knowledge that is the province of the musicologist; and of social practices, that is, the cultural institutions within which music is performed and heard, and which are the province of the sociologist.

Stefani's theory specifies a series of what he calls *codes*, which are viewed as correlations between the content and expression of particular cultural elements—in other words, as common understandings that relate sound events to cultural experiences that can be connected with them. These range from 'general codes', which represent the basic cultural conventions through which we perceive and interpret sound experiences, through 'social practices', 'musical techniques', and 'styles', through to the most detailed level of 'opuses', that is, single musical works or events. It would not be appropriate here to deal with these codes in any detail, but it is undoubtedly instructive to take the broader social context into account. This is particularly useful here in highlighting differences between commonly used models of music teaching, since these form the immediate context for the development of musical competence in many children.

Stefani also makes the distinction between 'high' and 'popular' competences. The former 'tends to approach music in a way that is specifically and autonomously artistic': it therefore considers the 'opus' level as most pertinent and the 'lower' ones to be less pertinent the lower they are. In contrast, popular competence displays an appropriation of music that is global and heteronomous ('functional'); consequently, it exploits mostly 'general code' and 'social practice levels' (Stefani 1987, p. 17). Some forms of music (for example, opera and 'classical' music) are primarily associated with high competence, some (for example, 'light' or 'popular' music in restaurants or shops) with popular competence, and some fall within a middle ground of common competence.

I have spent some time discussing Stefani's theory because the social dimension that it incorporates provides a useful stimulus for the examination of the prominent pedagogies in music education, and I should like to propose a conceptual model that is based on two dimensions (see Figure 6.1). This formulation draws upon some models proposed by Andrén (1988) and Olsson (1993) that were originally intended as descriptions of the ideological positions of particular educational movements; here they are adapted to a rather more specific description of

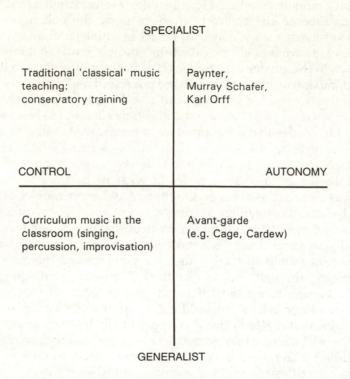

Fig. 6.1   A model of teaching methods in music education.

approaches within music education. The two orthogonal dimensions could be labelled in various possible ways, but I have opted for the terms 'specialist–generalist' and 'control–autonomy'.

In many cultures there is a long tradition of *specialist* education, within which talented pupils are given tuition, largely on traditional orchestral instruments, and reach high levels of achievement within the 'classical' tradition. This tuition is frequently provided by professional musicians who work with pupils from a relatively wide geographical region, and who deal with only a relatively small proportion of high-ability pupils, many of whom may go on to become professional musicians. This contrasts with what might be called *generalist* music education, which is based on the premise that music can be performed, appreciated, and enjoyed by all pupils at all levels. A high degree of conventional instrumental skill is not seen as a prerequisite for successful participation in music, and its absence does not in any way diminish the seriousness of purpose of the activity.

The specialist–generalist distinction is currently very salient in the UK. Since the introduction of the national curriculum in 1988, it is now statutory for all British children to follow courses in music up to the age of 14, which was not hitherto the case. A new body of teaching provision in 'general class music' or 'curriculum music' has accordingly emerged fairly quickly. Its aims are very different from those of the specialist music teacher, and new staff who are not primarily music specialists are being recruited and trained to teach it. The implications of the specialist–generalist distinction go well beyond the issues of teaching methods, as indicated earlier; they are also linked with questions about the relationship between serious and popular culture and the extent to which these are conveyed by different cultural institutions.

The other distinction, which intersects with this, has been labelled 'control–autonomy'. This refers to the extent to which particular educational practices emphasize creative improvisation on the part of the pupils, perhaps (but not necessarily) with relatively little emphasis on traditional instrumental technique, as compared with the reproduction of music previously conceived, and probably written down, by another composer. This is strongly related to the dimension of 'structuredness' which emerged in some of my own previous research on the dimensions of teachers' views of classroom activities in music (see Hargreaves and Galton 1992). This dimension can be applied to many aspects of classroom music teaching, including the teacher's implicit and explicit structuring of the lesson in terms of day-to-day planning and presentation, the degree to which the content, techniques, and media to be used are specified in advance, and the availability and variety of resources. 'Control–autonomy' can be thought of not only in terms of these aspects of the teacher's work, but also in terms of their corresponding effects on the pupils.

If we now conceive of these two distinctions as orthogonal dimensions, it becomes possible to identify particular pedagogical and/or musical techniques within each of the four quadrants. It is easy to locate traditional conservatory-based training within the 'specialist–control' quadrant since typical 'classical' conservatory training requires a great deal of detailed, high-level study of a relatively circumscribed repertoire of composed music. It is also possible, perhaps slightly more ambiguously, to identify the work of music educators such as John Paynter (for example, Paynter 1992), Murray Schafer (for example, Schafer 1965) and Carl Orff (for example, Orff and Keetman 1958) as representing both 'specialism' and 'autonomy'. These educators are firmly located within 'serious' specialist institutions, but are renowned for their advocacy of an approach that leaves a great deal of creative control in the hands of the pupils, and that therefore goes beyond the standard repertoire.

When we consider the two 'generalist' quadrants, it is easy to identify a good deal of the new material that is being produced in Great Britain to meet the demands of teaching general curriculum music at lower age levels (see, for example, Mills 1993) as being at the 'control' end of this continuum. Although the aim of techniques such as group singing, percussion, and improvisation is to encourage individual expression, it nevertheless takes place within a fairly constrained framework of conventional tonal music. A good deal of pop, folk, and rock music as they are used in the classroom could also be put into this category.

The most difficult quadrant to characterize is that representing 'generalist' music and 'autonomy', perhaps because this is by its very nature the broadest and most open-ended category. The obvious examples that spring to mind are the aleatory techniques of composers such as John Cage, or the 'scratch orchestra' experiments of Cornelius Cardew; these fulfil the description of 'generalist' by virtue of their non-reliance on conventional instrumental techniques. However, neither of these figures is associated with particular pedagogical techniques as such, and both would almost certainly resent being described as 'generalists' if this had any implication of being 'popular' rather than 'serious'. Furthermore, the absence of conventional tonality is by no means a necessary characteristic of music that might be produced by methods within this quadrant so that the categorization is made with a great deal of trepidation. This leads to the more general point that the scheme as a whole is approximate and provisional: it may well be possible to improve upon and refine it. However, the attempt to be more precise about the institutional context within which musical competence is expressed is worthwhile since it has a direct influence on psychological development, as we shall see in the next section.

2.2 Normative and expert development

The 'specialist–generalist' dimension in Fig. 6.1 is also very useful, when we return to the psychological domain, in making a distinction between two different aspects of the development of musical competence. The aim of generalist music education is to optimize what we might call normative development, that is, that which naturally happens to children as they grow up in a given culture regardless of any specialized attention or guidance, whereas specialist music education is consciously devoted to the development of high levels of musical skill or expertise, carried out by teachers and tutors who have particular ends in mind. In Chapter 7 Sloboda and Davidson deal with the latter; most of the material in this chapter deals with the former.

We should be careful not to make too strong a division between these two aspects of development. Davidson (1994) has pointed out some of the limitations of what he calls the 'talent' model of musical development, in which it is assumed that the flowering of the abilities of gifted pupils occurs more or less naturally, with little need for intervention by

adults. He points out that under appropriate conditions musically untrained children can display surprisingly sophisticated abilities, and that
musically untrained adults 'can solve musical problems at least at the
level of undergraduate music students who have years of performance
experience in their background' (p. 102). Davidson suggests that the
adoption of a developmental model is much more appropriate than
the adoption of one based on the idea of talent or 'giftedness', and the
pitfalls of the latter, as well as the problems associated with the predominant 'folk belief' that musical talent is bestowed in abundance on
certain gifted individuals, are explored in depth by Sloboda *et al.* (1994).

If the psychologist's aim *is* to study the emergence of very high levels
of expertise, however, then the specialist model of music education is a
more appropriate context, and different questions need to be asked
about musical competence. Issues of normative development need to be
set alongside those concerning the development of expert musical skills.
Sloboda (1994) points out that the study of skills, including musical
ones, gives rise to four general conclusions: that they are dependent on
the ability of the performer to detect pattern and structure in the
material; that the level of skill exhibited depends much more on the
amount of relevant practice undertaken than on any other factor; that
skills tend to become automatic, or unconscious, as they are practised;
and that they tend to be specific to certain domains of activity, and
therefore not to be susceptible to transfer to others.

Two methodological approaches have been particularly useful in the
investigation of expert musical development. Comparisons between
experts and novices have been used to illuminate some of the processes
underlying complex activities such as composition and performance
(see, for example, Ericsson and Smith 1991). Another promising approach is to carry out biographical studies of high achievers in music,
and two prominent studies (Ericsson *et al.* 1993; Sloboda and Davidson,
Chapter 7) have undertaken detailed analyses of the antecedents of
excellence in samples of conservatory students and pupils at specialist
music schools. These studies have led to some preliminary speculations
about regular stages in the development of musical excellence, and these
complement Manturszewska's (1990) model of the life-span development of professional musicians, which is itself based on biographical
data. However, our primary interest in this chapter is the explanation of
normative development, and it is to this that we now return.

2.3 Does artistic development proceed in stages?

This is a very difficult question for the developmental psychologist, and
one that has still not been satisfactorily resolved. Does development
proceed by means of the gradual accumulation of organized skills and

knowledge in a smooth, continuous fashion with age, or is it *discontinuous*, proceeding in a series of qualitatively different steps that are not necessarily accumulative? By far the best known exponent of the latter view was Jean Piaget, who put forward a very well known developmental stage model that needs no repetition here; some of the implications of his theory for musical development are discussed by Imberty in Chapter 8. The theory has had an immense impact on the way in which psychologists think about development as well as upon educational practice, especially in the design of curricula in mathematics and science.

However, it is probably fair to say that most developmental psychologists do not now believe that stages exist in the way that Piaget originally described them. There are two main reasons for this. The first concerns the functional coherence of the stages: Piaget saw them as integrated sets of activities characterized by precisely defined logical rules ('groups' and 'groupings'), which implies that the child's task performance within a given stage should exhibit certain common features regardless of the domain of that task. This claim now appears to have little support from the empirical research literature (see, for example, Beilin 1987), which suggests that activities within stages exhibit much greater diversity than Piaget proposed. The second reason is that the theory does not account adequately for cultural and environmental diversity in cognitive development. Whereas Piaget saw children's social environment as forming the raw material ('resistance') for assimilation and accommodation, such that cognitive development proceeded in a similar manner irrespective of the nature of this material, the predominant current view is that the environment also *shapes* the course of thinking rather than merely reflecting it.

Our main interest here is in whether developmental stages may or may not exist in artistic and musical development. There are two opposing viewpoints. One is represented by the theory of Parsons (1987), which is an explicitly Piagetian-style developmental stage theory that is based on research evidence from the visual arts. Parsons proposes that all children go through five stages of increasing cognitive sophistication, from 'favouritism', in which children simply take pleasure in art works with little cognitive discrimination, to 'autonomy', in which the artist is able to adopt a mature, reflective attitude towards the cultural value of particular works.

A contrasting theoretical view is that of Howard Gardner, who has elaborated what has been called a 'symbol system' theory of artistic development with his colleagues at Harvard Project Zero in numerous publications over the last 20 years or more (see, for example, Gardner and Perkins 1988). In brief, Gardner feels that there is no need to propose developmental stages for the arts because cognitive operations of the type described by Piaget are not critically important for many of the activities that artists carry out; in fact, he goes so far as to claim that 'the groupings, groups and operations described by Piaget do not seem essential for mastery or understanding of human language, music, or plastic arts' (Gardner 1973*a*, p. 45).

This theoretical debate has some important practical implications for the curriculum. If children do indeed pass through a sequence of stages, each one serving as a preparation for the next, then there is little point in attempting to introduce them to skills and concepts that exist at a higher level than that with which their artistic maturity can cope; but the implication of Gardner's view is that such considerations are for the most part irrelevant, since most children have achieved all of the essential characteristics necessary for 'participation in the artistic process' by the age of 7 years. In practice, educational objectives such as the 'statements of attainment' for the arts in the British national curriculum do implicitly adopt some form of age-based sequence, even though this is very unlikely to be built on a psychological stage model of the abilities underlying them. This problem of the extent to which we can distinguish between the cognitive abilities that underlie age-related changes in children's artistic behaviour, and their manifestation in the context of actual artistic activities leads to the next, related issue.

2.4 Musical competence and artistic development

The Piagetian-style stage theory of Parsons carries with it the implication that the stages apply across all art forms, that is, that certain changes in artistic thinking occur as a result of increasing age that in turn determine what happens in the visual arts, in music, in drama, in dance, and so on. Gardner's 'symbol system' view, on the other hand, which has been developed in his theory of multiple intelligences (Gardner 1983), proposes that developments that occur within particular artistic domains have no implications for those in any other since they demand completely different skills and techniques, which are applied to specific sets of knowledge and materials. In other words, we need to determine whether artistic developments are or are not *domain-specific*. This question is vitally important for the rationale of this chapter, since there is little point in setting musical development in the context of artistic development as a whole if the different domains are indeed independent of one another.

My own view is that these positions can be reconciled—that although medium-specific aspects of musical development clearly do exist, most notably at very high levels of skill and expertise, it is nevertheless possible to delineate general features of the course of artistic development that do exist across domains and that do display regular changes with age. This has been done by specifying aspects of thinking that underlie developments in each art form by identifying the cognitive rules and strategies which are present in artistic and musical development. One important concept in this approach, which has a long history within philosophy as well as psychology, is that of the cognitive *scheme*, or *schema*.

Cognitive schemes (schemata) comprise the mental 'models' or frameworks that we use to organize knowledge. Piaget proposed that we use them to take in or *assimilate* new knowledge, and that they are modified by the process of *accommodation* as a result of that assimilation. They are essentially co-ordinated sets of actions that can be observed in different forms of behaviour at different ages. They can be identified in many aspects of musical development, such as the regular patterns of physical movement in infants' rhythmic dancing, in the characteristic ways in which preschoolers' singing develops by the gradual incorporation of elements of the songs they hear around them, and in the ways in which people of all ages and abilities, including children, go about the business of musical composition and improvisation. Cognitive schemes are one way of describing the thinking processes that underlie different aspects of musical behaviour—perception, performance, literacy, and production—and they enable explanatory links to be made between these different aspects.

This theoretical question about functional linkages between the processes underlying the different systems in the arts has very clear practical implications. A debate has continued for some time in arts education about the extent to which arts subjects should be taught as an integrated whole, such that work in music and painting, for example, might be combined in project-based work with themes in drama or video. In opposition to this are those who believe that specialized skills should be developed in each of the disciplines and that fostering general aesthetic understanding should take precedence over the formation of inter-disciplinary links. Although domain-specific skills quite clearly need to be taught as such, it does seem not too unreasonable to suggest that these might also profitably be combined within particular educational activities, and this parallels the conclusion drawn above, namely, that medium-specific aspects of musical development can be identified within the context of general features of the course of artistic development which do exist across domains, and which do display regular changes with age.

3 THE COURSE OF ARTISTIC AND MUSICAL DEVELOPMENT

The descriptive model of artistic development proposed by Hargreaves and Galton (1992) originally arose from *Children and the arts* (Hargreaves

1989), in which acknowledged experts in each of the main art forms were asked to write an account of children's development in their areas primarily from the psychological point of view, but with a clear eye upon the educational implications. It soon became apparent that there were indeed common developmental progressions across the different domains, and our model was intended as a descriptive account of those progressions rather than as an explanatory theory. Each chapter in the 1989 book reviews and summarizes a wide range of empirical research in each domain, and more detailed reference is made to specific studies in our 1992 statement. The model can accordingly be regarded as drawing on an extensive research literature rather than as generalizing from a small number of studies.

In formulating it we were immediately faced with an important terminological problem: to use the term *stage* to describe these progressions, *à la* Piaget, would have raised many of the difficult issues that were discussed in Section 2.3. It would have implied that the stages did possess some degree of functional coherence, and we would have found it necessary to deal with the problem that Piaget's theory primarily emphasizes the drive towards logical-scientific thinking, which may well be quite inappropriate in the arts. Our ambitions were much more modest, and so we opted to describe the age-related changes as *phases* rather than *stages*. Having said this, because of the research on which it is based, the model clearly is based on the cognitive mechanisms that underlie each phase, and so there are obvious affinities with Piagetian-style stage theories.

In the original model we described five age-related phases, namely the *presymbolic, figural, schematic, rule systems,* and *metacognitive* phases, based upon research on drawing, writing, aesthetic perception ('cognitive aesthetic development'), and four areas of musical development, namely, singing, musical representation, melodic perception, and composition. The model has been presented in various conference papers and seminar discussions since then, and two important changes have been made as a result: the first and last phases have been renamed *sensorimotor* and *professional*, respectively. In this chapter I will concentrate on research on the four areas of musical development mentioned above, namely, singing, musical representation, melodic perception, and composition, and draw on research in other domains for illustrative and comparative purposes only. Table 6.1 shows the revised version of the model for these four areas alone, which is not, of course, to imply that developments in the other domains are any less important.

3.1 The sensorimotor phase

I have reverted to Piaget's original term for the developments that occur in the first 2 years of life since it provides a more direct description than

Table 6.1 Five phases of musical development (adapted from Hargreaves and Galton 1992)

Phase	Age (years)	Singing	Graphic representation	Melodic perception	Composition
Professional	15+				Enactive and reflective strategies
Rule systems	8–15	Intervals, scales	Formal-metric	Analytic recognition of intervals, key stability	'Idiomatic' conventions
Schematic	5–8	'First draft' songs	Figural-metric: more than one dimension	Conservation of melodic properties	'Vernacular' conventions
Figural	2–5	'Outline' songs; coalescences between spontaneous and cultural songs	Figural: single dimension	Global features: pitch, contour	Assimilation of cultural music
Sensorimotor	0–2	Babbling, rhythmic dancing	Scribbling; 'action equivalents'	Recognition of melodic contours	Sensory, manipulative

the earlier term 'presymbolic', which in a sense defines the stage in terms of what is absent rather than what is present. A second, pragmatic reason is simply that many people are familiar with Piaget's term. As it suggests, most of the major developments in the first 2 years of life involve the practice and development of physical skills and co-ordinations, and these are largely 'presymbolic' in the sense that abstract symbolism—the capacity to mentally conceive of or represent an object in its physical absence—is not yet present. In this section we shall need to consider how the forms of musical representation that occur later in childhood are rooted in early sensorimotor developments. Parents also play a vital part in mediating this important developmental transition, and in Chapter 7 M. Papoušek has provided a valuable account of the ways in which they do so.

One obvious illustration of this in the artistic domain is the scribbling movements that infants make on paper: these are not only seen in attempted drawings as such, but also in their 'story-writing', which has been described essentially as scribbling with verbal commentary, as well as in their attempts to represent musical stimuli (for example, clapped or tapped rhythmic patterns) by graphic means. In this latter area of research on 'musical representation', Goodnow (1971) and others have found that infants commonly produce 'action equivalents': their actions with the pencil on the paper do indeed match the timing of the pattern of sounds, but what emerges on the paper bears little resemblance to it. In Chapter 5 Pouthas discusses the function of 'motor rhythms' of this kind in the temporal regulation of infants' behaviour.

Sensorimotor activity is also clearly predominant in infants' musical 'composition', if we might use that term somewhat simplistically to refer to their activities with musical instruments. Swanwick and Tillman (1986) have suggested that these activities at this early age are largely concerned with mastering the means of producing sounds and with gaining physical control of them, which involves a good deal of intrinsic pleasure and enjoyment. They carried out a study of 745 compositions by 48 British schoolchildren between the ages of 3 and 9 years which ranged from making up simple patterns on maracas, chime bars, and other percussion instruments, through to instrumental improvisations based on short verbal phrases and sentences.

On the basis of their data Swanwick and Tillman proposed a 'spiral' model of musical development. This model has been described and evaluated in depth elsewhere (for example, Hargreaves and Zimmerman 1992); it complements our own model, focusing specifically upon musical composition rather than upon artistic production and perception more generally. In the sensorimotor phase, they suggest that there is a shift from *sensory* to *manipulative* musical behaviour—from explorations of the means of producing sounds towards an increasing control of the techniques of doing so. Infants' early fascination with variation of dynamic levels, as shown in 'strumming' on different instruments, gradually gives way to a more organized exploration of pitch, rhythm, and timbre.

The link with physical action is also apparent in infants' singing, and in their responses to music. Infants in their first year of life engage in a good deal of vocal play and babbling, and we shall see how this forms the basis for recognizable musical singing in the next section. Moog's (1976) extensive observations of some 500 or so preschool children also reveal some general trends in the physical response to music. Babies were found to sway and bounce rhythmically in response to music up to the age of 6 months or so, and the co-ordination between these movements and the timing of the music was found to gradually increase with age.

Research on children's perception of and memory for music has also been investigated experimentally, using some ingenious techniques such as the measurement of changes in heart rate and head turning as measures of discrimination (see the review by Fassbender in Chapter 3). In one study, Chang and Trehub (1977) played six-note atonal melodies to 5-month-olds, followed by versions of the melodies in which they were either altered by key transposition or by changes in melodic contour. Attentional reactions (measured by heart-rate deceleration) occurred when the babies heard the changed contours, but not when they heard the pitch transpositions, so it appeared that they did in some way recognize the shapes of melodies.

Subsequently, Sandra Trehub and her group (for example, Trehub *et al.* 1984) have experimented with further kinds of melodic transformation, including altering intervals with the contour preserved, octave transpositions of certain pitches, and changes in both contour and octaves. Trehub (1987) has reviewed this research, the results of which can be summarized under five main findings. First, contour is a critical feature of early musical perception; infants seem to use a 'global' processing strategy in which the broad shapes of melodies are extracted from their local details. Second and third, this contour information seems to be extracted from melodies regardless of variations in intervals and exact pitches, respectively; these do not yet appear to be critical in defining melodies. Fourth, however, interval changes can be detected in transposed sequences under certain conditions: and when this does occur, performance is best in sequences that conform to Western diatonic structure. Fifth, as with melodic memory, infants also seem to be able to recognize basic similarities between rhythmic sequences, and to do so irrespective of changes in the tempo of those sequences.

Babies seem to be able to detect the underlying structure of some simple melodies at a much earlier age than might have previously been thought possible. Their ability to do so is apparently superior with Western diatonic sequences than, for example, with atonal ones, and it can be significantly improved by training (Morrongiello 1992). The idea of 'global processing strategies' in musical perception as well as in generative artistic activity forms the essence of the figural phase in our developmental model, and it appears here to be present, in some form at least, much earlier than at preschool age.

3.2 The figural phase

The profound developmental change that occurs at the age of 18 months or so is that children acquire the capacity to *symbolize*—to conceive of objects, people, or situations that are not physically present. Piaget (1951) proposed a detailed account of what he called the symbolic or semiotic function, and elaborated upon the different areas of behaviour in which it is manifested. One of these is graphic representation, which is of direct relevance here: one central characteristic of preschool drawings is that they are *figural*; they depict the overall shapes or outlines of the subjects of the drawings, but the details within them are not yet accurate. A good example of this is the familiar 'tadpole figure', in which children appear to attach limbs to the head of the drawn person and omit the trunk. Children typically produce these up to the age of 3 or so, and there have been numerous explanations of the effect. One of the most longstanding is that drawings display 'intellectual realism'— that young children 'draw what they know, and not what they see'. This raises some complex issues, however, and explanations based on the cognitive and graphic strategies employed by children are now preferred (see for example, Cox 1992).

The main theoretical and empirical contributions to the study of children's graphic representations of music have been made by Bamberger (1982, 1991, 1994). At the heart of her work is the distinction between what she calls 'figural' and 'metric' drawings. In several of her earlier studies children of various ages, as well as adults, were asked to write down the clapped rhythm of the second and third lines of the nursery rhyme 'One, two, buckle my shoe' so that someone else could play it, or so that they could remember it themselves later. A *figural* drawing was described as one that conveyed the overall two-part shape or 'figure' of the sequence, which was seen as demonstrating an appreciation of musical expressiveness, and a *metric* drawing as one that accurately conveyed the number of claps, but that did not convey its musical sense to the same degree.

Children were found to use a number of ways to carry out this task, including the variation of the size, shape, and placing of the units they used to represent the taps on the page. They also invented their own

160   *David Hargreaves*

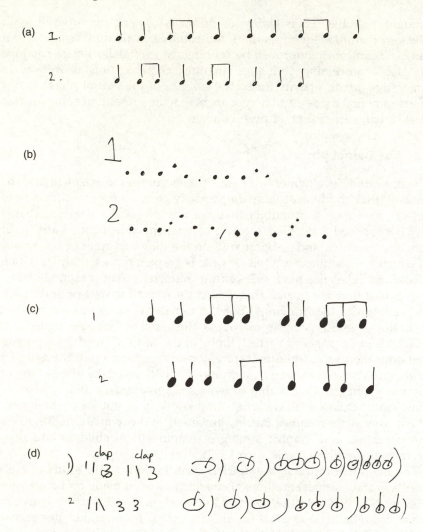

Fig. 6.2 (a) Notation of two rhythmic sequences. (b)–(d) Drawings of these
sequences by three 10–11-year-olds.

ingenious notations, including pictures, words or symbols: sketches of
pairs of hands actually doing the clapping, for example, were quite often
observed. Figure 6.2(a) shows the conventional notation of two short
rhythmic sequences (the first of which is Bamberger's 'class piece'), and
Fig 6.2(b)–(d) shows drawings of these by three 10–11-year-olds. These
have been deliberately chosen to illustrate the wide variety of types of
response, which raises the important point that artistic development not
only involves the gradual adoption of adult conventions, but also the
creative invention of new ones.

Bamberger has gone on to develop these ideas in much more detail, but the figural—metric distinction remains central to her thinking. In *The mind behind the musical ear* (Bamberger 1991), she adopts a novel form of discourse between herself, the children being tested, and two imaginary graduate students called Mot and Met, whose dialogue is designed to represent the figural (motivic) and metric forms of musical understanding respectively. Bamberger (1994) is anxious to point out that these understandings might represent different 'hearings' of a piece that are by no means mutually exclusive; it is quite possible for one individual to demonstrate both kinds of 'hearing' at different times, just as it is possible for performers to refer to different 'hearings' of a given work. The implication of our model is that 2–5-year-olds are more likely to make 'figural' than metrically accurate representations simply because of their level of development, and that these may well incorporate some metrical inaccuracy. The latter should decrease with age, and the educational implication seems to be that teachers should aim to convey both kinds of understanding music learning.

A good deal of research has been carried out on the development of singing in the preschooler, including the early descriptive studies of Moorhead and Pond (1978) and Moog (1976), and the more recent cognitively oriented developmental descriptions of Dowling (1984, 1988), Davidson (1994), and Davies (1992). The vocal babbles of the sensori-motor phase develop into articulate and recognizable songs in the figural phase, and these have been described as fitting into what might be called outlines, or 'song frames'. One of the central characteristics of these is that children's spontaneous vocalizations gradually come to incorporate aspects of the songs in the world around them, so that mixtures between the two emerge. Moog (1976) called these 'pot-pourri' songs, and an example appears in Fig. 6.3. This short song by a 3-year-old has three notable features. It is clearly based on the nursery rhyme 'Old Macdonald had a farm'; it has its own original words and melodic variations; and it combines two distinct key signatures—the first half is in G, but the second half drops down a tone into the key of F. This latter feature shows that, whilst tonality may be established within individual phrases at this age, it is still not fully stabilized across the whole song.

Davidson (1994) has developed an extensive database of the songs of some 69 children in cross-sectional studies, as well as the more detailed investigation of the nine children in his earlier longitudinal studies. On

I   wan da on – ly   poo poo poo   pee   pee   hee!

Fig. 6.3 Spontaneous song by a 36-month-old.

the basis of these results he has put forward a developmental view of children's ability to reproduce songs of the culture within the figural phase, and he uses the nursery rhyme 'Twinkle twinkle little star' as an example. His view is that the typical 3-year-old relies on the words of the song and that she can produce distinct pitches, but that these have no interval stability or tonal coherence; the song in Fig. 6.3 is a good example of this. By the age of 4 years, Davidson suggests that the child still relies on the text of the song, and that, whilst the reproduction of its melodic contour is improving in accuracy, it still does not yet possess overall coherence. Towards the end of this phase, by the age of 5 years or so, individual contours and intervals are reproduced accurately, but it is not until the schematic and rule systems phases that the parts of a song are organized into coherent wholes.

To summarize, Davidson's (1994) analysis shows us that the accurate reproduction of cultural songs requires a number of different abilities. These include the accurate singing of pitches with respect to the underlying tonality, the ability not only to reproduce the surface aspects of rhythm, but also to be able to relate these to the underlying rhythmic pulse, and the mastery of song forms, which include repetition, variation, and development. Although a significant minority of preschoolers can exhibit some of these abilities, they typically only begin to be established during the figural phase. Their subsequent development characterizes the next phase, leading to their description in Table 6.1 (following Davidson) as 'first draft' songs.

3.3   The schematic phase

Children's command of the conventions that are used by adult artists and musicians has increased considerably by the age of 5 years or so, and they may well also have invented some of their own conventions. This leads to the production of what might be called 'schematic' art works in which adult conventions are present, but not yet fully developed. One good example of this is the 'air gap' drawing that is typically produced up to the age of 10 years or so: children's landscape drawings often include a 'ground line' along the bottom of the page and a 'sky line' along the top in order to give some overall spatial organization, but the resulting 'gap' which persistently remains, and which children typically identify as 'air', means that the drawing is still not visually realistic (see Hargreaves *et al.* 1981). Artistic conventions are beginning to develop, but these are still not yet integrated into a coherent sense of style. In their musical compositions, correspondingly, Swanwick and Tillman (1986) suggest that children develop 'vernacular conventions', such as the use of simple melodic and rhythmic ostinati, in striving towards a coherent idiom.

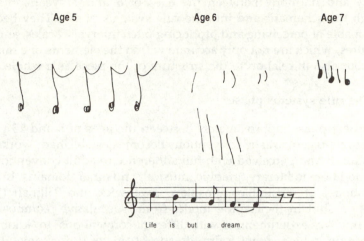

Age 5   Age 6   Age 7

Life   is   but   a   dream.

Fig. 6.4 Children's notations of the final phrase of 'Row, row, row your boat' at different ages (from Davidson and Scripp 1988).

In discussing musical representation, Davidson and Scripp (1988) have suggested that some consistent developmental changes can be observed in the transition between the figural and schematic phases, and these are illustrated by their examples of children's notations of the final phrase of 'Row, row, row your boat' at different ages (see Fig. 6.4). Five-year-olds typically record just a single dimension of the pattern in their drawings, usually the rhythm; whilst the number of notes or taps may be accurate, the melodic and temporal relationships between them are likely not to be. By the age of 6 or so some children will be able to represent more than one musical dimension at a time: in Fig. 6.4, for example, the drawing shows an understanding that the notes have different durations and that these form part of a common overall pulse. By the age of 7 years or so children not only can do this but can also include the shape and contour of the melodic phrase where one is present; they show what Davidson and Scripp call 'relations of systems'.

The same broad pattern emerges from research on children's perceptions of pitch, intervals, and tonality. In a study by Trehub (1985), for example, 4- to 6-year-olds correctly identified versions of 'Happy birthday to you' and 'Twinkle twinkle little star' in which pitch intervals and melodic contours had been changed as 'funny' rather than 'normal'. This is in line with the results of research on the acquisition of tonality and harmony (see, for example, Imberty 1969), which has investigated phenomena such as children's preference for consonant chords and intervals over dissonant ones, and their ability to recognize musically appropriate modulations and key changes. This evidence suggests that there is a gradual improvement in children's sensitivity to Western tonality and harmony between the ages of 5 and 11 years, that is, through the schematic and into the rule systems phase. They become fully capable of perceiving and producing pitch intervals, scales, and key signatures, which are not only accurate within the elements of a musical piece, but also in relation to the structure of the piece as a whole.

3.4 The rule systems phase

In this next phase, approximately between the ages of 8 and 15 years, the accurate use of artistic conventions becomes established: works can be produced and perceived with full adherence to adult conventions of style and idiom in literary, graphic, musical, and other domains. In their spiral model of musical composition, Swanwick and Tillman (1986) propose a shift in their spiral model from 'speculative' composition, which involves experimenting with different conventions, to 'idiomatic' composition, which shows a firm grasp of some of those conventions, during this phase. Swanwick and Tillman suggest that 'first attempts at musical speculation sometimes appear to be a kind of regression to earlier stages of manipulative insecurity' (p. 324); at first sight, 'speculative' explorations may appear less fluent than the by now well established 'vernacular' conventions of the schematic phase. However, they eventually become integrated into fully fledged styles and idioms.

The acquisition of adult conventions and styles is perhaps most clearly and explicitly shown in studies of the development of aesthetic appreciation in the arts. In the earlier description of our developmental model, the term 'cognitive aesthetic appreciation' was used to refer to the body of work that has investigated age-related changes in artistic perception in a number of domains, but primarily in the visual arts (for example, Winner *et al.* 1986). Parsons' (1987) theory of the development of aesthetic appreciation, for example, is specifically based on visual art. Parsons and others agree that, up to the age of 5 years or so, children tend to focus on the concrete properties of art works and the means of producing them; they are equally likely to be as concerned about who is allowed to play a musical instrument, for example, as about what is being played on it. Works in the visual arts are judged primarily in terms of their relevance to children's own lives, such as whether the objects portrayed are familiar to and liked by them. These might be described, in the figural phase, as 'egocentric' reactions to art.

In the schematic phase, visual art works are primarily judged in terms of their subject matter and the degree of realism with which they represent the world; pictures or drawings are considered to be successful if they accurately represent what they are supposed to, and this is much more important than any stylistic considerations. The small body of research on the development of style sensitivity in music has produced much less clear-cut findings with respect to the effects of age. Gardner (1973b) found 11-year-olds to be more sensitive to similarities and differences between extracts of classical music drawn from different styles than 14- and 18-year-olds, for example, and a partial replication of this study by Castell (1982), using popular styles, found that 8–9-year-olds appeared to be more stylistically sensitive than 11-year-olds. It seems likely that the cultural salience of the specific styles that are played to particular age/subject groups in these investigations can give rise to counterintuitive or conflicting results, and this is a promising area for further research.

Furthermore, music may well give rise to greater polarization of liking for different styles than does visual art, and such affective factors may exert a strong influence upon cognitive aesthetic judgements. LeBlanc's (1991) review of the literature on the development of musical style preferences leads him to suggest that, up to the age of 8 years or so, children might be described as 'open-eared' in the sense of being prepared to listen to and enjoy a wide variety of musical styles. As they approach adolescence there is a sudden and marked decline in the number of preferred styles, and a general concentration on different styles within pop music. As they approach early adulthood, LeBlanc suggests that there is what he calls a 'rebound' of open-earedness in that the range of preferences widens once again, and, still further ahead, in old age, this narrows once more.

3.5 The professional phase

Having mastered the conventions of particular art forms, some individuals are able to transcend them, producing works that display independence from conventional styles, and the capacity of self-reflection in relation to them. This advanced position, which is probably only achieved at the level of the professional artist, acknowledges that there are no absolute standards in art—that there is a sense in which rules exist in order to be broken.

The highest level of Swanwick and Tillman's (1986) 'spiral' model of musical development is what they call the 'metacognitive' mode. This term refers to 'thinking about thinking', that is, the capacity to reflect upon one's own thought processes. This may never be achieved by many, but, amongst those who do, two levels are identified. At the *symbolic* level, there is strong emphasis on the expressive and emotional power of particular pieces, composers, or performers, as well as the ability to reflect upon these experiences and convey them to others. At the *systematic* level this ability is present at an even higher level of abstraction and generality; self-reflection is guided by universal under- standings about music as these might be expressed in terms of musico- logical, psychological, or historical analysis, rather than through personal experience alone.

Many of the great composers, such as Stravinsky or Debussy, or the great innovators in jazz, such as Charlie Parker or John Coltrane, achieved their greatness by breaking the rules of the time rather than by following them, and created new styles or genres as a result. However, each of these figures had achieved mastery of the existing conventions before going beyond them, and this is an important part of real-life creativity. Of course, these great names represent only a tiny proportion of the population of musicians; many professional artists, composers, and improvisers have the capacity to work in a variety of styles, even if the effects of their innovations upon their peers are not as profound as those of acknowledged innovators. This is why I have replaced the term 'metacognitive' in the 1992 version of the model with 'professional'; even though it may be possible for an individual to reach this phase without being a full-time professional, the label is more useful because it refers to the stylistic flexibility of a much larger group of individuals.

Although musical composition is a very difficult area for empirical study, a small but growing body of research is enabling us to gain some insight into the development of musical competence at this high, expert level (see Sloboda 1988). In a comparative study of novice and expert jazz improvisers, for example, Hargreaves *et al.* (1991) demonstrated some clear differences in the approach to improvising a right-hand piano solo over a pre-recorded 'backing track'. The novices' improvisa- tions were firmly rooted in the physical and technical problems involved in playing the keyboard; in this sense, they resembled the sensorimotor strivings of infants that we described in the earliest phase, showing little evidence of any overall, abstracted plan of improvisation. The experts, on the other hand, clearly did approach the task with predetermined plans: but these plans were provisional in the sense that the experts had the ability to change direction as the improvisation proceeded. This flexibility in adapting a high-order skill to the demands of the situation is a commonly observed aspect of expert performance in many areas of skilled performance.

A very similar finding emerged from Davidson and Welsh's (1988) study, in which beginning and experienced students in a music con- servatory were asked to carry out a short composition exercise on the piano. Here again, they found that the beginners tended to work 'enactively' at the keyboard, whereas the advanced students tended to conceive larger-scale musical units internally before actually trying them out at the keyboard; this ability to work at a higher-order, *reflective* level is an important feature of the professional phase.

4 CONCLUSION

In the early part of this chapter I reiterated the often heard plea for a meeting between theory and practice, and set out some ideas that seemed to have some potential utility in this respect. Although it almost goes without saying that the study of human development needs to take account of the cultural, interpersonal, and educational context within which it occurs, psychological research has only recently and belatedly begun to reflect this fact. The other side of the coin is that teachers have a clear need for some kind of theoretical framework for their work, preferably based on empirical evidence, which psychologists and other social scentists ought to be able to provide. The need for such a framework is more clearly apparent in the arts than in many other areas of the curriculum (see, for example, Hargreaves 1989). The model outlined in the second part of this chapter is no more than a very large-scale and approximate map of the normative development of musical competence, but should at least provide some broad landmarks for evaluating the competences of individual children.

The distinction between generalist and specialist music education leads to certain tensions within the teaching profession. Music is perhaps unique in that it can be appreciated and enjoyed by all so that 'general' class teaching can be universally beneficial; at the same time, it demands highly specialized skills, training, and dedication for successful participation on the specialist level. This distinction between different pedagogies in music education is clearly linked with that between normative and expert explanations of musical development. When we consider the usefulness of these two types of explanation for teachers in the respective pedagogical traditions, however, we are forced to conclude that there remains a long way to go.

Teachers undoubtedly possess what might be called 'working theories' of pupils' musical development within both generalist and specialist teaching, but these are likely to be implicitly rather than explicitly formulated. We need research that renders these theories more explicit and that links them more clearly with the more abstract models available in psychological and educational research. We also need to develop and refine these theoretical models, since the research literature upon which they are based is clearly sparse and sketchy. This means co-operation on both sides: collaborative work between enquiring, research-minded practitioners and researchers who are willing to incorporate the insights of those practitioners into their thinking is probably our most important task.

ACKNOWLEDGEMENTS

I am indebted to Johannella Tafuri for her help in explaining the background to Stefani's theories, to Bengt Olsson for introducing me to the work of Andrén and for valuable discussions of the model of teaching methods proposed in this chapter, and also to three anonymous reviewers whose critical comments have greatly improved the chapter.

REFERENCES

Andrén, M. (1988). Studentideologier efter 1988 (Students' ideologies after 1988). In *Ideologi och institution. Om forskning och hoegre utbildning 1880–2000* (Ideology and institution. Research and higher education 1880–2000) (ed. S. E. Liedman and L. Olausson), pp. 197–217. Carlssons Bokfoerlag, Helsingborg.

Bamberger, J. (1982). Revisiting children's drawings of simple rhythms: a function for reflection-in-action. In *U-shaped behavioural growth* (ed. S. Strauss and R. Stavy), pp. 191–226. Academic Press, New York.

Bamberger, J. (1991). *The mind behind the musical ear: how children develop musical intelligence.* Harvard University Press, Cambridge, Mass.

Bamberger, J. (1994). Coming to hear in a new way. In *Musical perceptions* (ed. R. Aiello and J. A. Sloboda), pp. 131–51. Oxford University Press, New York.

Beilin, H. (1987). Current trends in cognitive development research: towards a new synthesis. In *Piaget today* (ed. B. Inhelder, B. Caprona, and A. Cornu-Wells), pp. 37–64. Lawrence Erlbaum, Hove.

Castell, K. C. (1982). Children's sensitivity to stylistic differences in 'classical' and 'popular' music. *Psychology of Music, Special Issue,* 22–5.

Chang, H. and Trehub, S. E. (1977). Auditory processing of relational information by young infants. *Journal of Experimental Child Psychology,* **24**, 324–33.

Cox, M. (1992). *Children's drawings.* Penguin, Harmondsworth.

Davidson, L. (1994). Songsinging by young and old: a developmental approach to music. In *Musical perceptions* (ed. R. Aiello and J. A. Sloboda), pp. 99–130. Oxford University Press, New York.

Davidson, L. and Scripp, L. (1988). Young children's musical representations: windows on music cognition. In *Generative processes in music: the psychology of performance, improvisation, and composition* (ed. J. A. Sloboda), pp. 195–230. Clarendon Press, Oxford.

Davidson, L. and Welsh, P. (1988). From collections to structure: the developmental path of tonal thinking. In *Generative processes in music: the psychology of performance, improvisation, and composition* (ed. J. A. Sloboda), pp. 260–85. Clarendon Press, Oxford.

Davies, C. (1992). Listen to my song: a study of songs invented by children aged 5 to 7 years. *British Journal of Music Education,* **9**, 19–48.

Dowling, W. J. (1984). Development of musical schemata in children's spontaneous singing. In *Cognitive processes in the perception of art* (ed. W. R. Crozier and A. J. Chapman), pp. 145–63. Elsevier, Amsterdam.

Dowling, W. J. (1988). Tonal structure and children's early learning of music. In *Generative processes in music: the psychology of performance, improvisation, and composition* (ed. J. A. Sloboda), pp. 113–28. Clarendon Press, Oxford.

Ericsson, K. A. and Smith, J. (ed.) (1991). *Toward a general theory of expertise: prospects and limits*. Cambridge University Press, New York.

Ericsson, A., Krampe, R. T., and Tesch-Romer, C. (1993). The role of deliberate practice in the acquisition of expert performance. *Psychological Review*, **100**, 363–406.

Gardner, H. (1973*a*). *The arts and human development*. John Wiley, New York.

Gardner, H. (1973*b*). Children's sensitivity to musical styles. *Merrill-Palmer Quarterly*, **19**, 67–77.

Gardner, H. (1983). *Frames of mind: the theory of multiple intelligences*. Paladin, London.

Gardner, H. and Perkins, D. (ed.) (1988). *Art, mind, and education: research from Project Zero*. University of Illinois Press, Urbana.

Goodnow, J. (1971). Auditory-visual matching: modality problem or translation problem? *Child Development*, **42**, 1187–210.

Hargreaves, D. J. (1986). Developmental psychology and music education. *Psychology of Music*, **14**, 83–96.

Hargreaves, D. J. (ed.) (1989). *Children and the arts*. Open University Press, Milton Keynes.

Hargreaves, D. J. and Galton, M. (1992). Aesthetic learning: psychological theory and educational practice. In *National Society for the Study of Education yearbook on the arts in education* (ed. B. Reimer and R. A. Smith), pp. 124–50. N.S.S.E., Chicago.

Hargreaves, D. J. and Zimmerman, M. (1992). Developmental theories of music learning. In *Handbook for research in music teaching and learning* (ed. R. Colwell), pp. 377–91. Macmillan, New York.

Hargreaves, D. J., Jones, P. M., and Martin, D. (1981). The air gap phenomenon in children's landscape drawings. *Journal of Experimental Child Psychology*, **32**, 11–20.

Hargreaves, D. J., Cork, C., and Setton, T. (1991). Cognitive strategies in jazz improvisation: an exploratory study. *Canadian Music Educators Journal*, **33**, 47–54.

Imberty, M. (1969). *L'acquisition des structures tonales chez l'enfant*. Klincksieck, Paris.

LeBlanc, A. (1991). Effect of maturation/aging on music listening preference: a review of the literature. Paper presented at 9th National Symposium on Research in Musical Behavior, Cannon Beach, Oregon, USA.

Light, P. H., Sheldon, S., and Woodhead, M. (ed.) (1991). *Learning to think*. Routledge, London.

Manturszewska, M. (1990). A biographical study of the life-span development of professional musicians. *Psychology of Music*, **18**, 112–39.

Mills, J. (1993). *Music in the primary school* (2nd edn). Cambridge University Press, Cambridge.

Moog, H. (1976). *The musical experience of the pre-school child* (trans. C. Clarke). Schott, London.

Moorhead, G. E. and Pond, D. (1978). *Music of young children*. Pillsbury Foundation, Santa Barbara, California.

Morrongiello, B. (1992). Effects of training on children's perception of music: a review. *Psychology of Music*, **20**, 29–41.

Olsson, B. (1993). *SÅMUS—Musikutbildning i kulturpolitikens tjänst?* Skrifter från musikvetenskapliga avdelningen, Musikhögskolan i Göteborg, Nr. 33, Göteborg, Sweden.

Orff, C. and Keetman, G. (1958). *Orff-Schulwerk music for children* (trans. M. Murray). Schott, London.

Parsons, M. J. (1987). *How we understand art*. Cambridge University Press, Cambridge.

Paynter, J. (1992). *Sound and structure*. Cambridge University Press, Cambridge.

Piaget, J. (1951). *Play, dreams and imitation in childhood*. Routledge and Kegan Paul, London.

Schafer, Murray R. (1965). *The composer in the classroom*. BMI, Toronto.

Sloboda, J. A. (ed.) (1988). *Generative processes in music: the psychology of performance, improvisation, and composition*. Clarendon Press, Oxford.

Sloboda, J. A. (1994). Music performance: expression and the development of excellence. In *Musical perceptions* (ed. R. Aiello and J. A. Sloboda), pp. 152–69. Oxford University Press, New York.

Sloboda, J. A., Davidson, J., and Howe, M. J. A. (1994). Is everyone musical? *The Psychologist*, **7**, 349–54.

Stefani, G. (1987). A theory of musical competence. *Semiotica*, **66**, 7–22.

Swanwick, K. and Tillman, J. (1986). The sequence of musical development: a study of children's composition. *British Journal of Music Education*, **3**, 305–39.

Trehub, S. (1987). Infants' perception of musical patterns. *Perception and Psychophysics*, **41**, 635–41.

Trehub, S., Bull, D., and Thorpe, L. A. (1984). Infants' perception of melodies: the role of melodic contour. *Child Development*, **55**, 821–30.

Trehub, S. E., Morrongiello, B. A., and Thorpe, L. A. (1985). Children's perception of familiar melodies: the role of intervals, contour and key. *Psychomusicology*, **5**, 39–48.

Winner, E., Rosenblatt, E., Windmueller, G., Davidson, L., and Gardner, H. (1986). Children's perception of 'aesthetic' properties of the arts: domain-specific or pan-artistic? *British Journal of Developmental Psychology*, **4**, 149–60.

7

The young performing musician

John Sloboda and Jane Davidson

1 INTRODUCTION

Individual development may be studied from a number of different perspectives. We find it helpful to distinguish three dimensions along which developmental studies may be ranged. The first dimension relates to the selection of the sample to be studied, the second is concerned with the selection of questions to be asked, and the third explores the type of observations to be made. A comment on each dimension will help to situate this chapter in the context of other approaches to musical development.

Research samples can be selected from different ranges of the total population. Much developmental research attempts to chart the typical capacities and changes that are to be observed at various ages. While this approach is undoubtedly useful in a variety of ways, it can tend towards conservatism in the examination of the capacity of individuals. Examination of the poles of a population distribution provides important information concerning the range of human potential. The focus in individual difference research, however, is generally on individuals at the lower end of the distribution, that is, those with lower levels of skill. Our approach, therefore, is expertise-oriented, in that it focuses on a statistically rare, but culturally desired, top end of the population distribution, the virtuoso performer. It asks not so much what is usual or average, but rather, what is possible. Our desired endpoint can be illustrated by three different individuals who all achieved virtuosity by around 20 years of age. Krystian Zimmerman is a classical pianist who, at the age of 19, won the International Fryderyk Chopin Piano Competition by playing with extreme technical and expressive brilliance (Polony 1991). Louis Armstrong was a jazz trumpeter who, from a background of extreme poverty and deprivation, with no formal tuition, established himself as a leading professional performer by the age of 23 (Collier 1983; Sloboda 1991*a*). Noel Patterson (NP) is an autistic mono-savant who, at the age of 20, was able to provide almost error-free performances of classical piano movements after one or two hearings, despite possessing very low overall intellectual performance (Sloboda *et al*. 1985). In each case, these individuals are representative of a wider population of high achievers (see, for instance, Howe 1989, 1990; Miller 1989; Radford 1990; Bock and Ackrill 1993). Our research focus is on young individuals who are performing at a level considerably above the average, and who may be on a developmental trajectory towards the levels of achievement represented by the three examples above.

Research questions can be motivated by different goals. The goal of much developmental research is what we might call exhaustive. For instance, the Piagetian approach to development aims to document in a detailed and comprehensive way the behavioural and cognitive competencies displayed by individuals at various ages and the way in which these develop over time. Research findings accumulated in this way have great archival and 'natural history' value, but they do not always promote greater understanding if there is no means of assigning different levels of importance to the data so accumulated. Our approach is strategic in that it focuses on uncovering the key factors that propel individuals towards the endpoint specified above, that of the virtuoso performer. We, therefore, make no claims to provide an exhaustive account of the development of performance ability, but rather to highlight some major contributory factors to the development of high-level skill in music performance.

Finally, research observations can focus on different aspects of a situation. Much experimental development research has focused on documenting changes in individual behaviour and thought without a clear characterization of concurrent changes in the individual's environment. That is, there has been a tendency towards the mechanistic, as opposed to the organismic. Our perspective has a high social component, with a focus on the relationship between the development of musical expertise and the external resources (material or psychological) that may be responsible for bringing it about. The approach adopted does not deny the importance of internal processes, but begins from a hypothesis that accomplishments that represent the upper end of the population distribution curve are the result of special circumstances applied to 'normal' individuals. Similar perspectives have been adopted by recent authors in relation to creativity (Amabile 1983; Weisberg 1986), intelligence (Ceci 1990), and skilled performance (Ericsson and Smith 1991).

2 THE CHARACTERISTICS OF EXPERT MUSICAL PERFORMANCE

Expertise in musical performance may be assessed along two broad dimensions, the technical and the expressive. Technical skills are those required to ensure accuracy, fluency, speed, and good control over such characteristics as intonation, evenness of sound, and timbre. Technical skills are necessary but not sufficient for satisfactory musical performances. When technically perfect performances of classical music are synthesized by computer according to exactly notated instructions, the resulting experience is dull and lifeless. The exercise of expressive skills within musical performance is what gives value to individual performances. This value resides, among other things, in the capacity of expressive performances to highlight to a listener important features of the music, for example, cadence points and phrase peaks (see Sloboda 1983; Palmer 1988, 1989), and is manifest in microvariations in the timing, dynamics, and pitch.

Recent research has established quite firmly that, although any one expert's use of expression may differ from any other's (Sloboda 1985*a*) thus allowing for artistic originality or idiosyncrasy, expressive performance is nonetheless rational or rule-governed. It is not arbitrary. There are five characteristics of expressive performance that attest to its rationality. First, it is systematic: that is to say, there is a clear relationship between the use of particular expressive devices (for example, slowing, accenting, etc.) and particular structural features of the music, such as metrical or phrase boundaries (Todd 1985). Second, expressive performance displays communicability, in that listeners are better able to infer structural features of the music when expression is present than when it is absent. Third, it shows stability. A given expert can very closely reproduce the same expressive performance on occasions that might be separated by some months (see, for example, Shaffer 1984). Fourth, expressive performance displays flexibility. An expert performer can attenuate, exaggerate, or change the expressive contour to highlight different aspects of the music (see, for example, Davidson 1993; Palmer 1989). Fifth and finally, it shows automaticity. An experienced performer is not always aware of the details of how an expressive intention is translated into action (see, for example, Gabrielsson 1988). This comes about through overlearning of consistent intention–performance mappings, which could not be established unless they were systematic and rule-governed.

The folk psychology of musical ability (see Sloboda *et al.* 1994) tends to attribute high levels of performance achievement to 'talent', conceived of as innate, genetically programmed superiority. There is, however, nothing in the nature of either technical or expressive skill that forces this interpretation. An illustration from the literature on general skill will help to explain the basis for this conclusion. In 1981 Chase and Ericsson published a seminal study on an individual with exceptional ability to memorize unrelated digit strings. At the time of publication, this individual (SF) was able to listen to 80 random digits, presented at a rate of 1 per second, and then verbally reproduce the sequence without error. By any standards, this is an exceptional ability, one which is shared by only a handful of individuals in the world.

What made the Chase and Ericsson study so important was the fact that it documented the process of acquisition. At the start of the study SF had the normal memory span of 7 (Miller 1956). Memory span increased over 200 hours of systematic practice of digit-span tasks. At the end of this period, span for other materials, such as recall of randomly sequenced letters of the alphabet, remained at seven. The effect was specific to the material practised, numbers. Clearly, the 200 hours of practice was instrumental in bringing about the final level of expertise. It would, however, be wrong to suppose that the 200 hours of practice was a sufficient cause. If we could persuade a large number of individuals to practise the same task for 200 hours, they would not all attain SF's level of performance. Indeed, Chase and Ericsson attempted to induce other subjects to practise the same task. All except SF abandoned the task after a short period because they were not able to sustain the appropriate motivation. This was caused, at least in part, by their failure to increase span beyond a plateau of about 15 items. In other words, perceived success enhanced SF's motivation to persist: perceived failure led to the demotivation of the others.

We could imagine an uninformed debate about the difference between SF and the other subjects to yield the conclusion that SF had some innate 'talent' for number memory, which accounted for his ability to increase his span to an unusually high level. Chase and Ericsson have provided data to show that such an explanation is superfluous. The detailed record of acquisition shows that the substantial 'breakthrough' for SF came when he realized that he could apply his existing knowledge in another domain to the memory task. As an athlete, SF was intimately acquainted with data on running times at various competitive events. Such times are coded as four-digit numbers (so, for instance, 3'49.2", signifies a time of 3 minutes 49.2 seconds). He found that he was able to relate the random numbers in the digit-span task to these running times, by grouping them in fours, and searching for a near running time neighbour. The sequence 3492 was coded by SF as 'near world record mile time'. So, rather than attempting to store 80 unrelated digits, SF was able to store 20 meaningful running times.

We believe SF's data have profound consequences for our understanding of high levels of performance in any area. The emergence of SF's skills reveal that expertise is predicated on the ability to detect and use structure in the material to be handled. Thus, prior relevant knowledge appears to be the principal predictor of developmental progress. Such relevant knowledge allows new data to be handled more effectively and increases the sense of success, which in turn leads to increased motivation for further cognitive effort.

The implications of these data for music performance are immediate. Music is highly structured, and much of the literature on the perception of music is concerned with elucidating the structures that people use to store and handle musical inputs (see, for instance, Bharucha 1987; Brown 1988; Butler 1989; Cohen *et al*. 1989; Palmer and Krumhansl 1990). The notion that performances are generated from a structural representation can account for both the stability and the flexibility of expressive performance. Stability in performance can be achieved by re-applying a small set of rules to a structurally marked representation, rather than by remembering a very large amount of analogue information about minute timing and other deviations (a probable psychological impossibility). Flexibility can be achieved by re-setting parameters on some of the rules, rather than by changing the representation of the piece.

If domain-specific structural knowledge is the key to high levels of skill, then a strong prediction is that, where such knowledge cannot be applied, performance will be degraded. This prediction has been confirmed in a large number of studies, including those concerned with music. For instance, Sloboda *et al*. (1985) showed that the outstanding performance and memory abilities of monosavant NP were quite specific to tonal music. Memory for a simple non-tonal piece from Bartok's 'Mikrokosmos' was much poorer than for a Grieg 'Lyric piece', despite the fact that the Bartok had many fewer notes than the Grieg, and was based on a repetitive ostinato melodic pattern. The Grieg, in contrast, had a very complex chromatic modulatory middle section, which posed few problems for NP.

Another strong prediction of the structural theory is that many errors in performance will be structure-preserving. Where errors in music performance have been studied, many of them have indeed been shown to preserve the musical 'sense', by deleting or adding ornamentation, substituting different notes of the same chord, etc. (Sloboda 1976; Sloboda *et al*. 1985; Palmer and van de Sande 1993).

A third consequence of the structural theory is the development of automaticity. The automatization of a rich knowledge of structure or pattern can lead to the experience and appearance of 'intuition', when a skilled performer simply 'knows' what to do, without being aware of any cognitive effort in producing a solution. This phenomenon has been observed in a wide variety of skills ranging from chess (Chase and Simon 1973) to taxi-driving (Chase 1983). Familiar patterns or stimuli elicit appropriate responses. We see no reason to attribute 'musical intuition' or 'playing from the heart' to any different source. Such phenomena come about when a musician has a large repertoire of expressive responses that can be mobilized in performance in response to specific musical structures without overt conscious deliberation.

3 CONDITIONS FOR DEVELOPMENT OF PERFORMANCE SKILL

There are two widespread myths about musical excellence. The first of these is that high levels of musical accomplishment are necessarily rare. The second is that these high levels of skill are predicated on particular unusual early musical attributes or capacities.

The first myth is readily dispelled by examining some non-Western cultures where musical achievements are much more widespread than in our own (see, for example, Merriam 1967; Blacking 1973; Marshall 1982; Feld 1984). Messenger's (1958, p. 20) account of the Anang Ibibo of Nigeria is representative.

We were constantly amazed at the musical abilities displayed by these people, especially by the children who, before the age of 5, can sing hundreds of songs, both individually and in choral groups and, in addition, are able to play several percussion instruments and have learned dozens of intricate dance movements calling for incredible muscular control. We searched in vain for the 'non-musical' person, finding it difficult to make enquiries about tone-deafness and its assumed effects because the Anang language possesses no comparable concept.

Criticism may be levelled at an observation such as this since the Anang Ibibo are being observed through Western eyes, and, therefore, concepts of ability may be completely different. However, Messenger (1958, p. 22) provides some support to his observation by stating, 'They will not admit, as we tried so hard to get them to, that there are those that lack the requisite abilities. This same attitude applies to the other aesthetic areas. Some dancers, singers and weavers are considered more skilled than most, but everyone can dance and sing well.'

Thus, the Anang Ibibo believe themselves to be capable of very high levels of musical achievement. Messanger's evidence does, however, require verification and controlled cross-cultural study would help to validate this currently anecdotal evidence.

Contemporary Western cultures may have features that are inimical to the widespread development of high musical achievement. However, even within Western society there are subcultures in which musical expertise is especially prevalent. They can emerge quite quickly, often as a result of deliberate efforts. For instance, in eighteenth-century Venice, certain orphanages, notably the famous La Pieta, established a cultural ambience in which musical expertise was valued and encouraged. This example reveals that, when ample opportunities for training were made available, environments were created in which a substantial proportion of the orphans became highly accomplished musicians (Kunkel 1985; Howe 1990).

The second myth receives little support from the available literature. Contrary to common belief, in early childhood the kinds of indicators of later ability that would be consistent with the notion of innate factors being important are conspicuous mainly by their absence. In an investigation of the early backgrounds of 42 notably successful young musicians, Sloboda and Howe (1991) discovered that very few of the individuals were reported to have displayed any overt signs of musical precocity. Indeed, attempting to as far as possible ask parents to recount the child's life in relation to measurable real-time events such as public music examinations, the researchers found there was no difference in the recollections of musician and non-musician parents. This suggests, therefore, that the parents' own knowledge of music or interest in music was not unduly influencing their interpretations of the child's behaviours. Sosniak (1985), who also adopted a chronological narrative method of data collection, interviewed 24 young American concert pianists and their parents. She found that, even after these individuals had been playing the piano for several years, there were few signs to indicate that they would eventually have more success than hundreds of other young pianists. That is, there were no distinctive behaviours observed in these children that differentiated them from other children.

A common folk belief has persisted that suggests that excellent musicians are likely to display absolute pitch from an early age (see, for example, Brunton-Simmonds 1969). In fact, this is a skill limited to a relatively small proportion of all musicians, and seems to depend on a particularly systematic exposure to musical stimuli in early childhood (Sergeant 1969). There is evidence to suggest that, with a sufficiently persistent approach, excellent pitch discrimination skills can be learned by any determined person (Cuddy 1968; Brady 1970). Levitin (1994) has argued that most measures of perfect pitch in fact draw on two independent abilities, pitch memory and pitch labelling (the ability to name a remembered pitch). When Levitin measured pitch memory in a task where pitch labelling was not required (singing well-known popular songs from memory), over two-thirds of an unselected sample of college students demonstrated some evidence of an excellent pitch memory.

Research evidence demonstrates that excellent pitch retention and reproduction is not the only musical skill that exists in 'hidden' form in the general population. Evidence reviewed in other chapters of this volume (Lecanuet, Chapter 1, and H. Papoušek, Chapter 2) suggests that most young children show sophisticated responses to music from an early age. In later childhood, most children are capable of discriminating musical sequences that fit the rules of tonal harmony from those that do not (Sloboda 1985b), and are able to make appropriate judgements of the emotional character of musical pieces (Gardner 1973). In adult life, provided that tasks do not require specialized musical vocabulary, notation, or long-term memory training skills, the structural judgements of non-musically trained adults are often very similar to those of the music-ally trained (see, for example, Bigand 1990; Deliège and El Ahmadi 1990). Thus, there is evidence that much learning about music and its structures is something that takes place normally as a result of exposure to the musical products of the culture. We may call this process 'encul-turation'. Learning through enculturation may, of course, occur at dif-ferent rates in different individuals, due to the amount and type of musical material heard, the type and degree of attention given to it, and so on. The point to be made here is that music performance ability builds on a very common human heritage, rather than a rare set of special characteristics.

4 THE STUDY OF YOUNG PERFORMING MUSICIANS

In order to discover something about the conditions for the develop-ment of excellence we need to find excellent performers to study. The logistics of the research process have led most researchers to adopt a retrospective approach, in which high performing individuals are inter-viewed about their earlier lives (for example, Sosniak 1985; Bastian 1989; Ericsson *et al.* 1993; Manturszewska 1990; Freeman 1991; Czikszent-mihalyi *et al.* 1993). We have adopted the same broad strategy, but have attempted to increase the reliability and validity of our data by a number of research strategies. First, we identified young people already judged excellent through competitive entry to a specialist music school. This allowed us to obtain information about childhood experiences as close as possible to their actual occurrence (rather than in adult life, as in several other studies). Second, we obtained corroborating data from parents wherever possible. Third, we asked all participants the same specific questions. Fourth, we arranged comparison groups who had clearly differential levels of musical achievement ranging from one group who had considerable public examination success on their instruments to one group of children who had actually ceased playing. These comparison groups were selected in order to determine which factors may dis-tinguish high achievers from those who were not so successful music-ally. Fifth and finally, we studied a considerably larger sample (119) of high achievers than in many previous studies. In total, there were 257 children in the sample, ranging from 8 to 18 years of age at the time of the interviews.

We drew on two methods of study. First, was a structured interview format based on the child's musical biography, which involved ques-tioning both children and their parents. This interviewing method enabled us to show respondents a choice of response categories for each question, and ask them to choose the single category that best specified their level of involvement or influence. The response categories were derived from the results of Sloboda and Howe's (1991) study in which open-ended interviewing techniques had permitted the interviewees to talk freely about their early lives. The interviewees had provided rich individual profiles from which Sloboda and Howe were able to sift out common themes and issues. Sloboda and Howe were able to code the interviewees' responses to make a quantitative analysis of the interview data. This facilitated the production of findings that were statistically generalizable across all 42 of Sloboda and Howe's interviewees.

We began the current study with the aim of producing generalizable data; therefore, we drew on the categories previously constructed. Since we were planning to interview young people with a broad spread of achievements in music, we needed to make provision for potential differences between those interviewed in Sloboda and Howe's (1991) study and our sample. To do this, we carried out pilot studies on children who had given up playing, adding new response categories to our questionnaire where appropriate.

Questions were asked about many aspects of the child's musical life including: early signs of musical behaviours such as singing, making rhythmic and dance movements, and displaying high degrees of attentiveness to musical sounds; quantities of formal and informal practice on each instrument learned; the roles of parents and teachers in practice and lessons.

Our second method of study was to collect contemporaneous reports of musical activities. This 'diary' was constructed to examine: quantities of practice and other playing done each day; the duration and content of lessons; major musical events such as examinations, concerts, or change of teacher. Participants kept these diaries for 42 weeks.

These two methods in combination enabled us to: (1) investigate the relationship between the retrospective estimates of formal practice and musical performance and objective measures of these activities in the 'diary' records; and (2) discover to what extent the amount and distribution and standard of current musical activity could be predicted by previous musical life-events.

The purely retrospective data revealed a number of interesting results. First, the 119 children from the high achieving group sang a recognizable tune on average 6 months earlier (around 16 months of age) than the children in the four comparison groups. Second, other preschool musical behaviours such as moving rhythmically to music, showing high attentiveness to musical sounds, and asking for involvement in musical activities did not differ between groups. Third, across all parent-initiated musical activities, the high achieving musicians experienced a greater degree of musical input from their parents. Finally, there was a significant relationship between the age at which children first sang and the number of parental-initiated musical behaviours. (See Howe *et al.*, in press for more details.)

We believe that the parental enrichment of the musical environment stimulated the early onset of singing in the most successful children. Indeed, anecdotal reports made by these children's parents were generally that there was no special behaviour apparent in the children. Also, it is important to highlight that the parent-initiated behaviours tended to occur from birth. This evidence would oppose any contrary interpretation of the results, such as that the parents responded to the child's early singing and encouraged it further. Thus, it seems that the presence of a number of early parent-initiated behaviours may constitute a musical environment conducive to those who go on to become specialist performers. The results also illustrate that, with the exception of the child's own early singing, none of the possible indicators of musical precocity (attentiveness to musical sounds and so on) are observed either more frequently or at an earlier age in the children who become good musicians than in other young people. This latter finding seriously undermines the previously described folk psychology view of innate musical talents.

Examination of the early signs of musical ability highlights the importance of parental involvement. Further investigation of the biographies of our sample showed that, once children begin learning musical instruments, parental involvement is critical as to whether the child persists or gives up musical activity. In Davidson, Howe, Moore, and Sloboda (in press) we discovered that high achievers had parents who were more involved in initial practice and lessons than the parents of the other subgroups. This parental involvement was characterized by regular feedback from the teacher, which often included being present in the lessons, and participation in practice activities. None of the other groups studied had equal levels of parent input. The group who gave up musical study had parents who hardly involved themselves in early lessons and practice.

The parents of the high achievers were not music performers themselves. Rather, they were, at most, people who enjoyed an amateur interest in music through listening. One factor that did distinguish the parents of the high achievers, however, was that their own listening to music increased once their child began musical study. Thus, it seems that the parents of the high achievers were committed supporters of their child's musical activities and demonstrated this support by becoming more involved in music themselves. Perhaps this support is most neatly encapsulated in a comment about initial lessons made by the father of a 15-year-old girl, 'I thought it was a wonderful opportunity for my daughter to start to play an instrument. I love music and admire the skills of the top performers, but I never had the chance to learn myself.

So, when Sophie started piano lessons, I used to sit in and try to help her. Now that she's older and lives away at school, I miss not hearing her play, so I've decided to start having piano lessons.'

Clearly, the child's musical activity was accorded high status by the parent. This suggests that the parent viewed musical ability as something admirable, yet difficult to achieve, that, therefore, required special attention. Treatment of the child as a 'special' person and the provision of support in musical activities may well, therefore, provide the child with the essential external motivation for high investment in music activity. Clearly, future research should investigate the value attributed to musical ability by parents in order to provide further support for the current finding.

Over time, the high achievers required less of the parental external support, and became more autonomous in their work and motivation towards practice. This was not the case for the children who eventually ceased music lessons. The children who gave up learning in their mid-teens received high levels of parental involvement in lessons and practice immediately prior to giving up lessons. It may be that the parents were attempting to coerce the children to persist with playing. One conclusion that might be drawn from this is that, unless external motivation develops into internal self-motivation by the early teenage years, it is difficult to sustain the commitment required to persist with musical instrument learning.

Next to parents, teachers are clearly the adults with the most direct involvement in the child's musical development. We examined the personal, teaching, and performance characteristics of each teacher using bipolar rating scales (friendly–unfriendly; good teacher–bad teacher, etc.) and discovered that the child's very first teacher was perceived differently by the groups in our study. The high achieving group perceived their first teacher to be chatty, friendly, and a good player, whereas the children who gave up playing tended to regard this person as unfriendly and a bad player. It is significant to note that, although the two groups of children perceived their teachers differently, the personal characteristics and performance qualities were linked—that is, children who saw their teacher as friendly also saw them as good players and vice versa. These associations are illustrated in the two following statements that were made by the children at the time they responded to the bipolar scales. Statement A is from an 11-year-old girl in the high achievers group; and statement B comes from a 12-year-old girl in the group who gave up.

A. My first teacher was really good at music. She let me climb the tree in her garden to get apples. I used to stroke her cats before and after the lessons. She was kind and I liked her.

B. I hardly ever heard Mrs X [the teacher] play the piano, but she was a horrible player. She used to shout and boss me around.

There are two possible interpretations of each of these citations. First, child A liked her teacher; therefore, her teacher was perceived to be good, regardless of whether in fact the teacher was or was not a good player. Second, child A's own favourable attitude towards music (that is, the child was enjoying success in learning) makes positive experiences more salient than negative ones. It could be this that makes the teacher good as well as nice. For child B, the teacher may or may not have been a proficient player, but the child disliked the lessons because of the teacher's overbearing attitude; thus, the child believed the teacher was a poor player. Or, alternatively, the child's situation with regard to music learning was negative and therefore focuses on all the negative experiences when asked to recall the teacher.

The link between personal and professional characteristics remained constant for the group of children who gave up, even in cases where the children had studied with a number of teachers over several years. These associations were always negative, bad personal traits always being linked to bad playing. This was not the case for the high achieving children. Looking at their current teachers, we discovered that the association between personal and professional characteristics no longer held. Students were able to recognize that a good teacher and player need not have a particularly sympathetic personality. As a 14-year-old boy commented, 'She's [my teacher] condescending, but she's a brilliant player and I've got a lot to learn from her.'

It seems that the boy is looking to his teacher as a role model performer. Her personal characteristics are less relevant. In the paper in which these results are reported (Davidson, Howe, Moore, and Sloboda, submitted for publication), we have accounted for the high achieving child's change from dependence on the personal characteristics of the first teacher towards appraisal of the professional skills of the current teacher in terms of the child's changing motivation. Initially, it appears that the friendly teacher supports the child and therefore increases the child's motivation to learn: 'playing for the kind teacher', as one child put it. With the current teacher, it appears that the child is aiming at improving her/himself. That is, there is a self-motivation to become a better player that does not depend so greatly on a teacher–pupil personal rapport.

Overall then, both teachers and parents have a vital role in generating and sustaining children's interests in and commitment to music. Our study develops ideas presented in previous work (see Sosniak 1985; Sloboda and Howe 1991) by showing that an important role of teachers and parents in the child's learning is to provide an initial external source of motivation.

We tackled the issue of practice in both the retrospective and the diary studies by asking children to quantify the duration of all their practical music activities (Sloboda, Davidson, Howe, and Moore, in press).

We examined two kinds of individual practice: 'formal' (scales, pieces, and technical exercises set by the teacher); and 'informal' (playing not for specific teacher-set tasks). Overall, we found that there were large differences in the quantities of practice being done across the different groups of children in our study. The high achievers undertook significantly greater amounts of 'formal' practice than the other study groups; the figures were similar to those reported by Ericsson *et al.* (1993) who had collected retrospective data from professional violinists and found that they had accumulated approximately 10 000 hours of practice by the age of 20. In our studies, an examination of cumulative 'formal' practice over the entire learning period revealed that the high achievers had amassed approximately twice as much practice time as the children who experienced only moderate levels of success, four times as much as the children who persisted with lessons but were not even moderate achievers, and up to eight times as much as the quantity done by the children who gave up lessons.

There were three principal areas of 'informal' practice: playing favourite tunes from a score; improvising; and non-specific 'fun' playing. We found that the higher achievers were more likely to do all of these forms of 'informal' practice than the children who ceased playing. This suggested that informal practice contributes to musical success. We are keen to point out, however, that this correlation does not necessarily imply causality. Indeed, both success and informal practice may be caused by yet another variable (for instance, a failure in another domain of the child's life).

One group in the study who had been unsuccessful in gaining a place at the specialist school (thus, were perceived to be slightly less successful than the high achiever group) engaged in more 'informal' practice than the high achievers. A hypothesis for future research might be to investigate whether too much 'informal' practice distracts from formal technical skill and repertoire acquisition.

Ericsson *et al.* (1993) found that the highest achieving performers practised at the same point every day. Our study contradicted this. We also found that practice was not of a constant daily quantity, with the tendency being for practice to increase before concerts and diminish over holiday periods. In addition, the elements of the 'formal' practice—scales, pieces, and technical exercises—were worked at in highly individualistic ways. For example, some individuals spent large quantities of time working on scales, whilst others focused principally on pieces. These variations were often influenced by teachers' instructions to assist a particular technical development. There were, however, an array of additional external factors that affected the distribution and types of 'formal' practice, which included having a defective reed or not being able to find a particular piece of repertoire.

The differences between Ericsson *et al.*'s results and our own may be based on the fact that Ericsson *et al.* drew on mainly German musicians whereas we studied British musicians; thus, potential cultural differences cannot be completely ignored. In addition, our sample of musicians was younger; thus, our musicians may not have developed the self-discipline of the 20-year-olds in Ericsson *et al.*'s study. Also, Ericsson *et al.*'s findings related to practice strategies were based on sampling of only 1 week's practice; therefore, their data may have been insufficient for accurate estimates of practice strategies.

In summary, our research to date has shown that the biographies of high achieving young musicians have particular features that distinguish them from other young people, and these provide useful indications of at least some of the determinants of musical expertise. These features include: (1) high levels of support and encouragement from parents who tend not to be musicians themselves; (2) perception of teachers by the young learner as being both good instructors and friendly people and by the older learners as people demonstrating high professional qualities; (3) an increasing self-motivation over the learning period; (4) moderate levels of informal practice, and very high levels of formal practice.

5   CAN EXPRESSIVITY BE LEARNED OR PRACTISED?

In relation to the data about practice discussed above, it is not hard to understand how technical achievement might be related to the amount of formal practice undertaken: the ability to play a passage quickly and accurately being a direct consequence of the amount of time invested in practising it. It is less easy to account for expressive performance expertise in terms of practice. Clearly, it is possible to practise the application of expressive intentions to particular musical works. Many performers know what they want to achieve expressively, but lack the technical facility to achieve it, and this must be addressed through practice. Is it possible to practise the creation or generation of expressive intentions in the same way?

Our current belief is that formal practice is just one form of relevant cognitive activity that is required to achieve expressive performance. It is likely that the creation of a repertoire of appropriate expressive intentions requires other additional types of activity. Although as observers we may, with appropriate analytic tools, be able to point to specific structural features of music around which expressive performance is organized, it does not follow that a conscious analytical awareness of these structures can guide expressive performance in real time.

It seems to us more likely that many expressive intentions are generated and monitored by the application of a gestural process that is verified against the recognized emotional (affective) outcomes of the performance. By gesture, we mean some perturbation of the sound stream that arises from, or in some way models, a bodily movement or a vocal sign that communicates emotion (for example, a caress, a blow, a sigh, a sob). This requires two kinds of activity: (1) a process of trial and error in generating alternative gestural responses; and (2) the application of a well-developed emotional reactivity to the aural outcomes of such experimentation. For instance, a performer might attempt a crescendo–decrescendo over a particular structure, monitor the emotional impact of this, and, if inappropriate, try another type of gesture. Structurally appropriate performance is thus mediated through awareness of the emotional effect of particular structurally determined events, rather than through analytical identification of such structures. This is, we believe, the intuition that commentators are trying to capture when they say that 'true' musical expressivity comes 'from the heart' or is 'instinctive'. It does not require formal analytical knowledge of musical structure. It requires a repertoire of gestures whose existence depends on general extramusical expressivity, and responsive sensitivity to those gestures.

Evidence for the primacy of a structure–emotion link comes from a number of research sources. Sloboda (1991*b*) has shown that musical passages that elicit strong emotional responses from trained and untrained listeners tend to share certain structural features. Most of these features concern the creation and resolution of tensions and expectancies of various sorts. For instance, appogiaturas or suspensions seem to be particularly effective at inducing emotions linked to crying. Enharmonic changes, and other similar violations of expectancy, seem to be associated with the emotions related to 'shivers down the spine' or 'goose bumps'. Expressive devices that intensify or exaggerate the tension- or expectation-provoking characteristics of these structures are likely to enhance their emotional effect. Musicians who have had many strong emotional reactions to these effects while listening to music may be better equipped to mobilize this knowledge when devising an expressive performance.

Research on emotional reactions to music (see Sloboda 1992, for a review) suggest that there are a number of childhood circumstances that determine the extent to which musical experiences will elicit strong emotional reactions of an appropriate kind. We may distinguish broadly between emotional responses to music that are determined by its content (of the type described above) and those that are determined by its context. Contextual responses may be both positive (as when the music is associated with some pleasant event, such as a party) or negative (as when the music is taking place in a situation of anxiety, threat, or humiliation).

A study by Sloboda (1990) of autobiographical memories of emotional responses to music in childhood showed that individuals with a life-long commitment to music were much more likely to report strong emotions in response to musical content than were those individuals who were not involved with music or considered themselves unmusical. The latter were more likely to report negative contextually based emotions. Significantly, nearly all such negative emotions were generated in pedagogical situations, where some attempt to perform or respond to the music was criticized by early teachers. In contrast, the individuals reporting content-based responses to music were most likely to have experienced the music in situations of low external threat (such as the home, the concert hall, alone or with friends, and without performance expectation). It seems as though some of the contextual experiences in the 'non-musicians' were strong enough to lead to disengagement from music, and caused experiences of anxiety to be triggered whenever later attempts to attend to musical content was made.

These data suggest how it might come about that individuals begin to differ in their emotional responsivity to music from an early age. It seems to be absolutely crucial to the development of musical expressivity that childhood is characterized by experiences of music that are pleasurable and unthreatening, like the instance of the friendly first teacher of the high achievers in our study. These experiences can be inhibited by some pedagogic regimes imposed by well-meaning teachers and parents.

There are indications in our data that young people who achieve high levels of expressivity in performance are more likely to have indulged in unplanned performance activities in early learning (that is, improvisation, free activity unrelated to lesson tasks). These activities (often described by both children and parents as 'messing about') may create more of the necessary conditions for expressive trial and error than highly task-oriented formal practice. They are also arguably more likely to generate the kind of pleasurable emotional ambience for new learning of emotion structure links, than are achievement-oriented forms of technical or repertoire practice.

It has been a source of some surprise and sadness that several young musicians we interviewed seem to have lost the ability to enjoy listening to music for its own sake. They are so focused on achievement, competition, and being the 'best' that they almost look down on listening to music for pleasure as 'a waste of time'. While it is certainly true that excellence will elude young people who cannot harness their love of music to hard, even gruelling, technical practice, we suspect that those individuals for whom music is 'all work and no play' will never achieve the highest levels of expressive performance. The achievement of the right balance between freedom and discipline is perhaps the single most challenging task for parents, teachers, and young musicians. Our data suggest, however, that the balance should be weighed heavily in favour of enjoyment until at least the age of 10.

Whilst we have no qualms about cautioning against the explicit creation of anxiety-provoking educational experiences for young children, we would not wish it to be taken that we are proposing that excellence can develop in an environment free of challenge. It is possible, however, that the best challenges are those that the individual seeks or accepts for him or herself. This may be one reason why there are some cases of outstanding musical achievement in the absence of early formal tuition. Two of the three individuals mentioned at the start of this chapter fall into this category, Louis Armstrong and Noel Patterson. It would be foolish to suppose that their musical learning was free from anxiety or challenge. But in both cases the particularities of their early lives meant that they were free from the critical attention of authority figures for much of the time. They both had many opportunities to try out musical effects in situations where mistakes were tolerated, if noticed at all.

These cases remind us that many of the conditions associated with exceptional development among the young musicians that we studied are culturally specific manifestations of enabling conditions that may present themselves in quite different guises for musicians of other cultures or ages. Even within contemporary Western society there are musical subcultures (such as the pop or folk cultures) that give rise to excellence in quite a different way from the conservatoire culture we have studied. For instance, there are few pedagogical institutions; teaching and learning take place in a much more informal way. These subcultures have received almost no serious psychological study. If our hypotheses about the development of excellence have any generality then we should be able to confirm them in a wide range of social contexts. Much work is still to be done.

REFERENCES

Amabile, T. M. (1983). *The social psychology of creativity*. Springer Verlag, New York.

Bastian, H. G. (1989). *Leben für Musik: eine Biographie-Studie über musikalische (Hoch-) Begabungen*. Schott, Mainz.

Bharucha, J. J. (1987). Music cognition and perceptual facilitation: a connectionist framework. *Music Perception*, **5**, 1–30.

Bigand, E. (1990). Abstraction of two forms of underlying structure in a tonal melody. *Psychology of Music*, **19**, 45–59.

Blacking, J. (1973). *How musical is man?* Faber & Faber, London.

Bock, G. R. and Ackrill, K. (ed.) (1993). *The origins and development of high ability*, Ciba Foundation symposium, no. 178. Wiley, London.

Brady, P. T. (1970). Fixed-scale mechanism of absolute pitch. *Journal of the Acoustical Society of America*, **48**, 883–7.

Brown, H. (1988). The interplay of set content and temporal content in a functional theory of tonality perception. *Music Perception*, **5**, 219–50.

Brunton-Simmonds, I. V. (1969). A critical note on the value of the Seashore Measures of Musical Talents. *Psychologia Africana*, **13**, 50–4.

Butler, D. (1989). Describing the perception of tonality in music: a critique of tonal hierarchy theory and a proposal for a theory of intervallic rivalry. *Music Perception*, **6**, 219–42.

Ceci, S. J. (1990). *On intelligence . . . more or less: a biological treatise on intellectual development*. Prentice Hall, Englewood Cliffs, New Jersey.

Chase, W. G. (1983). Spatial representations of taxi drivers. In *The acquisition of symbolic skills* (ed. D. R. Rogers and J. A. Sloboda), pp. 391–405. Plenum, New York.

Chase, W. G. and Ericsson, K. A. (1981). Skilled memory. In *Cognitive skills and their acquisition* (ed. J. R. Anderson), pp. 141–89. Erlbaum, Hillsdale, New Jersey.

Chase, W. G. and Simon, H. A. (1973). The mind's eye in chess. In *Visual information processing* (ed. W. G. Chase), pp. 215–81. Academic Press, New York.

Cohen, A. J., Trehub, S. E., and Thorpe, L. A. (1989). Effects of uncertainty on melodic information processing. *Perception and Psychophysics*, **46**, 18–28.

Collier, J. L. (1983). *Louis Armstrong: an American genius*. Oxford University Press, Oxford.

Cuddy, L. L. (1968). Practice effects in the absolute judgement of pitch. *Journal of the Acoustical Society*, **43**, 1069–76.

Czikszentmihalyi, M., Rathunde, K., and Whalen, S. (1993). *Talented teenagers: the roots of success and failure*. Cambridge University Press, Cambridge.

Davidson, J. W. (1993). Visual perception of performance manner in the movements of solo musicians. *Psychology of Music*, **21**, 103–13.

Davidson, J. W., Howe, M. J. A., Moore, D. G., and Sloboda, J. A. (in press). The role of parental influences in the development of musical ability. *British Journal of Developmental Psychology* (in press).

Deliège, I. and El Ahmadi, A. (1990). Mechanisms of cue extraction in musical groupings: a study of perception on Sequenza VI for viola solo by Luciano Berio. *Psychology of Music*, **19**, 18–44.

Ericsson, K. A. and Smith, J. (ed.) (1991). Toward a general theory of expertise: prospects and limits. Cambridge University Press, New York.

Ericsson, K. A., Krampe, R. T., and Tesch-Romer, C. (1993). The role of deliberate practice in the acquisition of expert performance. *Psychological Review*, **100**, 363–406.

Feld, S. (1984). Sound structure as social structure. *Ethnomusicology*, **28**, 383–409.

Freeman, J. (1991). *Gifted children growing up.* Cassell, London.

Gabrielsson, A. (1988). Timing in music performance and its relation to music experience. In *Generative processes in music: the psychology of performance, improvisation, and composition* (ed. J. A. Sloboda), pp. 27–51. Oxford University Press, London.

Gardner, H. (1973). Children's sensitivity to musical styles. *Merrill-Palmer Quarterly of Behavioural Development,* **19**, 67–72.

Howe, M. J. A. (1989). *Fragments of genius: the strange feats of idiots savants.* Routledge, London.

Howe, M. J. A. (1990). *The origins of exceptional ability.* Blackwell, Oxford.

Howe, M. J. A., Davidson, J .W., Moore, D. M., and Sloboda, J. A. (in press). Are there early childhood signs of musical ability? *Psychology of Music* (in press).

Kunkel, J. H. (1985). Vivaldi in Venice: an historical test of psychological propositions. *Psychological Record,* **35**, 445–57.

Levitin, D. (1994). Absolute memory for musical pitch: evidence from the production of learned melodies. *Perception and Psychophysics,* **56**, 414–23.

Manturszewska, M. (1990). A biographical study of the life-span development of professional musicians. *Psychology of Music,* **18**, 112–39.

Marshall, C. (1982) Towards a comparative aesthetics of music. In *Cross cultural perspectives on music* (ed. R. Falck and T. Rice), pp. 131–49. University of Toronto Press, Toronto.

Merriam, A. P. (1967). *The ethnomusicology of the flathead Indians.* Aldine, Chicago.

Messenger, J. (1958) Esthetic talent. *Basic College Quarterly,* **4**, 20–4.

Miller, G. A. (1956). The magic number seven, plus or minus two: some limits on our capacity for information processing. *Psychological Review,* **63**, 81–93.

Miller, L. (1989). *Musical savants: exceptional skill in the mentally retarded.* Lawrence Erlbaum Associates, Hillsdale, New Jersey.

Palmer, C. (1988). Timing in skilled music performance. Unpublished D. Phil. thesis. Cornell University, Ithaca, New York.

Palmer, C. (1989). Mapping musical thought to musical performance. *Journal of Experimental Psychology: Human Perception and Performance,* **15**, 331–46.

Palmer, C. and Krumhansl, C. L. (1990). Mental representation of musical meter. *Journal of Experimental Psychology: Human Perception and Performance,* **16**, 728–41.

Palmer, C. and van de Sande, C. (1993). Units of knowledge in music performance. *Journal of Experimental Psychology: Learning, Memory, and Cognition,* **19**, 457–70.

Polony, L. (1991). Sztuka odtworcza Krystiana Zimermana. In *Psychologia muzyki problemy zadania perspectywy* (ed. K. Miklaszewski and M. Meyer-Borysewicz), pp. 547–62. Frederic Chopin Academy of Music, Warsaw.

Radford, J. (1990). *Child prodigies and exceptional early achievers.* Harvester Wheatsheaf, London.

Sergeant, D. (1969). Experimental investigation of absolute pitch. *Journal of Research in Music Education,* **17**, 135–43.

Shaffer, L. H. (1984). Timing in solo and duet piano performances. *Quarterly Journal of Experimental Psychology,* **36A**, 577–95.

Sloboda, J. A. (1976). The effect of item position on the likelihood of identification by inference in prose reading and music reading. *Canadian Journal of Psychology,* **30**, 228–36.

Sloboda, J. A. (1983). The communication of musical metre in piano performance. *Quarterly Journal of Experimental Psychology*, **35A**, 577–95.

Sloboda, J. A. (1985*a*). Expressive skill in two pianists: style and effectiveness in music performance. *Canadian Journal of Psychology*, **39**, 273–93.

Sloboda, J. A. (1985*b*). *The musical mind: the cognitive psychology of music*. Oxford University Press, London.

Sloboda, J. A. (1990). Music as a language. In *Music and child development* (ed. F. Wilson and F. Roehmann), pp. 28–43. MMB Inc, St Louis, Missouri.

Sloboda, J. A. (1991*a*). Musical expertise. In *Toward a general theory of expertise: prospects and limits* (ed. K. A. Ericsson and J. Smith), pp. 153–71. Cambridge University Press, New York.

Sloboda, J. A. (1991*b*). Music structure and emotional response: some empirical findings. *Psychology of Music*, **19**, 110–20.

Sloboda, J. A. (1992). Empirical studies of emotional response to music. In *Cognitive bases of musical communication* (ed. M. R. Jones and S. Holleran), pp. 33–46. American Psychological Association, Washington, DC.

Sloboda, J. A. and Howe, M. J. A. (1991). Biographical precursors of musical excellence: an interview study. *Psychology of Music*, **19**, 3–21.

Sloboda, J. A., Hermelin, B., and O'Connor, N. (1985). An exceptional musical memory. *Music Perception*, **3**, 155–70.

Sloboda, J. A., Davidson, J. W., and Howe, M. J. A. (1994). Is everyone musical? *The Psychologist*, **7**, 349–54.

Sloboda, J. A., Davidson, J. W., Howe, M. J. A., and Moore, D. G. (in press). The role of practice in the development of performing musicians. *British Journal of Psychology* (in press).

Sosniak, L. A. (1985). Learning to be a concert pianist. In *Developing talent in young people* (ed. B. S. Bloom), pp. 19–67. Ballantine, New York.

Todd, N. P. (1985). A model of expressive timing in tonal music. *Music Perception*, **3**, 33–58.

Weisberg, R. W. (1986). *Creativity: genius and other myths*. Freeman, San Francisco.

8

Linguistic and musical development in preschool and school-age children

Michel Imberty

A great deal of psychological research in the past has been devoted to the development of musical thought in children. In France, Piagetian theory has contributed greatly to the construction by researchers of models of the development and function of thought in all its aspects, especially in music. This is somewhat paradoxical, as Piaget had little interest in the problems of language in general, and he only approached questions of temporal organization in the context of the construction of spatial representation, and was thus restricted to epistemological issues of physical understanding.

Since the early 1980s, another trend has had a significant influence on research in the psychology of music: the Chomskyan revolution has provided a greater insight into the similarities and differences between music and language, and hence between different potential models of the corresponding competences. This trend of thought has furthermore found support from neurophysiological research on the operation of the brain, with its very similar hypotheses concerning the interdependency of notions of grammar and of modularity.

I will thus begin by focusing on these theoretical issues, because it is on these that our concept of the child's musical development depends. I shall then go on to address some more concrete aspects of the musical cognitive behaviour of children.

1 THEORETICAL COMMENTS ON PROBLEMS CONCERNING THE DEVELOPMENT OF LANGUAGE AND MUSIC

1.1 Competence and equilibrium

Piaget had little interest in the problems of language because language does not pose any specific psychological problems in his theoretical system. Language is viewed as nothing more than an extension of sensori-motor activity through the mediation of imitation and symbolic play, which then makes up an integral part of the cognitive mechanisms that are formed as a result of the interaction between assimilation by the subject and accommodation of schemata to the environment. Language is nothing more than the necessary product of the progressive internal-ization of schemata that leads to operational thought and reflective abstraction.

Behind this very general idea lies one of Piaget's key concepts: struc-tures result from a process of self-regulation through which they are enriched and co-ordinated into increasingly complex and broad net-works of interconnections, under the constant influence of accommoda-tion. It is therefore unnecessary to retain the notion of specific innate structures corresponding to each of the large-scale functions since these develop from an organic minimum genetically programmed to be very general but at the same time to have a maximum of flexibility so that external influences are able to develop and transform the organism. Essentially, this minimum of genetic programming applies especially to the mechanisms of self-regulation, and not to the structures and opera-tions with specific content. In such conditions, human language does not require a particularly innate structure, but emerges progressively from the internalization of schemata and of representation.

This is clearly the point at which the ideas of Piaget and Chomsky, and of their respective supporters over the past 15 years, are divergent and incompatible. In Chomsky's view, language is a product of a specific *competence*, independent of other cognitive functions, and like every cognitive competence it is innate and ready to operate from birth. Learn-ing is thus simply an adjustment to the external reality, the environ-ment, a kind of running in and not the construction of new and complex structures. In this debate, which has lost none of its acuity today, the issue is the hypothesis of 'transference of structure' from the environ-ment to the organism upon which the Piagetian concept of self-regulation is founded. What does this mean? In Piagetian theory, this means that the schemata of regulation and the resultant structures are 'incorpor-ated' (or assimilated) by the organism, to its benefit, from elements present in the environment (assimilation, followed by accommodation, reorganization, etc.). In other words, in biological–genetic terminology, this means that a phenotype can become unstable and then take the place of a genotype under the effect of a mechanism that is entirely internal to the organism. This principle of regulation may manifest itself in the movement from one structure to another new and more powerful structure, this transference of structure being an expression of what is meant by *incremental equilibration*.

One can assume that, at the molecular level, biologists categorically deny the existence of such transferences of structure. Regulation always occurs between existing structures, not between a structure and a new, more powerful structure which would be built upon the existing one. However, from Piaget's viewpoint, there is nothing to suggest that the laws of the molecular domain are applicable; the complexity of mechanisms and of the organs of regulation is such that transference of structure is no longer impossible. 'In living organisms, there is an additional construction which is not programmed in advance, and which results from interaction with the environment' (Piaget 1985, p. 18). Biological order is a creative element through interaction with the environment.

1.2 Modularity and grammar

Whatever the reality, this is clearly the locus of the problem of defining the notion of *competence* as cognitive psychology understands it today. Since Changeux's *Neuronal man* (1983) and the *modular* models of Fodor (1983), which describe the operation of the central nervous system, the notion of competence has made a forceful comeback to cognitive psychology and, furthermore, in a new guise. For these authors, as for Chomsky, transference of structure from the outside to the inside of the organism is impossible. This leads to the adoption of a somewhat extreme position concerning language; as Chomsky comments, chimpanzees have a great capacity for intelligence, for manipulation of symbols, for causal representations, but, in the strict sense, *they do not speak*, because they do not possess the necessary competence, and nothing can ever enable them to gain this competence. Language, from this perspective, is thus independent of thought and of the functioning of operational structures.

The *modularity* model allows us to understand this hypothesis; according to this model, the human cognitive system is composed of physically separated subsystems (competences), each of which corresponds to a specific body of knowledge and of procedures. These subsystems are autonomous and may be modified without the entire system undergoing significant changes. Such a system is thus more economical and more effective than non-modular systems. Yet psychopathological observations of the effects of brain damage show that certain lesions are very specific and selective; the different forms of aphasia are an example of this. On the one hand, these result from disorders that only affect language; on the other hand, these disorders are often themselves independent from one another and only affect certain functions of language. All these phenomena remain independent of general knowledge. From Fodor's definitions of the properties of modular systems, it is apparent that these correspond fairly well to the properties of competences in the cognitive theories inspired by the work of Chomsky. Amongst these, four points stand out: (1) modules are linked to specific, identifiable neuronal systems that may be selectively destroyed in a particular way by a cerebral lesion; (2) modules have their own capacities to analyse their own memory resources: they are independent from other modules and from other more general processes; (3) the action or 'operation' of a module is very fast, automatic, and functional, and corresponds to a fixed neuronal architecture (circuit); (4) the integration of fixed knowledge in modules is guaranteed by central processes, which act on module output, but not on internal processes, which remain inaccessible.

All these properties may be equally applied to language, or more specifically to what Chomsky terms 'grammar'. A grammar is a collection of rules that describe a modular system of language functioning, in other words, a rule system that describes the subject's understanding of language in general and his/her own language in particular. A grammar is thus a model of the subject's competence. In answer to the question 'is there a relationship between thought and language, particularly, as Piaget contends, between sensorimotor intelligence and language?', Chomsky's response is unequivocal: 'no'. For Chomsky, the young child is able to do a great number of things at the point when he or she begins to learn to speak, but this is nothing more than a temporal coincidence and proves nothing more than that the 'competences' that the child exhibits outside the linguistic field may have a direct relationship to the acquisition of language. Admittedly, there are a large number of activities that can be understood as pre-linguistic or symbolic: the underlying problem is knowing whether these activities have the true characteristics of grammars, in other words, if they reveal the distinction between *surface structure* and *deep structure*, the specific properties of transformational grammar, and so on. Yet, according to Chomsky, there is no reason to believe that this is so. Thus linguistic competence bears no relation to any other cognitive functions. This is what is meant by his modular autonomy.

1.3   Integration processes and the development of the semiotic function

Clearly, Piaget's position cannot be reconciled with that of Chomsky as from the outset Piaget states that structures become enriched by development itself, and that the 'fixed internal nucleus' (which represents the universal grammar in the theory of generative grammar) comprises developmental capacities that arise only from experience provided by the environment. On the issue of the relationship between thought and language, Piaget's theory can be summarized thus: sensorimotor intelligence possesses or develops an *action logic* through the medium of assimilation to practical schemata and their co-ordination. These schemata differ from concepts in that they are not representations (they are not internalized) and, above all, in that they are defined *by comprehension*, not by *extension* (in the sense of the logic of classes). The child sees an object on a prop and pulls the prop to bring it towards him; there is a clear 'action category' of the genre of 'pullable objects' (which is comprehension), but the child cannot internalize the set of pullable objects, or the general conditions under which an object can be pullable: there is no extension.

The reason for this is that in order to have an extension the child must be able to represent the objects of the category, or more precisely of the class, and to relate the particular exemplar to other objects of that class. However, in order for this to happen, the child requires the *ability to imagine objects not present*. This ability is the foundation of all *semiotic functioning*, of which language is only a part, in the sense of being a specific system. By contrast, in the action plan itself, co-ordinations (an example being the relationship between 'placed on' and the action of 'pulling') already provide complex structures, which become enriched in the course of experience, and which comprise all kinds of forms (*morphismes*) that depend upon this *action logic* founded upon properties of order, of causality, and so on.

How may one thus move from an action logic to a conceptual logic in the context of language utilization? The answer is by qualitatively changing the concept of assimilation: it is no longer assimilation of an object to a schema, but assimilation of objects amongst themselves or of schemata amongst themselves from the viewpoint of representations that enable similarities and differences to be distinguished; it is no longer a case of putting them together, but of *representing* to oneself their particular similarities or differences. Of course, this only becomes possible once the child becomes able to represent an object that is not present; the child thus becomes able to apply 'reasoning' to representations. Yet one knows that this *object permanence* is a product of a reversible sensorimotor structure and thus of a structure that results from adaptation and compensation between sensorimotor assimilation and accommodation of practical schemata to objects. Thus the *representation* results from the emergence of a richer and stronger structure than those that one encounters before this sixth stage of development of sensorimotor intelligence, and at the same time it is the starting point of an *internalization of schemata in the form of mental images* that the subject will co-ordinate and organize into more or less complex networks throughout the next stage of development. It is in this context that language emerges, and, for Piaget, the semiotic function, which develops across the course of deferred imitation, imitation of objects, and symbolic play, brings some essential general cognitive structures into the realm of language functioning.

This brings us clearly back to the central issue: is there a transference of structure from the environment to the organism? Piaget's view is that development is a process that is genetically determined at the level of the principal constructors or structurers. In other words, self-regulation is a property genetically determined by structures. However, development is also at the same time an enriching, constant creativity, in short, *equilibration of structures is incremental*. Chomsky's opposing position is that development is not an 'enriching' process but rather consists of a progressive specialization, channelled by the environment. In his view, in order for a theory of the development of knowledge and of language to be valid, it should not account for a progressive construction; it should only account for the inner predisposition of the organism to choose a certain direction quickly and accurately. Essentially, learning is only learning to apply the correct disposition, at the most opportune moment; this explains the amount of attention that has been focused on the individual's *strategies* over the last few years in the field of cognitive psychology.

1.4   Language, thought, and operational logic

In practice, neither Piaget nor Chomsky are especially concerned with the interaction between language and thought. Piaget is certain that operations cannot develop without language, because the network of logical relationships cannot be built up without the *structured* and *structuring* support that language provides. However, conversely, at its most complex level, language cannot develop without operations, because the complex systems that it presupposes are only possible at a high level of internalization and of generalization, and grammar itself can only achieve such a degree of complexity and of organization because it relies in part upon operations. In other words, homomorphisms (at the least) are evident at a high level of generalization between grammar and formal operational thought. Chomsky's view is that language evidently results both from particularly linguistic functions and from more generalized functions of thought and abstraction, and it is sometimes impossible to distinguish between the linguistic and non-linguistic components of knowledge.

For instance, a number of studies (including those of Bronckart from 1977 onwards) have shown that word ordering in a phrase depends on complex intellectual mechanisms, which appear to originate in sensorimotor intelligence, in order to be learned and have its meaning understood. It is as if the child were developing a series of instruments—constructional procedures and discoveries—during this period, which it then applies in a recursive manner to its mother tongue. Spontaneously, from the point at which the child possesses several words, he or she produces two-component utterances, forming an intransitive SV (subject–verb) relationship on the one hand, and VO (verb–object) on the other. (These are what Piaget calls judgements of action and judgements of observation.) Next, the child produces more complex utterances combining the two types of simple structure, most significantly producing SVO phrases. When one attempts to follow how the child decodes a variety of messages deriving from the SV and SO structures, one realizes that he or she reapplies the SV and SO strategies, giving preference to SV (intransitive) above VO (X being acted upon), before combining the two, and eventually only by abstracting the positional order in relation to the verb by the application of a rule that seems to be almost universal around 7 years of age: the active always precedes the passive.

Yet in handicapped children this process of elaboration is retarded and this retardation is more significant the greater the intellectual impairment, which indicates the dependence of these strategies and the construction of rules upon cognitive development.

This is the site of all the problems of the nature and role of integration processes in modularity theory: in this context, Piaget's solutions concerning the incremental equilibration of structures still appear to be the most appropriate and satisfactory. It certainly seems that these integration processes are lacking in mentally handicapped subjects, and this deficiency blocks the regulations that lead to incremental equilibration. Indeed, as Chomsky says, linguistic competence bears no relation to intelligence since all handicapped people speak, but their language is not integrated and often does not permit abstraction and reasoning. This is a fundamental problem of elaborated language and of the area of semiotic functioning.

2 THE CONCEPT OF GRAMMAR IN MUSIC THEORY

2.1 Musical grammar and modularity

If one attempts to apply the above to music, it is immediately obvious that the real debate focuses on the issue of knowing whether the musical behaviour of the child derives from more general behaviour, certain characteristics and properties of which recur in musical behaviour, or whether, on the contrary, musical behaviour constitutes a separate, delimited entity, about which one can theorize without having to take account of any other activities, knowledge, and *savoir-faire* of the child. From the first perspective, there have been a large number of studies showing a more or less close relationship between motor activity and the development of rhythmic organization, language, and spontaneous vocal activity. This relationship is presented as the origin of musical thought itself, and, from a theoretical perspective, the Piagetian model seems to be dominant.

On the other hand, the last few decades have seen a body of work emerge, inspired by Chomsky, that has attempted to define the concept of *grammar* in music and to simultaneously give it an abstract form-alization and a neurophysiological support through hypotheses of *modularity*.

The existence of modular systems for musical perception and under-standing has been proposed by Fodor (1983), by Gardner (also 1983) and by Jackendoff (1987). According to Fodor, there are modular mechan-isms for the processing of pitch (melody) and for the processing of temporal organization (rhythm) that are differentiated and very specific. However, the reality is far more complex: according to several recent studies summarized clearly in an article by Peretz and Morais (1989), everything depends upon the level of musical information processing. At the more elementary—and earliest—levels, the hypothesis of two distinct modules, one for pitch and one for duration, seems to be appro-priate. However, at higher levels of musical information processing and memorization, it must be recognized that there is a dependence between the two modules, and this calls into question the appropriateness of the modular hypothesis, *at a minimum because one might consider that tonality in general can be defined as a modular system* (in the sense of a scalar struc-ture of notes with fixed intervals, rather than in the restricted sense of classical tonality) (Imberty 1993).

2.2   Experimental facts and theoretical doubts

This hypothesis is illustrated by some recent research related to two types of facts, which I will return to in more detail later. The first type of fact concerns the problem of the tonal organization of pitch in a musical context. One could assume that, in this instance, pitches are codified into different forms of early sensory codes. The subject establishes links with a body of knowledge on pitches used in musical traditions: notes organized according to a fixed schema of intervals that repeat them-selves at the octave and a polarization around a reference tone, the tonic. These properties are sufficiently general and may constitute properties of musical perception in general. On the other hand, these properties of musical scales determine pitch organization in music for non-musical subjects just as well as for musical subjects (Bharucha 1984; Bharucha and Stoeckig 1986, 1987). These results were foreshadowed by Francès' experiments in 1958 on memory for tonal and atonal melodic sequences. His resuls showed that non-musical subjects exhibited an equivalent degree of success to musical subjects when memorizing tonal sequences, but that they had far more difficulty in retaining atonal sequences. This indicates that non-musical subjects also have an understanding of tonal organization, and that this understanding intervenes at a perceptual level. However, for the musical subjects the opposite is true; they have a level of processing that corresponds to memorization of sensory pitch, and this type of processing enables them to detect changes in atonal sequences despite the lack of tonal reference, which makes the task more difficult. The interdependence of two subsystems (sensory codification of pitch and tonal codification) is thus apparent for all subjects, regardless of their level of musical training, and may even be a fundamental principle of perception. It is not the case that, when this co-ordination becomes difficult, modular functioning appears at the sensory level of pitch organization, because the musical system no longer corresponds to certain minimal requirements of the tonal system. But dependence and co-ordination appear to be very general; other research has effectively demonstrated that tonal understanding of pitch may also affect temporal organization.

The tonal system as a whole thus appears to exhibit all the characteristics of a modular system, and pitch and duration are only particular aspects of this. Automation of organization, independent of training or of any kind of action or influence on the subject's capacities, is also an element as is the fact of its early appearance in the psychological development of the child. We will discuss this further shortly, and it constitutes the second type of facts which enable the modular character of tonality to be established. A different body of research shows that the independence and autonomy of modules—particularly at the level of collections of neurones in the central nervous sytem—probably have limits that are not entirely compatible with Fodor's theory. For instance, hemispheric specialization is less clear for music than for speech and, as early as 1974, Bever and Chiarello showed that musicians and non-musicians processed melodies in opposite hemispheres. The viewpoint that musical perception and understanding are based upon very generalized mechanisms is still plausible, above all at the higher levels of processing. The important issue for research will be to understand how higher-level cognitive activities are co-ordinated from the functioning of modular systems. This issue is still problematic today and in music the modular model can only explain the phenomena of perception and memorization of notes or very short sequences, in other words, very simple material.

2.3 Psychological implications of the generative theory of tonal music

The attempts to develop formal systems called *musical grammars* are related to this perspective, of which the prototype is undoubtedly the *Generative theory of tonal music* presented by Lerdahl and Jackendoff in

1983. This theory is based on a hierarchical description of the tonal system and the structure of tonal phrases, a description that is also, hypothetically, a description of the functioning of musical memory in general. The authors propose that tonal music is a generalizable example of the organization of human musical thought. This means that the strong hierarchic nature of tonal music is at the same time a property of that music, culturally determined, and a *psychologically and biologically determined* requirement. A relationship should thus exist between the structure of tonal music and that of cognitive musical functioning, and the rules of tonal grammar would constitute a particular case amongst the more general cognitive laws.

But in what sense? The reality is that theory wavers between a modular and an interactive conception: on the one hand, the rules of tonal music should be the expression of the functioning of a specific, autonomous musical system and one should be able to find in the brain the neuronal modular system that corresponds to this (this is the hypothesis according to which grammatical rules are also 'natural' mental procedures, a collection of particular *inner and universal competences* for music); on the other hand, tonal grammar is a particular case of a procedural system used to organize knowledge in memory and to activate it at a high level of generalization and complexity. In short, both perception and comprehension of music should be dependent upon far more general mechanisms that apply to other fields of human activity.

This idea originates from Chomsky's linguistic theory and shares its sense of ambiguity and, according to this theory, the grammar of language represents a model of the linguistic *competence* of the subject, and describes its knowledge about its own language. The grammatical rules thus correspond to the mental operations of the subject in speaking. Amongst these rules, some are common to a large number of natural languages, perhaps to every language, and they describe man's innate biological capacity for language in general. Conversely, other rules are specific to a group of languages or a single language, and these would represent particular competences, subsystems enclosed within the general grammar, that is, within the general linguistic competence.

How might this type of competence, which one might call by analogy the *tonal musical competence* of the subject, operate for music? Lerdahl and Jackendoff's main hypothesis is that, in order to understand and memorize a tonal musical phrase, the listener attempts to locate the most important structural elements, reducing the musical surface to an economical and strongly hierarchical schema. The principle is thus that the listener effects mental operations of simplification that enable him not only to understand the surface complexity but also, if in addition he is a performing musician, to reconstruct this complexity from the simplified schema, or even to produce other musical surfaces, other phrases of the same type, by reactivating this memorized structure. These are the progressive reductions, which are simultaneously procedures of musical analysis and actual mental procedures, that the authors assume constitute the essence of tonal competence, a competence that must therefore be an *innate neuronal modular form*. However, we still lack the neurophysiological proof of such a hypothesis.

Yet one finds here again the notion that musical *grammar* is a collection of rules that provide an adequate description of the operation of competence, being understood as an aptitude or combination of human aptitudes for music. In Lerdahl and Jackendoff's theory, these aptitudes are primarily concerned with tonal music, and this constitutes a limitation of their model which I have examined elsewhere (Imberty 1991*a*).

3 AN EVOLUTIONARY MUSICAL GRAMMAR OF CHILDREN: A KEY CONCEPT FOR RESEARCH INTO THE COGNITIVE PSYCHOLOGY OF DEVELOPMENT

3.1 The concept of evolutionary grammar

Observing children's musical behaviour, and in particular their improvisations, is a good way of clarifying the appropriate psychological content of the notion of musical competence. In psycholinguistics we have known for a long time about the concept of *children's grammar*, which tends to model the actual linguistic behaviour of children according to the presuppositions of generative theory. However, such grammars also tend to distance themselves from the corresponding classic Chomskyan concept by the fact that they only represent the formalization of language at a given age.

The concept of *evolutionary grammar*, which I will briefly summarize here and which I have formulated elsewhere (Imberty 1984, 1989), implies that the rules that are hypothesized as corresponding to the mental operations of the subject comprise fixed 'compulsory' elements, which describe general, stable processes, and also 'non-compulsory' elements, which describe processes of structural evolution that can be seen in the course of the child's psychological development. To simplify, the 'compulsory' elements of the rules may describe constant processes, operations that characterize the fixed core—perhaps innate?—of musical competence, whereas the 'non-compulsory' elements describe the programming of changes, structural evolutions that lead to the final form of competence. One can see that this represents an attempt at a theoretical synthesis of the viewpoints of Piaget and Chomsky that cannot be explored further here.

3.2 Pitch and duration

In music, one can start from a fairly well established but interesting semiological proposition made by Lidov (1975) that describes the tonal musical phrase in terms of rules concerning at the same time pitches, durations, and general temporal organization. The principles of this are *orientation*, *perfection*, and *dependency*.

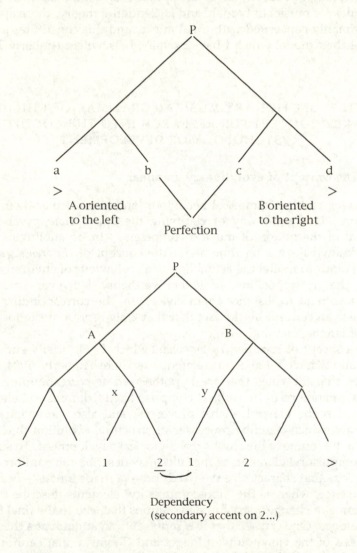

Fig. 8.1 Orientation, perfection, and dependency.

Orientation defines the location of the tonal accent in a musical phrase or a member of the phrase in relation to the subunits which constitute it. If a member of a phrase A can be broken down into two subgroups *a* and *b*, orientation would define the relationship between *a* and *b* in relation to the tonal accent of A. If *a* precedes *b* and the tonal accent of A is at *a*, A would be called the *left-hand member* of the structure at a superior level P from which A is derived; A would be otherwise described as '*oriented to the left*'. If the tonal accent of A is at *b*, A would be the *right-hand member* of this same structure P from which A is derived, and A would be therefore called '*oriented to the right*'.

Perfection defines the progression, in a unit of a given level, of an ordered sequence of two subgroups belonging to the level immediately beneath, one oriented to the left, one to the right, in a particular order. Tonal accents are thus situated at the start and the end of the unit under consideration (Fig. 8.1). *Imperfection* would be the succession, in a given unit, of two subgroups oriented in the same direction, whether it be left or right.

And, finally, *dependency* characterizes the means of linking lower level units in a *perfect* structure (Fig. 8.1): when this results from the succession of two units *x* and *y*, *x* oriented to the left, *y* to the right, the final element 2 of *x*, and initial element 1 of *y* (adjacent elements in the succession), may be of relatively equal or unequal tonal weight. When they are of unequal weight, there is a *dependency* of *y* in relation to *x* (if 2 of *x* is more important than 1 of *y*) or of *x* in relation to *y* (if 1 of *y* is more important than 2 of *x*); in the opposite instance (equal tonal weight) there is a *parallelism* between *x* and *y*.

3.3 A potential model of an evolutionary grammar of melodic structures in children

I shall not elaborate in detail on the research outlined in my articles of 1981 and 1983, but will restrict myself to presenting the *evolutionary musical grammar* of children that may be derived from Lidov's hypotheses on orientation and perfection and the conclusions that can be drawn from my most recent observation and experimentation.

3.3.1 The first and second rules

Each musical sequence produced by the child, whether it be a spontaneous production or an imitation of a model, consists of two basic elements, which give rise to the formulation of the general rule

$$Sm \longrightarrow P + C.$$

Sm designates the musical sequence, P is a pivot, and C a dynamic process of *filling-in*. P corresponds to a phenomenon that has been shown by several researchers investigating the period between 3 and 6 years of age; the musical sequence is constructed around an interval of fixed boundaries, within which the child carries out all kinds of vocal movements whose actual sounds do not have fixed pitches. Sometimes one can detect 'ornamentation' around the notes that restrict the pivotal interval. These ornamentations also have no precise pitches.

It should be explained that the pivot is not always melodic in nature and sometimes, even relatively late in development (for instance, improvisations from children of 7 or 8 years old; Imberty 1981), the only significant landmarks in the structure are rhythmic ones, or even accentual ones. The sequences are thus divided into as many fragments as there are 'weighted' accents, which always bear the sense of ending the preceding fragment. This importance of *orientation to the right* is a fundamental marker of the temporal *irreversibility* of the musical sequence from a cognitive point of view: all the weight of the sequence is deferred until its end, making any connection to a potential subsequent sequence impossible. A great deal of research into the ages between 3 and 6 years has shown that this type of structure is extremely common in spontaneous production of music, but less common in reproductions of models suggested by the adult where the model provides a clear suggestion of a melodic pivotal interval, whether by frequency of repetition or by perceptual 'weighting'.

This first rule can be further defined by the second rule:

$$P \longrightarrow Pr + (Pm)$$

where the arrow indicates 'rewrites itself', Pr indicates 'rhythmic pivot', Pm indicates 'melodic pivot', and the brackets () indicate that this part of the rule is not compulsory, in other words, as a consequence of the developmental considerations outlined above. From the point of view of developmental psychology, one can say that the melodic pivot (Pm) becomes more frequent, occurring in 75 per cent of productions around the age of 6 (see Lucchetti 1992 on this point).

3.3.2 *The third rule*

The following rules constitute the cognitive rules concerning the structures which begin to develop around the age of 5 and which are followed from 6 years to at least 8 years by a period in which the child begins to conceive of the duration of a musical sequence independently from its concrete contents in a progression fixed by an irreversible sequential order. The third rule is concerned with the phenomenon of orientation defined by Lidov, as follows,

Pr —→ > to the right + (> to the left).

The rhythmic (or dynamic) pivot necessarily implies a final (to the right) accentuation (>), as well as an optional accentuation to the left, whether it is at the start of the sequence or at a tonal or dynamic point preceding the final accentuation, in order that the sounds before this point in the sequence are not themselves accentuated. This rule thus implies an extremely simple structure consisting of *two accentuations*, and *only* two, that outline a formal symmetry that defines for the first time an order in the rigorous sense of the term, as temporal symmetry cannot be defined in any other way than by a sequence of types (*a, x, a*). In this ordered succession, the term *x* may be a filling-in as much as a sound element with a determined structure, and the sequence as a whole may be purely dynamic. Sequences constructed in this way are still very short in duration.

Thus, the melodico-rhythmic structure consists of the addition of juxtaposed fragments, oriented to the right, and then progressively oriented to the right and the left at the same time. There is no organic relationship, no 'order relations' (see Imberty 1989, 1990) between these fragments; they simply constitute ordered series that are independent of one another. This phenomenon persists beyond the age of around 6 years, and there is a high degree of consistency between results obtained from different researchers. Moreover, every researcher insists on individual differences that are underlined by differences in environment and especially in education. Nevertheless, the constituent basis of these structures can be considered as being part of the general musical competence of the subject, a competence whose manifestation depends on factors of experience and of environment.

3.3.3 *The fourth and fifth rules*

The fourth and fifth rules are concerned with clarifying what the pivot consists of when it is an interval. The fourth rule is

Pm —→ limitations + (fourth, fifth, variable).

This means that the melodic pivot (pivotal interval) is defined by two boundaries that delimit it in the range of pitches, and that this interval may be a fourth, a fifth, or a more extended interval. With children above 6 years, I have myself observed that this pivotal interval is often a fourth or a fifth and, more rarely, a third. In contrast, Michel (1973), as well as Moog (1976), comment that there does not seem to be any preponderance of certain intervals in favour of others in younger children, and that the pentatonic or the tetratonic structures do not appear to have any privileged basis.

The fifth rule clarifies the definition of the boundaries of the pivotal interval such that

Boundary $\longrightarrow$ > + definite pitch.

The boundaries are always accentuated and functionally equivalent (not hierarchical), as they necessarily act as conclusions.

3.3.4   *The sixth rule*

The sixth rule concerns *filling-in*. This rule is important in that it comprises all the elements that enable us to understand how filling-in is, in fact, the dynamic basis of all the musical structures produced by the child. The rule is

C $\longrightarrow$ \$.(> to the left + (boundary)) . indeterminate interval . . > to the right + (boundary).

Filling-in consists of a progression, in this order (\$.), of a series of intervals of indeterminate or variable pitch and with an accentuation to the right that may eventually be *a boundary of* a pivotal interval. Filling-in may begin—but not necessarily—by an accentuation to the left, either within the boundary of a melodic pivot or not.

All that is known about the productions of the very young child can be summarized in this rule of *filling-in*: an essentially dynamic process, it may initially comprise a continual vocal glissando falling within a duration bounded by an initial and a final accentuation, or even simply with a final accentuation without the beginning being marked as such. Between 3 and 6 years of age, filling-in increasingly falls within a pivotal interval whose limits have a precise pitch, and which are equally used for a final accentuation or sometimes also for an initial accentuation. But in this period, one finds virtually no sequences—spontaneously produced—that go beyond the framework of rules that I have just outlined. In particular, fragments are juxtaposed without relation, the child progressing *gradually* (according to Piaget's terminology), moving from one fragment to the next with no intention of linking them together in any way.

The fragments that make up a sequence are thus successive without order, and order only intervenes within these fragments. One could thus say that, between 3 and 6 years of age, *simple order schemata* are being used, in contrast to the *articulated order schemata* that begin to emerge from 6 years onwards and last until about 8 or 9 years of age. At this age *order relations* begin to take shape. The distinction between these is important: *order schemata* constitute the collection of intuitions that the subject has of temporal succession without being aware of the constituent elements of such succession. It is thus a case of intuitions that are essentially of a sensorimotor or representational nature and whose contents cannot be dissociated from the ordered sequences themselves. For instance, the child is capable of reproducing a short melody in its entirety, but, if he makes a mistake, he cannot continue from where he left off, as the sequence only exists globally, and he must start again from the beginning. Similarly, there are no privileged temporal events, for instance, no structured beginning or ending events—signs of the conceptual unity of the sequence. If one stops, it is because the sequence is complete. The final event is only a final event after the event; it is not that which follows all the others, but only exists in the temporal prolongation of the sequence as a whole. On the contrary, the *relational order schemata* organize the logic of the succession in a contained timespan independent of the elements contained within it. Each event, each note or chord, for example, has a place defined in relation to the collection of other events, that is, at a deep level as represented by a *syntax*. This organization of musical time is only possible after time in general has been itself organized in this way, that is, according to an *operational* mode, to recall the Piagetian term. I have shown that this is only possible following the start of *formal operations* and the consequences of such operations on representations of time and space. As for the *articulated order schemata*, these correspond to the still intuitive identification of privileged events in the temporal order, and they regulate progress, as for instance the identification of opening or closing formulae, particular pivots, and so forth. But these events still have only a 'presyntactic' function, they are still indissociable from the sequence (melody, for instance) of which they constitute the perceptual framework. Further details of this can be found in my research (Imberty 1989, 1990).

4 THE DEVELOPMENT OF TONAL COMPETENCE AT SCHOOL AGE

I will only make a few observations that will help in the understanding of the significance of the *evolutionary grammar*, the model that I have just outlined.

4.1 The importance of dynamic aspects in the organization of melodic sequences

The primary observation that can be made between 6 and 8 years of age concerns both the melodico-rhythmic structures of the production and reproduction of models and an understanding of tonal harmonic structures.

In the context of melodico-rhythmic structures, as a consequence of the distinction suggested earlier between simple order and articulated order, one can say that primary cognitive organization of the musical phrase begins to take shape at this age. In effect, a structure that one can already see with certain 6-year-old subjects and that is most evident at 7 years of age, in spontaneous productions and also in reproductions of a model (Imberty 1982), takes the form of 'three positions' with accentuation to the left, central accentuation, and final accentuation. Between the initial accentuation to the left, from the boundary of a pivotal interval, and central accentuation, we frequently have a jump of a fourth or a fifth, then an ornamentation around the upper note of this interval. Finally, without repetition of the central accentuated note and often in a chance manner, a filling-in appears that leads one to the final note, accentuated tonally. This is most frequently the initial note, the lower of the pivotal interval.

Two new properties of musical competence are exhibited here: primarily a neat symmetry that derives from a *purely dynamic tendency*, provoked by the alteration of ascending motion (initial) and descending motion (final). In short, the third rule is reinforced by this phenomenon: orientation to the left and ascending motion; orientation to the right and descending motion. Most researchers (for example, Moog 1976; Michel 1973; Ries 1986; but also Leibold as early as 1936*a*, *b*) have remarked on the greater frequency of descending intervals in children's productions, and such intervals appear to be privileged realizations of the filling-in with orientation to the right. Here symmetry signals the beginning of a much greater and more complex ordered temporal succession.

Thus one can easily understand that from this point a certain *temporal reversibility* begins, and an expectation of that which will eventually become the hierarchy of tonic–dominant–tonic.

In the context of harmonic understanding, I have shown elsewhere (Imberty 1981) that, before 6 years of age, the child is not sensitive to any harmonic reference points; each interrupted tonal musical harmonic phrase is for him complete. But from this age onwards, a particular reaction emerges that confirms the evolution of order schemata; in order to appear complete, the musical phrase must be terminated on a *strong rhythmic accent*. On the one hand, one can remark again that structural organization always begins with the location of dynamic or rhythmic elements, not by the selection of particular intervals or tonal 'degrees'. And one can also remark that orientation to the right again plays a privileged role in an irreversible musical time. However, at around 8 years of age, every cadential formula, perfect cadence, or imperfect cadence ending on the fifth degree, is considered to be a satisfactory conclusion of the musical phrase: tonal functions are recognized, but are not differentiated in a functional sense. The function and the situation of points of accentuation in the phrase are defined in the phrase, at the start and at the end, and, if need be, some of them are perceived in the middle of the sequence. The order is thus defined between the points of tonal attack and the other notes and chords, but the order between these points themselves is still not yet defined.

4.2 The origin of the tonic–dominant–tonic relationship

It is at this point that the second observation applies: between 8 and 10 years of age, the melodic structures of spontaneous productions are articulated into segments that are henceforth dependent on one another. This is produced by a *differentiation* at the level of central accent of the preceding structure (Fig. 8.2); thus, in particular, the pivotal interval at the start is a fourth or a fifth and the upper limit takes on the sense of an intermediary accentuation that ends (oriented to the right) the first sequence and appears then at the note that follows a secondary accentuation (dynamic accentuation or a longer duration), which takes on the sense of an orientation to the left of the second segment, with which the final note of the phrase as a whole is in symmetry. In short, the central emphasis that inheres in the two segments is split up into the last note of the first segment and the first note of the second, thus *articulating the sequence* of the two segments. At the same time, the primitive process of filling-in has a tendency to disappear in favour of the use of intervals of fixed pitches. It is in this sense that we can speak of the setting up of *articulated orders* that define an integral order within the perceived or produced sequence. The only remaining element is the setting up of a hierarchy within the limits of the pivotal interval for the emergence of the tonal schema of tonic–dominant–tonic.

In fact this appears earlier in the context of perception and comprehension of melody than in that of harmony. Between 8 and 10 years of age, virtually every child becomes capable of producing musical phrases where the tonic and the dominant have a clearly identifiable role, even if sometimes the system employed is not that of classical tonality, but a pentatonic or tetratonic system. I have found in my own research instances of children's improvisations where the pivotal interval was a major second and where the lower note played the role of dominant and the higher note that of tonic. In contrast, in a harmonic context it is clear that the hierarchization of functions does not become integrated until around 10 years of age; only at this age do children become capable of understanding that a tonal phrase concluded on an imperfect cadence at the dominant is not complete. Thus, this is the beginning of *tonal reversibility*, which is so difficult for younger children to conceive and which is highly cognitive in nature.

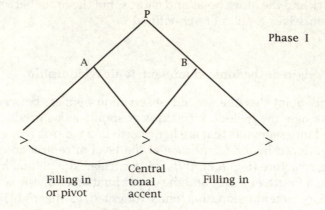

Phase I

Filling in
or pivot

Central
tonal
accent

Filling in

(may constitute a
dominant function
without a hierarchy with
the tonic function)

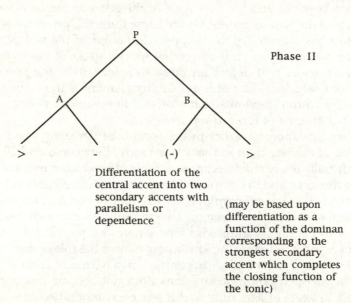

Phase II

Differentiation of the
central accent into two
secondary accents with
parallelism or
dependence

(may be based upon
differentiation as a
function of the dominan
corresponding to the
strongest secondary
accent which completes
the closing function of
the tonic)

Fig. 8.2 Filling in and differentiation.

5 CONCLUSION

In relation to the debate at the start on the nature of tonal competence, and on the modular character of tonality, one can see that the evolutionary grammar presented here, by virtue of its agreement with empirical findings, comes very close to qualifying the hypothesis of a neurophysiological innateness of cognitive structures that engender the grammar of tonal music. This is probably nothing more than a particular instance—itself particularly sophisticated—of more general systems that bring into play at an early stage dynamic phenomena linked to the experience of vital energy in the body of the subject. Filling-in, a central phenomenon, is first the exteriorization of a motion that exerts its energy in the larynx–pharynx region, in the muscular tensions and relaxations that regulate the vocal cords. Furthermore, when one takes as an object of study the improvisations produced by children on whatever instruments (percussion or others), one can see that the earliest productions are at first the expression of a veritable interplay of the body with the instrument (Mialaret 1990). Filling-in is thus a primary dynamic process in musical organization, prior no doubt to all the phenomena of elementary formal construction that one can find in the work of the Gestalt psychologists and that provide the starting point for the work of the authors of *A generative theory of tonal music.*

This is doubtless, from a psychological point of view, a point of weakness of such a theory. But it is also an issue which points again to the limits of the eternal parallelism between language and music.

REFERENCES

Bever, T. and Chiarello, R. (1974). Cerebral dominance in musicians and non musicians. *Science*, **185**, 537–9.

Bharucha, J. J. (1984). Event hierarchies, tonal hierarchies and assimilation: a reply Deutsch and Dowling. *Journal of Experimental Psychology: General*, **113**(3), 421–5.

Bharucha, J. and Stoeckig, K. (1986). Reaction time and musical expectancy: priming of chords. *Journal of Experimental Psychology: Human Perception and Performance*, **12**, 403–10.

Bharucha, J. and Stoeckig, K. (1987). Priming of chords: spreading activation o overlapping frequency spectra. *Perception and Psychophysics*, **41**, 519–24.

Bronckart, J. P. (1977). *Théorie du langage, une interprétation critique.* Mardaga, Brussels.

Changeux, J. P. (1983). *L'homme neuronal.* Fayard, Paris.

Francès, R. (1958). *La perception de la musique.* Vrin, Paris. (2nd edn, 1972.)

Fodor, J. (1983). *The modularity of mind.* Cambridge, Massachusetts.

Gardner, H. (1983). *Frames of mind, the theory of multiple intelligences*. Basic Books, New York.

Imberty, M. (1981). Acculturation tonale et structuration perceptive du temps musical chez l'enfant. In *Basic musical functions and musical ability*, Publication of the Royal Swedish Academy of Music, no. 32, pp. 81–107. Royal Swedish Academy of Music, Stockholm.

Imberty, M. (1984). Può il concetto di grammatica esserci utile per l'elaborazione di una teoria della percezione musicale presso il bambino? Paper presented at Analisi musicale, computer, grammatica, Convegno internazionale, Modena (1982). Published in *Quaderni della Rivista italiana di Musicologia*, **8**, 255–71.

Imberty, M. (1989). Lo sviluppo del pensiero musicale nel bambino. In *Tre-sei anni, l'esperienza musicale* (ed. A. Talmelli). Paper given at Convegno Nazionale della SIEM, Como. Published in *Musica Domani*, **71** (suppl.), 25–35.

Imberty, M. (1990). La genèse des schèmes d'organisation temporelle de la pensée musicale chez l'enfant. *Les Sciences de l'Education*, **3–4**, 39–61.

Imberty, M. (1991*a*). Le concept de hiérarchie perceptive face à la musique atonale. *Communicazioni scientifiche di Psicologia Generale*, **5**, 119–33.

Imberty, M. (1991*b*). Stabilité et instabilité: comment l'interprète et l'auditeur organisent-ils la progression temporelle d'une oeuvre musicale? (Analyse, mémorisation et interprétation). *Psychologica Belgica*, **31–32**, 173–95.

Imberty, M. (1993. Teorie musicali e teorie della memoria. In *Memoria musicale e valori sociali* (ed. M. Imberty, M. Baroni, and G. Porzionato), pp. 8–32. Ricordi, Milan.

Jackendoff, R. (1987). *Consciousness and the computational mind*. MIT Press, Cambridge, Massachusetts.

Leibold, R. (1936*a*). *Akustisch-motorischer Rythmus in früher Kindheit. Eine struktupsychologische Studie*. C. H. Beck'sche Verlagsbuchhandlung, Munich.

Leibold, R. (1936*b*). Eine neue Entwicklungstheorie des Rythmus. *Zeitschrifte für pädagogische Psychologie*, **37**, 161–5.

Lerdahl, F. and Jackendoff, R. (1983*a*). An overview of hierarchical structure in music. *Music Perception*, **1**(2), 229–47.

Lerdahl, F. and Jackendoff, R. (1983*b*). *A generative theory of tonal music*. MIT Press, Cambridge, Massachusetts.

Lidov, D. (1975). On musical phrase. *Monographies de sémiologie et d'analyse musicales*. Université de Montréal, Montreal.

Lucchetti, S. (1992). L'esperienza musicale nel periodo prescolastico. In *Alle origini dell'esperienza musicale*, Collab. della SIEM (ed. S. Lucchetti and S. Bertolino), pp. 7–73. Ricordi, Milan.

Mialaret, J. P. (1990). Propositions pour la description et l'analyse de productions musicales instrumentales spontanées chez le jeune enfant. *Les Sciences de l'Education*, special number, *Education musicale et psychologie de la musique*, **3–4**, 145–66.

Michel, P. (1973). Optimum development of musical abilities in the first years of life. *Psychology of Music*, **1**, 14–20.

Moog, H. (1976). The development of musical experience in children of preschool age. *Psychology of Music*, **4**, 38–45.

Peretz, I. and Morais, J. (1989). La musique et la modularité. In *La musique et les sciences cognitives* (ed. S. McAdams and I. Deliège), pp. 393–414. Mardaga, Brussels.

Piaget, J. (1985). *Equilibration of cognitive structures: the central problem of intellectual development*. Translated by Terrance Brown and Kishore Jullian Thampy. University of Chicago Press.

Ries, N. L. (1986). An analysis of the characteristics of infant–child singing expressions. *Replication Report, XVIIth International Congress of the ISME*. Innsbrück, Austria.

Index

accentuations 205
acoustic deprivation, fetal 17–18
acoustic stimuli, *see* auditory stimuli
action logic 195
aesthetic appreciation 164–5
age
  absolute thresholds and 60–2
  artistic development and 151–3
auditory sensitivity and 68–9
  frequency discrimination and 64–5
  masked thresholds and 62–4
  temporal discrimination and 125–6
  time-conditioned behaviours and 132
airborne acoustic stimulation 12
  fetal responses 13, 14, 15–17, 18–19
air-coupled acoustic stimulation 12
  fetal responses 13
air gap drawing 162
Ammensprache, *see* infant-directed speech
Anang Ibibo of Nigeria 176
animals
  auditory communication 40–1, 42
  cultural precursors 49
  play 46–7
  singing 42
animal studies
  intra-uterine noise 5–6, 7
  prenatal auditory deprivation 17–18
  prenatal auditory function 10, 11
anticipation
  of motor action over sound rhythms
    137–8
  by neonates, of temporally predictable
    events 120–1
aphasia 193
Armstrong, Louis 171, 187
arousal state, modulation of 94–5
articulated order schemata 206, 207
artistic competence
  course of development 154–67
  development 145–68
  developmental stages 151–3
  musical competence and 153–4
  see also musical competence
arts
  aesthetic appreciation 164–5
  education 154

atonal melodic sequences 198–9
attention
  head-turning procedures and 62
  modulation by infant-directed speech
    94–5, 96
attenuation, *in utero*
  of auditory stimuli 5–6
  of speech 7–8
auditory evoked potentials 10
auditory grouping/segregation, by infants
  70–5, 76, 89
auditory pattern perception, in infants 68,
  69–70, 76–80
auditory sensitivity
  infants 46, 57–70, 89
  neonates 46
  prenatal 9
auditory stimuli
  fetal behavioural studies 11–12, 18–20
  infant studies 58
  integration with temporal information
    127–8
  in utero attenuation 5–6
  localization by infants 56–7
  neonatal preferences 22–4
  neonatal responses 20–4
  rhythmic, discrimination by infants
    121–5
auditory stream segregation, in infants
  71–4
auditory system
  maturation in infants 68–9
  prenatal maturation 8–10
  prenatal sound exposure and 17–18
automaticity, in expressive musical
    performance 173, 175
autonomy-control distinction, music
    education 146, 149–50

babbling
  canonical 105–6
  variegated 106
baby talk, *see* infant-directed speech
behavioural observation audiometry 60
behavioural state
  fetal, acoustic responsiveness and 14–15